Wendy Steele

CW01498964

Wendy Steele lives in Essex but dreams of a new life up a mountain in Wales.

She worked in the City, BC (Before Children) but since 1999 has indulged her creative side, training in natural therapies, belly dance and writing. Publication of dance articles led to writing courses, and summer school, producing her first novel as well as her current non-fiction project, Wendy Woo's Tummy Friendly Cook Book.

Wendy lives with her partner, Mike, three growing children and four cats. She says her favourite days are those spent as a human being, as opposed to a human 'doing'.

Find out more at wendysteele.com

Destiny of Angels

**First book in
the Lilith Trilogy**

Wendy Steele

www.wendysteele.com

Published 2012, in Great Britain,
by Phoenix & The Dragon

ISBN 978-0-9573169-0-4

British Cataloguing Publication data:
A catalogue record of this book is available from the British Library

This book is also available as an ebook
Please visit
www.wendysteele.com
for more details.

This book is dedicated to my dad,
Alexander Eric Steele (1915-2008).
Much loved, much missed, but always in my heart.

"Seek out those who have wronged you but do not seek revenge. Offer them the bread of angels and the opportunity of redemption and together we will watch them destroy themselves on the sweetmeats of demons."

Lilith, the Dark Goddess.

Jo Mel

Power to the sisterhood!

love

Wendy Steele

17th July 2012

June

1

As the sat nav brought her closer to familiar territory, Angel's heart beat a tattoo of remembrance, igniting her brain with childhood images. Streets of identical post-war houses, neat little front gardens all three metres square and then the road to the school, lined with poplars, forcing into the blue firmament.

Angel joined the queue of cars as parking attendants in orange high-viz jackets walked down the line, signalling with airport precision. Exquisite anticipation tingled on her palate as she parked her matte black Mercedes convertible and stepped out onto the playground.

It was a warm June afternoon - perfect for tennis, thought Angel. The pale blue sky, barely interrupted by squishy cumulus puffs, was deepening to a shade of cerulean as Angel sashayed to the doors. Bare-legged and bare-shouldered, the warmth of the sun increasing her inner glow, while the soft, red silk folds of her wrapover dress swished as she walked, gently fanning her at every step. Delicate French polished toes peeped out from her red Jimmy Choos.

A banner in the school colours, bottle green and gold, announced the Centenary as Angel entered. No amount of airing could dispel the odour of pubescent teens that clung to every locker and wafted around the school, tickling Angel's nostrils with memories.

The main hall thronged with people like an army of ants, skittering apart, joining and separating again as they sought their peers amongst the nest. From panelled walls, balconies and window sills, signs stating dates and showing arrows guided and funnelled the throng to their destinations. Angel's peer group sign directed her into the sunny quadrangle, a whole corner of which had been set out with chairs and garden tables for her year group. Already a number of people clutched plastic glasses of varying sizes and smiled as they conversed. She'd felt the looks in the main hall - some curious, some lustful, many jealous - and she felt them again as she walked into the quad with her head held high and her willowy frame held confident and unabashed. Upon glimpsing her, men stood silently and she treated them to an all-encompassing gentle smile, swishing her long dark hair from her face. As one, they relaxed and resumed their conversations, still glancing in her direction but attending to their present tête à tête.

She scanned the minds in the quad picking up thoughts here and there. Fear, doubt and panic bounced around the airwaves as she tuned into the different frequencies but the consensus and most prolific thoughts were those of self-image. She ensured her mind was guarded as she flicked through the channels, careful not to float an opinion on the air. The range of female jealousy directed at her, as the quad began to fill up, ceased her indulgent sortie of the minds around her and Angel closed her senses to her gift.

"Angel? Angel, is that you?"

Angel turned on her elegant heel and watched as a pretty blonde arrived in her eye line.

"Wow! Angel! You look amazing! It's Jenny, 'member? Let's get you a drink and find a seat. I can't believe it!"

"Hello," said Angel, as she was guided by the elbow to the refreshments. She embarked on a quick search in the filing cabinet of her mind, delved into the archive and found what she was looking for. "Jenny, it's good to see you. How's Tim?"

Jenny spun round in amazement, full cup in hand, sloshing sweet liquid onto her fingers. "You remember me? And my brother?"

"Of course!" laughed Angel, "We *were* friends!"

Jenny's blue eyes sparkled and she stifled a giggle. "We were, weren't we? But we lost touch so quickly. You disappeared - what happened?"

They wandered from the drinks table, found seats by a rhododendron and Jenny chatted while Angel nodded and smiled. Angel listened and digested the words she heard but Jenny's thoughts ran much deeper than the social whitterings she divulged but before Angel could speak a giant of a man blocked out the sunlight.

"Who're you keeping to yourself now?"

Jenny's smile dissipated. "Don't you remember Angel?" she said.

The man's large, pale face crumpled with the effort of recollection. His bloodshot eyes squeezed to pinpricks as he scanned the image before him and attempted to remember. He brought the pint cup to his saggy lips and disgorged its contents, causing a tidal wave to quake his heavy neck. Sweat prickled his brow and painted dark patches under the arms of his light blue polo shirt.

"The only Angel I knew…Fuck, it *is* you!" He pointed one pudgy finger from a hand covered with gold sovereigns. "Well, I'll be buggered!"

Angel sensed the disgust emanating from Jenny but gazed at the puffy digit and smiled up into the beaming countenance. "It's Rob, isn't it?"

Disbelief winked on his face for a second. "Hey, course it is! Course you remember the big man! Hell, wait 'til Vincent hears about this!"

"I beg your pardon?"

Rob reached for his phone. "I gotta Facebook ol' Vinny boy and let him know who I'm talking to, 'specially with you looking alright 'n' all!"

"And how are you, Rob?" said Angel, still smiling. "What have you been doing with yourself?"

"Me?" said Rob, thumb working on his phone. "Bit of this, bit of that. Been in the car trade, bit of property, you know how it is?"

"Oh, I do!" said Angel. "Lovely to see you," she added, standing up and opening her purse. "But I should really take the opportunity to mingle. Jenny," Angel smiled down at her and handed her a card, "we must catch up properly. Mail me."

Angel reapplied her red lipstick in the mirror above the basin.

"Flavour of the moment, ain't cha?" said a female voice, emerging from the cubicle after the flush. The voice belonged to a small, buxom female, voluptuous yet wiry, with striking, short blonde hair atop a flouncy, tight cotton summer dress. Under the pressure from her ample breasts, the 'sweetheart' description of her neckline was more accurately portrayed as 'sex toy'. She bent over to re-lace a wedged sandal to her ankle and lower leg, revealing inadequate underwear.

"I beg your pardon?" said Angel, lipstick still poised.

"They can't get over you. Always out to steal the limelight, weren't ya?"

"Me?"

"Yeah, you, and don't try that Little Miss Innocent act on me!"

"I'm sorry, I really don't understand and I don't recognize you either, sorry."

The smaller woman folded her arms, sending more sagging flesh from its mooring. "You know who I am, you little tart! Always trying to steal my man, you were."

"Clare? Gosh, Clare, you were a brunette at school! Of course I remember you! Sorry - took me a while. You weren't in mine and Jen's classes."

"No, well, I wouldn't have been, would I? You pair o' geeks deserved each other, but I won't forget you tried to steal my man." Clare glared up into Angel's beautiful face.

Angel laughed lightly. "Oh Clare, are you serious? I have no recollection of what you mean. It was fifteen years ago! Look, I thought you said I was a geek - how can I have been some sort of man eater?"

Clare's eyes softened slightly and the corners of her mouth twitched but she rallied and folded her arms tighter before adding, "Well, I won't forget," before picking up her silver studded bag and leaving.

Clare looked up as the tube train pulled into the station. Four more stops. She wouldn't forget. He was hers and then *she* came along and that's when it all went wrong. Okay, he got someone else pregnant but he was hers, should have stayed hers. They could have been good, the two of them.

The summer sun dipped below the horizon. The doors opened at the next stop, letting in a cool breeze to ruffle the sweat-filled haze within. Two more stops to go. She wouldn't forget. Every day she thought of what might have been. Was it really fifteen years? The doors opened again. Six casually dressed young men boarded, their banter not ceasing and the tallest nodded over at Clare. She smiled back and they turned away, laughing, snippets of 'old tart' and 'slapper' reaching Clare's ears. She pulled her knees and shoulders together but couldn't make herself smaller. I won't forget, never, she thought.

"Just on the left, mate. Cheers."

Rob clambered from the taxi and thrust a crumpled note through the window.

"Yeah, 'course I want change!" He secreted the coins in his pocket and turned to face his house. The fading light reflected off the white PVC, including columns on the porch, as he fumbled for his key. He gave up, banged on the door and yelled, "Trees! Open up! Trees!"

Eventually a tiny, orange-tanned teenager let him in, turned and made her way upstairs.

"Trees! Te-re-sa! Don't you wanna drink wiv your ol' man?" A door slammed above him.

Rob bounced off the hall walls to the kitchen and selected a tall glass, and then a second, much shorter one. With the latter inside the former he staggered upstairs, opened a door, turned the key with fumbling fingers and fell onto the bed.

"How did it go?"

"You shouldn't have waited up. I said I was going to pop into Mum and Dad's to see Tim."

"I had a doze and then heard your car. You look shattered."

"It's been a long day. Look, I know it's late but I'd love a bath."

"I'll run it for you. Kettle's boiled. Finn woke once, bad dream but Scarlett's been sound asleep since 6pm. She'll probably make it through. I know you said try to keep her going 'til 7pm but she wasn't having it."

"Oh, Scott, you are a poppet!" said Jenny, flinging her arms around her husband's waist.

"Steady on, don't get excited. I've an early start in the morning," said Scott, gently peeling her from him. "I'll run your bath," he added, taking the stairs two at a time.

Jenny's head sank down and her shoulders curled forward, choking the breath in her throat. In an instant she threw back her head, her eyes moist, and took in a great gasp of air before levelling her features and reapplying her smile. She kicked off her shoes, locked the front door and climbed the pine stairs.

The sun was finally setting on Angel's right hand side as she turned into the driveway. She put her foot down and sped through the dusk to arrive, grinning, with a skid at her front door. A young man appeared, descended the steps and opened the driver's door before the engine noise fell. Angel alighted, smiling at the beautiful, blond face and chiselled cheekbones. She licked her lips as she walked round him and started up the steps. Halfway up she turned back.

"Aidan?"

"Yes, Mistress?"

"I would like some company this evening."

"Yes, Mistress."

The small brown door was almost hidden by the bill posters and graffiti slathered across the empty shop fronts. As her key turned in the door, the smell of urine welcomed her home. Up two flights, stuttering over empty bottles, newspapers and syringes, Clare stood at the door to her flat and searched through her keys. A warm, rank odour greeted her as she closed the door behind her and leant on it. She scrambled for the phone in her bag as it vibrated against her hip.

"Hi, Freddie," she said. "Yeah, sure, yeah, course I can. Give me 'alf hour, lover."

The voice in the phone became louder and more insistent. "No, no, honestly, no problem. I'll be ready in ten." The voice ceased abruptly and Clare stood looking down the hallway. Moisture welled up in her eyes and she bit her chapped lip. The sudden saltiness in her mouth was like a slap in the face and she hurried to her bedroom, throwing clothes under the bed and scurrying dirty plates and glasses into the kitchen. Back in her bedroom, she sprayed perfume over herself and the bed, straightened the dingy covers and sat at her dressing table, painting on a Scarlett smile until the banging on the door started. She hurried to cease it.

"Fred! Oi, Freddie, you know the rules! Cash through the letterbox, then you can come in."

The bashing ceased and was replaced with muffled curses before five rumpled £10 notes arrived through the letterbox. Within moments, Clare had grabbed the notes, secreted them in the tin in the bottom of her wardrobe and opened the door.

"Freddie, my love. Come in, come in, let's be 'avin' you, lover."

Most of the photos were grainy and blurred but some had come out well. Rob knocked back a shot and poured another from the sticky bottle as the computer uploaded the file from his phone. His shirt and trousers lay scrumpled around him as he sat in his boxers, watching the screen, one hand on the shot glass, the other rubbing his groin. Finally the set of pictures were ready to view in slide show mode. Two shapely legs disappearing under a skirt or crossed elegantly at the knee, then hips, breasts, lips and finally Angel's face looking straight at him, her tongue licking her top lip.

Rob began to stroke as the images, like a heavenly conveyor belt, flashed past on the screen. Sweat ran down his chest and his breathing rasped and quickened as he beat out the rhythm of lust.

Jenny sank to her chin in bubbles and let the silent tears flow. She'd had a nice day and a nice chat with Tim. She cried harder, allowing her chest to heave and let out those built up frustrations that ate away at her insides. And now back to her nice house and nice family. But it wasn't nice, was it? It was a sham, a lie, a falsehood....She closed her eyes and ducked under the water.

As she dried herself, she took stock of her pale skin, a little pinked by the sun, and ran her hands over her body. It was still taut and smooth despite two children and she lingered on her small, pert breasts as she looked into the misty mirror. She rubbed her towel on the glass and a sad, pretty face looked back at her. Oh, to have a face as full of life as Angel's! She dropped her nightdress over her head as she remembered the brief meeting and a bubble of excitement burst in her stomach. Did she really want me to email her? she thought, running a comb through her blonde curls, or was she just being polite? No - Angel remembered her, and she'd given her the card. She'd mail her tomorrow. No, that might come across as too keen. Maybe Monday. Or should she wait a week?

The huge oval white china basin on gold-clawed feet stood on a marble plinth in the centre of the room while the steps and floor around it were carpeted with a lush, white pile. Cushions the size of double beds graced one side of the room whilst on the other, a chaise longue was draped with silk, satin and glorious fluffy towels.

Angel lay resplendent in her bath, her dark tresses clipped above her head, while the scent of jasmine and ravensara permeated the air. Aidan stood before her in his black suit, smiling as he watched her stroke the perfumed water over her body. She stopped, crossed her arms across her breasts and looked up coyly. "I think I'd like you to be naked too."

"Of course, Mistress," said Aidan, immediately pulling off his black neck tie.

"No, Aidan," said Angel. "You are in charge tonight."

"Ah," said Aidan, slowly unbuttoning his shirt. "So you've no experience in these matters?" His trousers fell to the floor and he was naked.

Angel blushed and shook her head.

"Then let me teach you," he said, stepping into the bath. "Gently?"

Angel shook her head again slowly, her innocent gaze fixed on his jade green eyes.

"I see," said Aidan. "Then I shall teach you a proper lesson."

"Yes, Master," said Angel.

2

Angel lay in bed with Aidan's sleepy breathing soothing her, as she recalled her day at her old school. A warm glow spread over her as Jenny's kind, gentle face appeared in her thoughts, her only friend from school and yet, a friend she had dismissed along with the pain. It would be good to meet up and find out how the bright confident Jenny of fifteen years ago had fared since school. A round puffy face interrupted her musings and then an angry one, filled with pent up hate and malice. Rob and Clare forced their way into her musings – two of the perpetrators of her childhood agony. She'd faced them at the school as a woman, not a child and yet, the pain was still there. Old thoughts resurfaced and sought to rebuild the neural pathways she'd carefully deconstructed. Unwelcome thoughts strove to remake a route to undermine her confidence. She saw them coming and closed them down, constructing her own roadblock but, the fact that a brief meeting could bring back the pain of her youth, reinforced her belief in continuing the course she was on. They were on. She and her friends, the new 'family' she had made.

Angel snuggled into Aidan and recalled the Full Moon ritual that had set her on this path. She heard the music beginning softly, a background hum resonating around the cavernous walls, filling her body with the weight of the earth and the primordial depths of the universe. As the regular beats of a gong tolled, she and her friends, cloaked figures in the gloom, walked forward into the circle, mere shades of them visible in the monstrous candlelight. Vast battalions of head-high, wrought iron candlesticks stood to attention, circuiting the cave, dripping and dribbling light into the abyss, where fool's gold and quartz glistened in the walls but no sunlight could pervade. Upon the altar, flanked by two flaming braziers, the tools of the ritual were set out, glistening, sparkling and smoking in turn. An ornate carved owl sat on a pentagram in the centre.

Words escaped from the communal hum and as the energy rose, the figures walked slowly clockwise, heads bent upon their steps. They stopped and shook back their hoods and Angel, Aidan and Sophia stepped forward into the middle of the circle. She saw herself, hair like a jet black waterfall, stood before the altar, arms raised, palms open to the sky, as Aidan and Sophia, in their roles of Priest and Pythoness, took turns to cast the circle, first with an ornate sword, then a bowl of water and salt.

Angel heard herself complete the circle, "And I consecrate this circle with the incense of Kyphi[1]," turning from the north and making her tour of the circle, stone bowl in hand, filling the air with smoke.

The Pythoness, Priestess and Priest held hands before the altar as the ritual continued, the air in the cave hanging heavy and expectant, screaming with anticipation. The chill of the night seeped into the cave as the sun set in the world outside. Angel spoke the familiar words, feeling the energy

---

[1] See Glossary

in her blood begin to quicken. Her skin prickled, her
fingertips tingled and she was wakened by the energy from
another world. Her disciplined mind sought for the Path and
she opened herself up as the quarters were called: earth, air,
fire and water. The sphere of power encompassed them all
and the Priestess began her invocation while the smiling
faces of her companions glowed around her, joining the
union, beseeching the Goddess to join them in their work.
Angel saw her cloak fall to the earth before the altar, as she
stood tall in her black gown, flecked with gold and the
yellow citrine on a simple cord hanging in the curve of her
breasts, glistening in the fiery glow.

Within the sphere of power, the Tree of Life[2] appeared -
the witches' Qabalah[3], a map of the Universe, a framework
upon which all experience, both physical and spiritual, could
be understood and upon which Angel had concentrated her
study for the past three years. Upon the Tree hung ten
coloured vibrant discs - the Sephirah[4] - which were linked
together by thirty two pathways that blazed and dazzled like
a crystal cobweb. Over many years she'd searched for
answers to her questions among gurus, prophets and
magicians but not until she placed this knowledge upon the
framework of the Qabalah, could she begin to understand
this immense source of knowledge. Not until she'd begun to
understand had Lilith[5] come into her life and begun to shape
her future.

Her mind returned to the Full Moon ritual and the
Qabalah hanging in the air. She focused on Path thirteen,
where the outline of another disc shimmered like an
architect's draft superimposed on the map, sometimes there,

---

[2] See Glossary

[3] See Glossary

[4] See Glossary

[5] See Glossary

other times fading into nothingness. The image of the Tree was suspended in the air before them all, a map of the complex journey ahead simply portrayed for them to see.

As she watched the Qabalah resonate and grow, the sphere of power expanded with energy, announcing the presence of an Egyptian god. They were all familiar with the wise and learned Thoth[6], in his white pleated kilt, the head of an ibis upon his shoulders and, upon his head, the lunar disc and crescent. He was the Dweller on the Threshold, the first obstacle upon the Path, through whom Angel, as Priestess must convene to ensure their journey be a safe one.

Angel recalled herself balanced and prepared, as she opened her mind for the Dweller on the Threshold to read, displaying her resolute intent for him. He scrutinized her thoroughly and then, once satisfied, Thoth welcomed her to the astral plane, admitting her entrance to the paths she sought and allowing her access to the others who dwelt there. She watched his countenance change, the disc and crescent upon his head beginning to glow and he became the Doorkeeper, the protector of her physical body, a vital accessory for the journey ahead, keeping harm from her as she opened the door and stood upon the Path.

Angel loved the first step upon the Path and she snuggled deeper under the covers next to Aidan, allowing the recollection to flood over her. She enjoyed all her Path workings, whether alone or with her friends. Years of practice had perfected her craft so the process flowed through her with ease. Every step she took washed her mind with new visions and with each experience, greater understanding followed. Standing on the threshold of infinity was an awesome freedom while the power at her disposal was electrifying but more exciting was the realization that

---

[6] See Glossary

she carried this power with her, reinforcing her belief in a fine line between reality and imagination.

A yawn brought her into her bedroom but she brought her mind back to the ritual, determined to revisit it all before she slept.

Back in the cave, her feet firmly planted on the ground in Malkuth[7], the tenth Sephirah at the bottom point of the Tree of Life, the physical plane here on earth, and with the owl from the altar in her hand, Angel began her evocation.

"Oh Dark Moon Goddess, patroness of all witches,

Dark are thee, black on black, lips red as rose, kissing the entire Universe,

I open myself to thee.

Infuse me with your wisdom and power,

O fulfiller of all lust, seer of desire!

We stand before you, willing and eager to hear your command!

First of all women – Lilith!

Queen of the Magic!

KI-SI-KIL-LIL-LA-KE!"

She felt Lilith consume her, a fiery glow spreading up from her toes, quickening her blood and energizing her mind until she buzzed and vibrated with the power of the Dark Goddess. Angel welcomed her presence and accepted her into her body and mind as an intimate friend, mentor and guide. For years she'd communed with Lilith on the dark moon and she relished the perspective Lilith brought.

Within the cave, black filled the sphere of power, not darkness but old black, the black before existence from the edge of time. Black filled the lungs of the followers, seeping into their bodies, awakening their ancient urges.

And the Priestess, now the Dark Goddess, turned to the figures in the circle and spoke.

---

[7] See Glossary

"I welcome your summoning, independent humans. I welcome you with the arms of the first Goddess."

Six figures knelt before their Goddess.

"Rise - you shall not kneel before me, for we are as one. Each of you vibrates with creativity and verve, ready to learn. I know it and feel it. I say to you, do not stray from the power of your nature. It is your lust for life that keeps you strong and directs you upon the Path!"

"Thank you, Great Goddess," they intoned as they stood.

"Eons pass, yet humankind still hurts and rejects that which is too beautiful, too strong or too confusing to understand. My children, you have been damaged thus but brought together, you can heal yourselves and gain far more than you have lost. I have returned to this physical plane with a task for you. Travel the Paths set out and experience each Sephirah in my name, seeking answers as you progress. Your destination is Daath and there you will find the truth."

As the Great Goddess spoke through her, Angel saw the discs upon the tree obtained a third dimension and became spheres, glistening and vibrating to her voice and, at the mention of Daath, the outlined disc on Path thirteen became clearer and brighter, adding an eleventh Sephirah to the Tree.

"Seek out those who have wronged you but do not seek revenge. Offer them the bread of angels and the opportunity of redemption and together we will watch them destroy themselves on the sweetmeats of demons. Follow me, for I shall show you the true Path to unlimited knowledge and infinite understanding. Do this in my name and the pleasures too, I shall bestow, shall be beyond your understanding."

As Angel opened the bedroom door the yellow citrine at her throat pulsed and glittered, its vibrant power visible within the depths of each quartz face. She saw the corridor before her, wide and high with seven doors, each marked with a glyph.

Angel felt Lilith within her. Strength and independence exuded from her and she felt full of instinctive lust and desire. Red hair in ringlets cascaded over her shoulders and from her feet to her waist the flames caressed and energized her. Power sizzled through her veins as Lilith's voice filled her head and her blood. "You have stepped upon the Path and carry your true intent. Now it is time to choose."

Angel stepped up to the first door and sensed a broad, fair man at her side. Eli stood smiling as he offered her his arm. Angel took it and leant into him, grateful for his presence at her side. Together they opened the door. They were beneath the ocean and as they walked across the shifting sea bed, shoals of strange fish flashed past them and rocks rose from the surface, grew legs and fins and sculled away. The water became murkier as they walked until they came across a vast mound on the ocean floor. Angel's heart beat faster as they placed their hands upon it and felt movement beneath their feet.

Curling and slithering, black-suckered tentacles emerged from the mound encircling them until the great sea beast, Leviathan[8] loomed above them. Eli lifted his arms to the great razor-toothed mouth and called its name, and with one almighty roar from the beast, Eli was consumed.

A tall handsome man with hazel eyes that twinkled with mischief stood beside Angel. Jed smiled at her as he took her hand and Angel held it tightly as they entered through the door. The stench of foul excrement invaded their senses and they staggered before leaning on each other for support. The grey walls around them disappeared into infinity and the space around them was filled with riches beyond calculation. Piles, mounds, stacks and heaps of gold bars, precious gems and money, all surrounded a throne, whereupon sat a

---

[8] See Glossary

monstrous demon with horns that touched the sky and pointed nails that sliced the air with every gesture. Behind his throne, banks of computer screens showed the world's money markets while at his feet minions scurried. Every time one of them slowed down, he pierced it fiercely with a fingernail.

Jed lifted his arms and cried out the demon's name. "Belphegor[9]!"

Belphegor pointed his finger and sent a bolt of power through Jed who, smiling, disappeared in a flash of red light.

In front of the third door stood a petite young woman. Gentle wispy curls encircled her tiny face, and she looked fragile, but determined. Maddy grasped Angel's hand and they opened the door. They entered a dark room and stood breathing quickly, sensing the smell of death and the silence of dull, lifeless air. As their eyes readjusted, walls rose around them and golden statues began to emerge, the heads constantly changing as they watched. Each statue was a priceless treasure with precious jewels for eyes and extravagant adornments of gold, silver and platinum. One of the statues stepped forward and began to grow, its one sapphire eye the size of an ocean liner and its teeth diamonds the size of skyscrapers. It waved its countless limbs, showering gems like confetti over the ground.

Angel lifted her arms to shield her face but Maddy, fearless and smiling, raised hers to the beast and cried, "Mammon[10]!" With a flick of its tail, it sent a cascade of diamonds and Maddy disappeared, engulfed in a shower of gem stones.

---

[9] See Glossary
[10] See Glossary

At the fourth door a young blonde woman, beautiful and smiling, stood by Angel's side. Sophia held out her hand and Angel took it, excitement and trepidation taking turns in her brain. They opened the door together. A bright summer's day greeted them. Lush grass crushed between their toes and a warm, gentle breeze caressed their hair. Upon the hillside, sheep grazed beneath the early sun's warmth but another light was forming in the firmament, growing bigger and brighter. White light began to pervade the golden scene before them, scouring the colour from the land. Whiter and brighter it grew, obliterating the sun, and from this light stepped a great horned demon, flexing his wings as he towered above them.

Angel let go of Sophia's hand to shield her eyes from the piercing glare and watched in awe as Sophia raised her arms and opened them to the beast, crying, "Lucifer[11]!" The white light surrounded her and she was gone.

At the fifth door, a dark, gentle giant of a man stood beside Angel. Zac put a strong arm around her as she opened the door. The enormous room before them was set with vast banqueting tables and illuminated by a host of chandeliers. The smells of the feast lingered in their nostrils as they walked between tables piled high with food. Angel's heart clamoured with expectation as she walked behind Zac, fearful of what awaited them but confident in her companion. At the end of the hall a huge, muscular beast rose before them, its head as big as a house and its forked tail as long as a tube train.

The scales covering its body glistened red and black as Zac stood and called it: "Beelzebub[12]!" With a crack of the forked tail, Zac was consumed.

---

[11] See Glossary

[12] See Glossary

Angel stood with Aidan at the sixth door. His beautiful smile sparkled in his jade eyes and Angel felt confident and calm as they entered the doorway. A roar from the distance beckoned them forward and out of the darkness came the monster. The beast before them had three heads - bull, ram and man - sprouting from a gigantic neck. Its body was that of a man but blue, and scaled with dragon wings, and it had the tail of a serpent. It stood as tall as a pyramid and the energy within it pulsed through its every scale. On seeing Angel, the beast smiled and bowed.

Aidan called him: "Asmodeus[13]!" and the beast devoured him greedily.

"This is your final choice," said Lilith, as Angel stood before the seventh and final doorway. "Choose carefully when you enter, for this door changes you and your life forever."

Angel sensed every cell in her body awakening. Dense blue pigments seeped into her skin. Scales began to form and from her back, the wings of a butterfly began to metamorphose. Angel hesitated at the doorway and woke up.

---

[13] See Glossary

July

3

Angel loved hot summer days, the days that scorched the earth and scoured the tarmac, making the reality of the world vibrate and shudder in an opalescent haze. Jenny was already outside the restaurant, shifting nervously from foot to foot. Her navy maxi dress, dotted with white daisies, looked cool enough but its oversized billows clung to hot flesh while the white cardigan induced more heat to rise to her throat and face.

In the cavernous depths of the London restaurant, cool air blew freely as they were seated at Angel's table. Delicately painted oriental screens afforded them privacy and once drinks were ordered and food was chosen by Angel, they sat sipping margueritas.

"So how are you, Jenny? I know you're a mum and a wife, of course, and you work…?" said Angel.

Jenny nodded and began recounting her life since leaving school, while Angel opened her mind to the true thoughts behind Jenny's words. Though it came naturally to her, Angel endeavoured to restrict this talent to minimum usage, believing an individual's thoughts to be private and personal but she was curious to know the real content of Jenny's life this past fifteen years and, with the feelings she'd sensed at the centenary celebration, feelings her friend was still inadequately trying to hide, she justified her dabble into another's privacy. Jenny with her children, smiling and laughing, Jenny at work in her tabard, smiling in the playground. Scott in the arms of another man.

"Why the look?" asked Jenny.

"Look?"

"Just then. Your face changes when you're thinking about something. It always has! Sometimes you'd go off into another world!"

"Really? I didn't notice. Well, I wouldn't, would I!"

They laughed. "Something struck me, that's all," said Angel.

Food arrived and they sipped and picked while the silence hung between them. Angel relaxed. She kicked off her sandals under the table and laced her loose hair into an intricate plait while Jenny concentrated on her chopsticks.

"So how are you really, Jen?"

"Like I said, I'm ticking along just fine."

"And Scott?"

"I love my husband," said Jenny hanging her head and prodding in her bowl.

"But you know it's over, don't you?"

Jenny looked up, tears welling in her eyes and nodded.

"How long can you go on living like this?" said Angel.

Jenny shrugged. "I don't know."

Tears and jasmine tea followed and Angel soothed and calmed her old friend. Maybe she'd said too much too soon. Her gift allowed her so much incite and information if she allowed it that it was tricky balancing a desire to help with the need for discretion.

"Feeling a little better?" she asked, passing Jenny a huge pink cup.

"Yes thanks."

"Sip some tea. You'll be fine," said Angel.

"You've changed so much," said Jenny.

"We all change."

"I haven't! Well, I don't think I have."

"Sure about that?"

"Well, I'm older!"

"And wiser?"

"I've not thought about it, to be honest."

"You don't think about *you* at all!"

Jenny looked up from her cup.

"Sorry, I've spoken out of turn," said Angel.

"No you haven't, tell me."

"How often do you meet friends for lunch?" asked Angel.

"Never," said Jenny, returning to her cup.

"How often do you go for a walk, read a book, attend a class?"

"Well, I do…"

"On your own?"

"Okay, I don't, but…"

The next words committed Angel to a path she wasn't sure she should take, but she took the first step anyway. It was too late now. She'd witnessed first hand the pain in Jenny's mind and she wanted to help her.

"Jenny, you should get out more and take time for yourself. Everyone deserves a break sometimes, and spending an hour with friends is good for you. Why should you have to justify 'time out'? Making decisions for yourself gives you a chance to find yourself again so you can *be* yourself."

"But who *am* I?" said Jenny.

"I don't know, Jen. Only you can find yourself, but, I can tell you how I found *myself,* if it will help."

"Yes, tell me. I'd like to know."

Elbows on the table, Angel supped as she spoke, telling her tale in a calm, factual and unemotional manner as if she'd learned it to recount upon request. "Father got the call to go to South Africa, and Mother went with him. I was shipped to Mother's only sister in Wales. Within three months, Aunt Alice was dead of a coronary and Mother and Father's bodies were found, burned in their own car."

"Oh my God! I'm so sorry!"

"Don't be. It's been fifteen years, remember."

"All the same.…"

"Jenny?"

"Hmm?"

"It doesn't matter. I know that sounds harsh but try to understand. I arrived late in my parents' life, proclaimed 'an angel', but realistically I was an intrusion in their dual happiness. When they died, I felt little loss. Father wouldn't have dreamed of turning down the post in South Africa even if I'd asked. The church was his vocation, his life, and Mother did what he did. They were in it together. I always felt an outsider, kept at a distance, not part of their lives. I've spent years coming to terms with their rejection. It gets easier with time. Aunt Alice was an awkward, argumentative woman." Angel grinned. "Easy to fool. I was a resourceful teenager."

Angel put down her cup and began stroking her plait of hair, occasionally brushing the loose end against her cheek. "I was the sole living relative. Father was an only child and his parents had done well out of the war, while Aunt Alice had never married. I inherited money and property from both sides of the family. There were some legal wranglings as I was so young but without boring you with details, I lived on in Wales with a substantial income and then took possession of my fortune at eighteen."

"It sounds so....unbelievable! From schoolgirl to property millionaire!"

"I wasn't a millionaire then," said Angel, "But I met some extraordinary people over the next few years and built up a circle of friends and advisers and they helped me. I learnt about finance from them and then went on to develop business strategies of my own. I've read and studied and I've travelled, which I love, but my true home is in Wales now. I've grown fond of the place. I have a house there, on the edge of Snowdonia. So that's how I've ended up here and now! No family ties, just good advisers and close friends.

Travel and work I can do when I choose to, and time - time
to catch up with an old friend."

"It's sad and yet so exciting! You've not come from Wales
today?"

"No, my house in Surrey."

Jenny put down her cup. "It sounds amazing, Angel! So
what do you do? No, don't answer that, I'm being silly. You
don't have to *do* anything!"

"Oh, but I do, Jenny," said Angel. "I live."

A black silk shift caressed her skin as Angel sat cross-legged
on a cushion in the centre of a chalk circle marked upon the
painted wooden floor. Four candles burned around her and
the smell of cedar mixed with vanilla pervaded her nostrils
as she shut her eyes and regulated her breath. Her mouth
began to form words, silently spoken, rising from her,
reaching out beyond the circle to the zenith beyond the stars,
until she felt and welcomed the presence within her and
ceased her active tongue.

She saw herself seated on a throne. Not regal and
sumptuous but a harsh, dark seat, violent and old, hewn from
the rocks that began the Universe. There she sat, and though
her hair was brighter than a freshly split conker and flames
licked and caressed her limbs, she knew that it was she,
Angel who sat, crowned and isolated, high above her
minions. Angel, wearing the bright white crown of her
destiny. She watched through burning eyes as the figures
climbed the steps below her, until her friends reached her
and sat at her feet, awaiting her command.

She beckoned Eli to stand before her, his gentle, fair face
relaxed and subservient to her wishes. Angel spoke, and she
knew the words were hers, her truth and intent honestly
sprayed upon her lips.

"From this moment forth your will be guided by my
demon Leviathan. Through his eyes, see the power of envy,

but use the love in your heart to promote kindness in its place. Bend no man's will but offer only as a gift the benefits of your understanding upon this plane. Keep your feet firmly in the earth and from this journey, your eyes will be opened and the secrets of Malkuth will be shown to you. I present you with this wish of mine for you. Will you accept it?"

"I will," said Eli.

"So mote it be."

Jed, tall and handsome, stood before her.

"From this moment forth your will be guided by my demon Belphegor. Through his eyes, see the power of sloth but use the love in your heart to promote diligence in its place. Bend no man's will…"

And the ceremony continued, and to each of her friends Angel presented her wish: to Maddy, the demon Mammon, to see the power of greed but to promote charity; to Sophia, the demon Lucifer, to see the power of pride but to promote humility; to Zac, the demon Beelzebub, to see the power of gluttony but to promote temperance; and finally to Aidan, the demon Asmodeus, her husband, to see the power of lust but to promote chastity.

Once commissioned, her friends stood before her, smiling and excited, eyes shining, prepared and keen to begin their journey. Angel stood and lifted her arms, palms open. She felt the surge of power through her physical body, the presence of the Divine.

"Binah! Queen! Mother of all that exists and all that will exist!

Mother of the Earth and all that is earth!

We seek your Divine and Infinite Wisdom

As we step upon the Path!

Guide our steps and replenish our intent!

Protect us and nurture us!

Show us our true Self and we will see!

Glorious Mother and maker of Form!

Imbue us with the Force to do thy will!"

Angel opened her eyes but there was no light in the room.
Darkness fell on her body, pushing and squashing it,
squeezing the breath from her lungs. Enormous and
deafening in its silence, the darkness enfolded her and took
her and she felt herself lifting, rising from the earth, on and
on, upwards, higher and higher until she hung, drifting in the
blackness of nothing. Out of nothing came the universe. She
watched the earth emerge from the great darkness of space
and there, below her, she saw the sphere turning, day and
night, light and dark painted on its surface. She watched the
seasons unfolding, fields planted, growing, harvested and
then fallow until new seeds were planted again. Upon a hill
she saw a tiny acorn nestle into the soil. She heard the shoot
break from its dark confinement, seeking firm foundations,
and she felt its contact with the warm, rich earth. Her body
filled with warmth and light and the four candles were alight
around her once more.

Shivering, she rose and went to the curtain, just as the
curve of the sun began to rise in the sky like a lilac balloon.

4

"You can't say that!"

"Why?"

"Because you've never met her!"

"Look, I'm just saying," said Scott, "she's not your sort of
person."

"How do you know?"

"She's loaded, by all accounts. Houses all over the shop.
How can you have anything in common?"

"But we were best friends!"

"Yeah, but you're not now. She's moved on."

"And me?" shouted Jenny.

"What?"

"What about *me*?"

"What about you? She's moved on and you haven't," said Scott, turning to the array of bottles lined up on the table next to him.

"Well, maybe I should have! Or ... or maybe I could!"

"Jenny, you're being stupid," said Scott, not looking at her.

"No, I'm not!"

Jenny stood in front of Scott's deckchair in her swimsuit and shorts, hands on her hips, feet widely spaced, and continued to shout him down, while Scott refused to be ruffled.

"I'm not stupid, I'm being serious!"

"No, you're not," said Scott, carefully reapplying the sunscreen to his nose and face before moving down and changing bottles for chest and arms. "You're trying to pretend that you and Angela have something in common."

"Angel, her name's Angel," said Jenny, through gritted teeth, "And I'm not pretending anything. She's invited me down to Surrey for the weekend, remember."

"And I've said you're not going. She's a bad influence. You came back last night all overexcited and full of stupid ideas," said Scott, stroking and massaging his torso as he spoke. He changed bottles and began to smear lotion on the flesh not concealed beneath his miniscule black Speedo trunks.

"So it's stupid to expect a husband to want to make love to his wife?" said Jenny, quietly.

Scott looked up. "Don't go there, Jenny. We've been there, okay, and we made our decision. It's not easy for me either, you know."

Jenny gulped as salty tears flooded her face and mouth. Not easy for him! To love and lust after her own husband, knowing he didn't want her, and there he sits, almost naked in the garden with the children at her mum's! Not for the first time, she considered taking what she craved, but she knew it wouldn't work. She ran, crying, into the house.

"Cheers!"

"Cheers, mate!"

Rob and Justin sat in the beer garden at one of the white plastic tables under a huge umbrella and simultaneously reached for their boxes of cigarettes.

Justin was the first to speak. His close-cropped black hair glistened, a hint of grey at the temples, while his blue eyes shone brightly, his dark lashes the perfect foil to show them off. "I was well surprised to hear from Vincent. Haven't heard from him in years. Is he still coming?"

"Should be, should be, haven't heard otherwise," said Rob, dragging on his cigarette, blowing smoke out of the corner of his mouth as he spoke.

"You two keep in touch?"

"Yeah, kind of, see him every couple o' months or so."

Justin nodded and leaned back in the white plastic chair. His khaki shorts and tight vest showed off the deep, rich tan covering his body and the layers of muscles on his torso. His arms and shoulders were adorned with intricate Celtic tattoos that spiralled and twisted around the inflated musculature. "So what've you been up to?"

Rob, red and sweating in long, navy shorts and a white football shirt, filled in some details.

"So it's just you and Teresa now?"

Rob nodded. "It's not so bad. Barely see her, only when she wants money. She doesn't get paid much at the hairdressers - when she bothers to turn up!" Rob chuckled, "She's a good kid. She'll be okay."

"Vince said you'd seen Jenny and Angel? Can't really remember them."

"Yeah, " said Rob, pointing his pudgy index finger with purpose, "now that's what really got me thinking. Nearly fifteen years on, would you believe it!"

Justin finished his cigarette, flicking the butt on the ground, and reached for his pint. "Believe what?"

"Angel! And Jen looks pretty good, but I've seen her a few times over the years. Teresa went to the school where she worked, but Angel!"

Justin smiled. "Vince said you said she was hot, so now, on the strength of seeing two good looking women, you want to organise a party?"

"No. Yes. Maybe. Look," said Rob, "the morning after the school bash, it just came to me: why not have a party 'n' get our year back together again? We could even make it fancy dress! And there's Angel, of course. You gotta see Angel! Can you remember the last time you saw her? I'll get another," he said, standing up.

"Make it a pitcher. Save ya legs!" said Justin. Angel, Angel Parsons, Parson Parson's daughter, he thought, watching Rob's huge backside wobbling to the side entrance of the pub. Justin automatically lit a cigarette and tried to picture her, but he couldn't. He didn't remember much about the final year at school. Except the pussy. There for the taking from so many girls, especially after the Spring Dance. He didn't remember fucking Angel and he still couldn't picture her. Angel and Jenny? The geeks from 5M1. A picture of blonde curls and suspicious blue eyes appeared from his memory. Ah, Jenny. Her older brother was a twat, he recalled, but Angel?

Rob blundered into his thoughts. "You'd think there was a drought on! Bar's fuckin' heavin'!" He deposited two large golden jugs on the table before flopping into his seat. A flatulent echo resonated against the plastic. A few drinkers on the tables around them cheered and Rob lifted his glass to accept the recognition. He lit a cigarette.

"Saw Clare too," he said.

"Clare? Clare who?"

"You don't remember? Clare Maloney. Clare of the double D bangers, most accommodating bangers too!" recalled Rob. "She followed you around. She was mates wiv Danielle and Tiffany."

Recognition lit a spark. "Fuckin' hell, yeah, Clare," said Justin. "I remember! I was fuckin' all of them at one point!"

"But Clare told everyone…."

"….I was her boyfriend! I remember, bloody hell. How is she?"

"Honestly, not good, mate. Looks well old. Still got the bangers, but the face…" Rob looked down and shook his head sadly. "Tiffany not see her anymore?"

"How should I know?" said Justin. "She does what she likes."

"You two….?" said Rob.

"What?"

"Still together?"

"We're still married, if that's what you mean."

"Of course, and you've kids."

"Yeah, we have kids. To be honest, I've never thought the youngest, Chelsea, is mine, but the others are."

"Really?" said Rob, glass halfway to his mouth.

"It's no big deal," said Justin, smiling. "Keeps Tiffany happy 'n' off my back, so who cares?"

"But bringing up someone else's kid!"

"What! Look, Tiffany chooses to ignore my little…indiscretions. I'd be a fuckin' hypocrite if I started laying down the law!"

"But you still sleep together?"

"Mate, what is this? Yeah, and sometimes, if I've not had it for a bit, we have sex, okay. Its just sex," said Justin.

"Okay, cool," said Rob, his free hand flattened, mimicking 'lower' over the table, as heads around them turned. "Just interested."

Justin took a mouthful of lager. "You seeing anyone?"

"No, not at the mo. Too busy to think about it. When would I fit a woman into my busy life?" said Rob, grinning.

"So you want to host a party?" said Vincent. "Well, I'm your man!"

Pleasantries over, the three men soon returned to the reason of their summoning.

"So you're the man to organise a party?" said Rob, eyes watering with concentration as his hand missed his pint again.

"Of course I am, Rob."

"Yeah, yeah, the man with the contacts, that's Vincent," said Rob, winking at Justin. He aimed for his pint again and grabbed it with a cheer.

"Okay, so Rob seems to think we should see Angel again," said Justin, locking his gaze on Vincent.

"You think she's hot?"

"Scorchin' hot, according to Rob, but I haven't see her and can't recall her face from school and do we trust *his* choice in women?"

Justin and Vincent looked at Rob as he slouched back in his chair, nursing his glass on his belly, eyes closed and chins rumpled.

"The photo didn't look bad," Vincent admitted, reaching for his phone in the pocket of his cargo shorts. His spare hand unfastened both buttons of his navy polo as he scrolled down, revealing a flat, heavy gold chain at his throat that matched the one on his wrist. His manicured nails soon found the photo and he spun the phone to Justin across the table before sipping at his pint.

"Oh fuck!" said Justin, almost jumping in his seat. "Those eyes! I remember her!"

"Yeah, thought you might," said Rob, back in the conversation now.

"She's the one you stitched up at the Spring Dance," said Vincent, smiling as he surveyed his nails.

"Yeah, yeah!" chuckled Rob. "Like a kipper!"

"I think it was a koi carp, actually," said Vincent, smiling up at Justin, "but who cares, eh Just?"

Justin stared at the screen, occasionally pressing a button to keep it alight. Angel. Angel Parsons, looking straight at him - through him, almost. His guts twisted and he shivered, nausea quivering in his throat.

"You okay?" said Rob.

Then it was gone and Justin smiled up at his companions. "Yeah, great. Anyway, it was your idea, Vince."

Vincent sat back, twisting his glass on the table, surveying the bubbles and froth and condensation before lifting it half way to his lips. Eyes of pale silver blue shone out from beneath auburn eyebrows, topped with close cropped hair, while his pale, pock marked skin, pulled tight across his cheeks, began to pucker as his smile spread from ear to ear. "And a bloody good idea it was too! Cheers!" he said, and drank to his mates.

"Yeah," said Rob. "She knew nuffin'! Believed the whole shebang! You were ace, Just. She never suspected a thing!"

Justin nodded and smiled, raised his glass and drank deeply, the mercurial liquid traversing his guts.

"So it would be interesting to meet her now, wouldn't it, Just?" said Vincent, his eyes seeking Justin's.

"Course," said Justin. "But what if she doesn't show? Do we want a party enough if Angel doesn't turn up? And it's not a party, as such, is it? Or not just a party. I'm just sayin' it *would* be fun to meet up with a few old flames but how are we gonna contact everyone and all that?" Justin finished, red in the face and out of breath.

Vincent raised his eyebrows. "It's no big deal. I can sort out the invites, venue, catering, booze but I'm not running the whole show. If you want to do it, we're all in it together."

"Sure," said Rob. "Sure, mate, course we'll help. I'm your man if ya need a van or ought. Got a couple o' good lads who'd help settin' up. What you reckon?"

"Sounds good, Rob," said Vincent. "'Bout you, Just?"

"Have I ever let you down?" grinned Justin.

August

5

The sun had nearly reached its zenith as Eli escorted Jenny into the conservatory. Angel sat, her feet resting on a pale green beanbag, notebook on her lap, manicured nails tapping at the keyboard.

"Jenny, welcome!" she cried, putting the notebook on a side table and getting up, "Thank you, Eli. Would you ask Sophia to bring tea and some fruit, please. Come and sit," said Angel, to Jenny, "Make yourself at home."

They sat in mahogany chairs carved with luscious sinuous snakes and mythical beasts that wound around them. Pale green velvet padding helped to provide a sumptuous, comfortable seat.

"It's like a throne," said Jenny.

"Far more comfortable," said Angel, "Get those feet up. Good for the ankles in this hot weather."

Jenny did as she was bid, and sighed.

"Relaxed?" said Angel.

"Oh yes," said Jenny, sighing again. "This is … this is so…beautiful."

"I like a conservatory," said Angel. "There's another, much larger one, along the back of the East Wing."

The chairs were arranged so easy conversation could be accomplished with a mere glance of the head so they chatted and Jenny divulged the complex strategy needed to ensure her arrival and short stay. Tea and fruit arrived and as the young women left, Angel answered Jenny's look.

"It's a big house, Jen. Sophia likes to cook so she and Maddy help in the kitchen, and Aidan manages the grounds with Jed," she said, indicating the men now naked to the waist in the flowerbed. "Aidan's my partner and his passion is gardens so, why not experiment in mine? Eli and Zac work in security as well as being trained masseurs and fitness coaches."

Jenny's face remained bewildered as she fumbled with the sugar tongs.

"We've all been friends for years. We're more like a family really, each of us using our special talents to help the others," said Angel, helping herself to tea while she scanned Jenny's face for a response. She opened her mind a little and sensed Jenny's fear like a terrified bee, hot and buzzing in a fathomless jar.

"Tell you what, after tea I'll show you round so you'll feel more at home. Then we'll choose what to do for the rest of the day."

Angel's maxi dress, a cotton silk mix in peacock tones, swung from her shoulders as she walked from room to room while Jenny scuttling behind her, craned her neck back to view opulent ceilings and awesome skylights as Angel gave her a tour of the house. She heard Jenny's intake of breath as they entered the ballroom whose formal green walls, adorned with occasional trompe l'oeil panels depicting architectural columns wound round with greenery, were overseen by magnificent chandeliers. Fireplaces at each end of the room were banked high with tinder and logs, ready to be lit.

Back in the hallway, Angel opened a small wooden door and took Jenny's arm. "The pool room," she indicated. Starting indoors beneath catacomb-like arches and flowing out into the garden, the pool finished horizontally across the skyline.

Jenny gasped and Angel squeezed her arm. "Shall we?"

"What, swim? Here, now?"

Angel's laugh rang out with girlish abandon. "Of course. Only if you'd like to."

"But...I...I didn't bring a costume or a towel or..."

"There's no need. We have everything here, and you don't need swimwear in a private pool," said Angel, guiding her to a decked area furnished with cane chairs and a table, half in and half out of the sunshine. She turned to face her worried-looking friend and locked eyes with her, retrieving a few memories from her mind and offering them to Jenny. Jenny and Angel in the snow, building a huge dragon and Jenny flying down the hill on an old tin tray. Jenny and Angel on the swings in the park and Jenny flying so high she almost fell. Jenny and Angel in the woods, collecting feathers and hazel nuts and Jenny climbing a broad oak and shinning along a horizontal branch to hang by her knees. "When we met in London, Jen, you said you wanted to find yourself again. You could start here. It's safe. You can relax."

"It's like, it's like...swimming on top of a mountain!" said Jenny as they sat in their robes in the sun. "Certainly cold enough!"

They laughed easily. "I rarely heat it in the summer as it's so refreshing," said Angel, "but there's a roof that comes over, and it's heated in the winter. Fun?"

"Oh yes, thank you," said Jenny.

Angel opened her mind and sought for Jenny's fear again. She found the bee still buzzing but less frantically. Now, it was taking in the scenery.

"Skinny dipping in a strange pool on a Saturday afternoon. How did it feel?"

"Good," said Jenny, bobbing for the straw in her drink. "What's this?"

"Like it? It's a fruit blend with a tiny touch of vodka."

"It's lovely. Thank you so much for inviting me."

"No more thanks. I'm so glad you could come," said Angel.

They sat looking out over the gardens as the sun beamed down its summer love.

"Jenny, can I be honest?"

"Of course."

"I can feel your pain, the pain inflicted on you by others but only because I've known it myself. You need to let it go," said Angel, removing a chunk of orange from the lip of her glass and nibbling it. "I carried my pain for too long and then, alone in the world, I realised I'd been given a blank canvas. A new start. No one knew who I was, or who I'd been, so I could be anyone I wanted. I've worked through a lot of the pain. It's taken time, but I like who I am now."

"Mmm, me too. Not that I didn't like you at school," said Jenny, draining her glass to the bottom. "But you positively ooze confidence and style now. I'm getting used to it."

"And you could get used to this?" said Angel, wafting a hand at the world in general.

"Me? Oh yeah! Not going to happen though, is it?"

"Why don't we ensure we have the best girls weekend ever?" said Angel, ignoring the question. "Let's be fifteen again, but fifteen with what we know now."

"Now that," said Jenny, stifling a giggle, "is a very dangerous combination." She nodded towards Aidan and Jed, appearing in their eye line from the garden.

"I like danger," said Angel.

Minutes later, the four of them were splashing in the water.

"How's that?" said Angel.

"Mmm," said Jenny.

They lay naked, bodies pressed against white towelling and a smaller towel draped over their buttocks, and abandoned themselves to the strokes, pulls and thumps of an expert massage. Essential oils tickled their noses and they relished the oily bliss on their flesh. Having swapped

tailored black suits for tunics and trousers of pale blue, Eli
and Zac had been transformed and Angel and Jenny
surrendered their muscles to powerful hands.

"Well, who would have thought?" said Jenny.

"What?" said Angel, turning to face her.

"Me. Now. This. Fuck, the vodka's got my brain!"

"No, the sunshine's relit your inner child," said Angel.
"Fun, isn't it?"

"Oh, yes," said Jenny.

The phone in Jenny's bag grumbled again.

"You could answer it," said Angel.

Still in their towelling robes, Angel and Jenny curled up
on the sofa in front of the log fire in the elegant lounge.
Swathes of midnight blue curtains swamped the windows,
though night hadn't yet declared itself outside. The dark blue
ceiling and walls accentuated the feeling in the room of
winter evenings, roasted chestnuts and toasted crumpets.

Comfortable, cosy, relaxed and glowing, the real world
felt a lifetime away. "I don't want to," said Jenny.

"Fair enough," said Angel. "I thought you might like to
speak to him as the new you - or is that the old you, but with
newer bits!"

They laughed together and in that moment Jenny felt
brave - brave and new. She picked up the silent phone. "Four
missed calls and two messages," she said, calling up her
mailbox. Scott's scratchy voice, simmering with irritation,
enquired how she was, what she was doing and spurted out
mundane family whitterings. "Shall I?"

Angel shrugged and began to work on the fire, leaving
Jenny to face her fears. Smells from the grate seeped into the
room, cedar, sandalwood and juniper and Jenny breathed in
the fragrance, feeling her shoulders relax.

"Hi there," said Jenny. "I'm fine. Yes, journey was fine.
Yes it's been hot here too. Yes, I know, but I won't let her

unless she wears her hat. No, no, I'm not saying that…."
Jenny held the phone further from her ear as the ranting
continued, half listening yet more intent on Angel and the
fire. Smoke steamed off one log before the wood came alive
with golden sparks and crackled into roaring flames. Purple,
green, red, gold, blue - all the luxurious colours soared and
wrapped and intertwined amongst the wood and a pungent
waft caught the back of Jenny's throat.

"Scott, stop. Scott! Do you know something?" said Jenny.
"No, I don't want to hear it. No, shut up! Listen, I'm taking
two days off to catch up and relax with an old school friend.
Scott, shut up! I don't care what you think! I'm taking two
days for me, because I deserve it. I'm *not* deserting my
children *or* being a terrible person. Goodbye!"

Angel's lap was full of Jenny's curls as they re-ensconced on
the sofa. Angel rearranged them à la Rosetti as she spoke.

"I think you've identified the cause of your pain, Jen."

Jenny nodded. "You're right and every day for two years,
it's got worse. It's like having a hole in a tooth. I try to leave
it alone, manage quite well when Scott's at work, just the
occasional flick of my tongue over it but, as soon as I'm near
him…"

"Then, while you're here, let's take Scott out of the
equation. He's holding you back. I can feel it. Let's indulge
'Jenny'. Let's have a party."

"A party? What, here? Now?"

"Why not? What could be more fun in a child's life than a
party?"

"I don't know," said Jenny, frowning. "I didn't like them
much. Never won the pass the parcel, and that's before you
got a prize in every layer," she said, leaning up on her elbow
and sipping her drink of choice, vintage champagne. "I
wasn't mean enough for musical chairs, and strawberry ice
cream makes me puke."

Angel laughed, an earthy, rip-roaring laugh that Jenny
loved. "I meant a more adult one, though you shall have
games if you want to," she said, stroking Jenny's arm. "I
thought we could dress up."

"Fancy dress?" said Jenny, "I don't know."

"I'll be more specific: a themed party. A Venetian masked
ball, or an Egyptian court, or an Edwardian soiree...."

"Or a Roman orgy. Fuck, did I say that out loud?"

Halved by an organza curtain and pastel fairy lights, the
ballroom shone like a wooded glade. Greenery drooled over
towering candlesticks and oozed over the floor. The single
chandelier was unlit by electric light but glistened and
twinkled to the tune of four candles at its quarters. Long low
tables and cushions embraced the walls while coloured
lanterns defined a large circular space in the centre of the
room. And then the music began.

Standing in the doorway, Jenny felt the drum in her heart.
Each beat bypassed her ears, reached inside her and drew her
into the dance. She stepped forward once and then again.
One step at a time, and with every step her senses expanded.
Sweet smells registered on her taste buds and incense
seduced her eyes until the beat began to quicken and she
drank it all in. She felt the story of the flute brush her skin,
softly clad in rosebud voile, where it stroked her bare
shoulders, drew the curves of her breasts and, feather light,
caressed her legs, making her toes tingle.

A tiny lilac fairy scampered into the circle on her toes,
smiling and beckoning for Jenny to join her. The beat moved
Jenny's feet, one step at a time, while the flute roused her
body and she began to move. Her arms floated up and down
in endless waves, weightless as if strung by a puppet master,
and then she laughed as the tinkling bells loosened her
throat. Maddy laughed too, and fairies of lilac and rose
circled and twirled in the candlelight.

More fairies joined the circle. Shades of green, blue, peach and cream turned and twirled, mixing and touching, laughing and smiling as the music lifted them. Green eyes of autumn, blue of ice, wings tipped with diamonds, hair threaded with ribbons, the sweetness of frankincense and the tickling of champagne like the tendrils of a summer breeze drew Jenny in and included her in the dance.

The music began to quieten, first the bells and then the flute, until just the drum beat remained. Sophia drew Jenny gently to the cushions where Jed sat, naked bar a skirt of green felt. His long legs were shaggy with tan fur and Jenny smiled as she leaned into him.

Only two dancers remained on the floor, still stepping to the beat of the drum. Aidan, clad like Jed, his chest bare and a skirt of felt over his furry legs, stepped around the edge of the circle, his head bowed, while in the centre danced Angel. While each fairy wore a single colour, Angel wore them all and yet none of them, as the folds of her iridescent dress reflected and fractured the light. Step by step the beat quickened and changed its rhythm, forcing Aidan to step faster, dance faster, lifting and turning him in its wake, but all the while Angel stood unfolding, turning and stepping slowly, always careful not to meet the eyes of her suitor. As Jenny watched the dance unfold, she was in a fairy glen. She smelt the greenness of summer on the wisp of a breeze and the warmth of the sun through the foliage. Jed took her hand and they joined the Queen of Summer in her dance.

"Thought I'd find you here," called Angel, dropping her robe and walking into the pool. She waited until Jenny drew level, then swam breaststroke next to her. In silence, they freed their aching muscles and loosened their minds.

"I fancied a swim to clear my head," said Jenny, towelling herself down and wrapping her robe around her. "I don't feel hung over. Just a little muzzy and confused."

"I've had breakfast sent to the East Wing conservatory. It's a lovely spot to catch the morning sun," said Angel, wrapping the soft towelling around her and scrunching up her natural dark brown curls. "Shall we?" She offered Jen her arm and they strolled through the quiet house.

"I've been thinking," said Jenny. "Was last night real?"

"What do you think?"

"Well, that's the problem," said Jenny. "It felt real last night - I think - but looking back, it feels hazy and odd."

Angel opened the door to the vast orangery that sprawled around the south and east of the house. Luscious vines clung to walls and trellises, while pots were abundant with greenery and fruits, tickling the palate with smells of citrus. They ducked under the undergrowth to a table set with coffee, fruit and croissants.

"Talk as you nibble," said Angel, tearing off a hunk of croissant. "Talk it through and see where it leads you."

"Okay," said Jenny, knife poised balancing a blob of glistening marmalade. "It started before the dance. All day I'd felt these tingles in my arms and legs and even my head. This sounds nuts!"

"No, it doesn't, go on."

"Well, the tingles seemed to enliven me, energize me somehow. I'd never have believed I could be so relaxed splashing in a pool with strangers, men at that! But no guilt, and it felt natural. And then the dance. I felt like me but in retrospect....Oh I don't know!"

"That's fine. Do you remember dancing?" said Angel, sitting back holding a white pottery bowl steaming with fresh coffee.

"Yes, yes I think so."

"And how did it feel?"

"It was wonderful! No embarrassment or worries. My arms and legs, all of me felt in tune with the music and the people. I remember feeling arms holding me and swaying with me gently and stroking me. It felt like love." Jenny stopped, sadness obliterating the sun, tears welling in her eyes.

Angel reached forward and took her hand. "It was real, Jenny, all of it, especially the love. You made it so, we all did. It's complicated, but I can try to explain if it helps."

Jenny's tears subsided and she nodded, munching her croissant and pouring orange juice into a tall slim glass.

"The concept of reality is a question for quantum physicists to ponder but for us, let's think of it as choices. How did you feel when we met last month in Chin Chin's?"

"I was nervous," said Jenny, blushing. "But then I really enjoyed myself and it was lovely catching up. No, more that that. I felt I had my old friend back."

Angel smiled. "And?"

"And not just my old friend, but a friend who'd done more and been to places I could only dream of, and yet she still wanted to be friends with me. I felt warm, loved and happy."

"I am glad," said Angel, sincerely. "but how long did the feeling last?"

"It faded a little on the train home," said Jenny, "and once I was indoors…and then Scott."

"So once home, back in your home life, how did the lunch date feel?"

"Hey, you're right! It felt unreal, as if it almost happened to someone else! Why was that?"

"I don't have all the answers, Jen, but as I said, it all comes down to choices. You chose to meet me for lunch, to be 'Jenny on her own', going up to town. It wasn't a usual reality for you but you chose it, in the same way as you chose to react the way you did when you got home."

"You mean, let the feelings of disappointment, stagnation and sadness back in?"

"Yes, and yesterday and last night you chose the reality you experienced."

"So somewhere another Jenny, in another reality, didn't go to the ball?" said Jenny, laughing.

"She didn't even come for the weekend!"

"So last night I was choosing the reality I experienced?"

"Yes and no," said Angel, "We helped create the reality for you, but you chose how you interacted with it."

"You mean the lights, the music, the ambience?"

"You've got it," Angel nodded, "It's like putting on a Buddhist chant if you want to relax, or Led Zeppelin if you want to play air guitar!"

Jenny laughed before adding, "But now I have to go home."

"But you can still choose," said Angel. "You always have a choice, however hard it may seem." Angel opened her mind once more and sought for Jenny's fear. She found the bee, still buzzing but this time hovering over the flowers, curious and sensitive to the delights they withheld but wary of the consequences of immersing its body in pleasure.

"I've a lot to think about," said Jenny, "But thanks, Angel, thanks so much."

"Please, don't," said Angel, shaking her head. "It's been lovely to have you here. I'd like to think I've helped but…I sensed a longing in you, Jen, even at the school. You were hiding behind your beautiful smile and all I saw was sadness and pain in your eyes. I'm just….I just hope I haven't made it worse." She twiddled a ringlet from her hair and bit her lip as she looked at Jenny.

"No, oh no!" said Jenny, putting down her glass and reaching for Angel's hands. "I needed you, I can see that now. I needed it all laid out in front of me. I've known my life's a mess for a long time, Angel, and I've been sitting back and allowing it to squash me, suffocate me, the real me, the old one with the new bits!" They laughed, but Jenny continued. "No, but seriously, you've given me the confidence to face things and not bury them any more."

Angel shook her head. "I gave you nothing, just the time and space to choose your own reality. It's all up to you now. Everyone makes their own choices."

One woman chewed like a raptor, occasionally stopping long enough to swig from a diet drink can while the other devoured the all day breakfast in front of her.

The masticator looked around her at the stained yellow walls, rickety, chipped melamine tables and assorted chairs, most with the stuffing on view.

"Sure this is the place?"

The eater nodded and spoke between mouthfuls, "Uh ha. She said she might be delayed."

Tiffany checked her almost-Rolex watch and sighed. "Haven't got all day, you know!"

"Haven't you?" said Danielle, turning to a plate of butter encrusted processed white bread. She carefully folded each slice, mopping bean juice from her plate.

"Why couldn't we meet at hers?"

A pause ensued as the sixth and final slice mopped carefully, not missing a drop. "Said she was in the middle of decorating."

"Do ya reckon?"

Danielle shrugged, surfacing from her plate with a sigh and reaching for her mug of tea. She began measuring in spoonfuls from the sugar cellar.

"Not good for you, all that sugar."

"Not good for you, all those chemicals," said Danielle, still counting.

Tiffany sighed, looked at her watch again, and retrieved her mirror from her almost-Gucci bag. Routine surveillance began. Eyebrows, still smooth. False lashes, still intact. Blue eyeshadow, abundant. Cheeks, highlighted. Lipstick, perfect. No, a little more gloss maybe. Tiffany applied the necessary embellishment and continued. Teeth, clean. She tipped the mirror. Tits, magnificent. She tipped again. Fringe, just a little tweaking. Hair, perfectly straight.

"Do you have to do that *all* the time?" said Danielle.

"I don't!"

The bell over the door clanged and with the merest glance, Tiffany was out of her seat and at the counter at the same time as the two young builders.

"No, you first," she said, her smile and breasts like a flashlight in a forgotten cellar.

The men smiled and mumbled and she smiled back, leaning back on her wedges, relaxed and welcoming. Their order of 'take out' however, proved her efforts fruitless and she ordered another diet drink with a sigh and went back to the table.

"Can't you stop thinking with your fanny for one second?"

"Can't you stop thinking with your belly?"

The next clanging of the door announced Clare's arrival. She stood, worried and dishevelled, scanning the tables in panic before Danielle recognised her and raised her arm. Clare nodded, bought coffee from the counter and tentatively joined them. Smiling pleasantries, the tallest of tall stories and giggling reminiscences led them to a hush. Unsaid words filled the air, knocking on the ears, demanding the mouth to spurt forth.

"So you're in recruitment?" said Danielle, taking in the shabby cardigan that failed to disguise an even shabbier dress.

"Yeah, how 'bout you?" said Clare, pulling the bobbled acrylic to her throat.

"Taking time for a career change at the moment," said Danielle. "Looking for a new direction."

"Yeah, right," said Tiffany, trying to produce a sneer with botoxed brow and filled lips. "Sitting on your arse, you mean."

"Thanks for that," said Danielle. She looked at Clare and smiled a grimace. "I've had a tough year. Not been well. Had to give up my job. It isn't easy to start again, 'specially when money's tight, something some people wouldn't know about."

Clare returned her smile. "It ain't easy. On your own. Work's…on and off, you know. I do my best," she said, rallying to her own cause. "I've never been a shirker."

"While some people can rely on someone else…" said Danielle.

"Stop talking like I ain't 'ere!" snapped Tiffany. "Danni, you're a fine one to talk! Okay, so you fink I've got a cushy number, but you're not backward in coming forward when I'm handin' out freebies!" Her anger brought colour to her cheeks, heating the air between them. "It ain't my fault you got dumped and left high and dry! No one knew he'd do that, not even you by all accounts. I always said he was too fuckin' smart, fancy words and fancy suits, but you wouldn't listen! Stop whingein' and find yourself a real man!"

"What, like Justin?" The words stampeded from Clare's mouth before she could stop them. Her body shook and sweated under the prickly acrylic.

Tiffany paused and looked at Clare, then at Danielle. Time had expanded Danielle's face, or at least that which could be seen beneath rolls of useless fat, while Clare's face looked ravaged by a holocaust, lined, strained and scared. Danielle was a natural brunette but the non-styled hair and the increasing grey threads added nothing to smarten or enhance her countenance, while Clare had sought solace in seeking to be a blonde bombshell. Unfortunately, the straw-like yellow mass on top of her head, black roots showing through, proclaimed her scarecrow rather than movie star. Tiffany hadn't been first in line when the brains were handed out but she summed up this train of conversation swiftly and succinctly. "Let's not do this. This ain't mates' talk. It's in the past."

"But he said he loved me." Clare's voice was tiny and raw, forced to her mouth by the nauseous pain in her belly. She hung her head.

Danielle touched her hand. "He said he loved all of us."

"But it wasn't his fault," said Tiffany. "He told me once," she leaned forward, "he thought she'd put a spell on 'im, after the Spring Dance." She nodded as her audiences eyes widened. "Every offer, every girl, every opportunity. He couldn't resist. He said it was her eyes. Ferocious lust, he called it."

"I'm not blaming him, or you," said Clare, looking up. "I know it was *her*. Told her as much at the school reunion."

"Really?" said Danielle, intrigued. "What happened?"

More drinks and toasted teacakes pampered the speakers and produced comfortable conversation.

"So although I'm married to 'im," said Tiffany, "you're not missing much. I learnt a long while ago not to hang around waiting for 'im to be *my* man. He's a worker, I'll grant you that, good builder, pretty good father - but good husband? I don't fink so."

"So how do you feel about seeing her again?" said Clare. "I mean, this is why you called, right? To see about this party?"

"I called 'cos we 'aven't spoken in ten years, Clare. Justin came back from the pub 'avin' spoken with Vincent and Rob, and your name came up," said Tiffany. She paused, stroking her fringe to her face. "I thought it was long enough. I…we wanted to see you. We were good together once."

Clare smiled, displaying her missing teeth. Lines ran from the sides of her mouth and eyes, scoring her dry skin, and tears gathered in the folds. "I've missed you both," she mumbled.

"Come on," said Danielle, "we're here now. Skeletons aired 'n' ready for a new start."

"Yeah," said Tiffany. "We should be a gang again, like the old days."

"You mean 'All for one and one for all!'?"

Tiffany looked bemused. "I was finkin' more like Charlie's Angels!"

September

6

Jenny sat at the kitchen table as rain fell in rivulets down the window distorting the view of the garden like a weird glass in a hall of mirrors.

Alone in the house she had time. Time to herself. She'd come back from Angel's full of ideas and plans but the pressures of full time care of the children and the housework, shopping, washing, all of it, had become her reality again. She'd wanted to talk to Scott, but she didn't know where to begin, as trying to have a conversation without causing offence or it ending in an argument had been beyond her these past two years.

Jenny stopped rain gazing and flicked the switch on the kettle and as the rumbling began, her silence and therefore her thoughts were interrupted and she began clearing the drainer of the washing up.

The problem was, she didn't know where to start and it was too easy to fill her time with domesticity rather than face up to her predicament. A pang of inspiration hit her and she reached to the back of a top cupboard and found a mug. It was big, red and a little chipped but the writing and picture were still visible. 'You're a star!' it declared and she filled it with black coffee and a smile. Angel had bought it for her all those years ago, after the Spring Dance. Her mind drifted back and another idea broke the surface. She placed the mug on the table and scampered upstairs, returning at the same pace carrying a wooden box the size of a boot sized shoebox. With a key from her key ring, Jenny's box was open and she began revisiting her happy memories as the clouds outside disgorged the last of their booty. She laid the treasures on the table before her. Each brought a joy she'd forgotten and a warm calmness settled on her shoulders. Children's drawings, feathers, shells and home-made cards covered the table and photos, curled and fingered but still full of life and love, smiled up at her. Her parents' wedding, Tim as a baby, Jenny and Tim on donkeys at the seaside, photos of Finn and Scarlett, nan, grandpops, Scottie the dog and Figaro the cat. Angel and Jenny before the Spring Dance.

Jenny gazed at the young girls, posing for Tim's camera in the hallway at home. Her own radiant skin and sparkling innocent eyes smiled back at her and while Angel's stance was nervous and awkward, her brown eyes were not. All seeing eyes looked out from the photo, hiding all knowledge from those who looked into them but confident in their own secret wisdom. While Jenny stared intently at the faces, she recalled Angel's recent words, how she'd known as a child she wasn't welcome in her parents' life and how their loss, then and now, was no great one to her. Bagpuss, the marmalade cat jumped onto her lap and she stroked him as she thought about her own childhood and how lucky she was, about her children and all the aspects of her life that made it special. 'Count your blessings' Nana Ward used to say so Jenny did.

The rain stopped teaming down the window and weak autumn sunlight lit the table with a yellowish glow. At the bottom of the box lay the final envelope, the last of the treasures in the box of memories. Held in her hand the envelope trembled as she opened it. Tears ran down her face as she read Scott's only love letter but the envelope retained a further missal, dated ten years after the first. How long had it taken him to pluck up the courage to write this? How long had he felt that their life, their marriage was too much to bear? How long had he lied before telling her the truth and changing their lives forever? But he did. No discussion, no arguments, then or now. His way or no way and as her thoughts mingled, grew, went off at a tangent and shouted to be heard, Jenny felt the anger rising from her stomach in increasingly painful waves of nausea. She'd agreed to his demands, but why? As if slapped in the face with a wet cloth, Jenny raised her hand to her cheek and it glowed, raw and aching beneath her touch. Because I let him, because I love him, them, everyone. Because I didn't want anyone to be upset. A howl drew abreast the nausea waves and pulled ahead, forcing her jaws apart and all the tears, the pain and hurt came crashing out. As Bagpuss leapt free of the torrent, Jenny ran and curled up on the sofa, heaving sobs racking her chest, her limbs shaking and her heart bleeding.

Finding the house unlit on their return, Maureen Parkes insisted on going in first, an easy task as the children were both asleep in their car seats. She found her daughter sleeping soundly on the sofa, it's throw curled around her like a nest. In the fading light she saw the memory box open and empty, surrounded by its treasure. She refilled it carefully, smiling at a photo here and a picture there.

Bumps and chinks from the kitchen roused Jenny from her slumber and her mum hurried over to greet her.

"Oh, Mum!"

Maureen held her and rocked her as she sobbed, stroking Jenny's hair while tears ran down her own cheeks.

"I can't Mum! I can't do this any more!"

"I know, love. I know."

Colin Parkes sat in his car with a mug of tea, Vivaldi on the radio and his grandchildren snoring softly behind him. He'd not questioned Maureen why he needed to stay with the children; Jenny needed to talk to her Mum and this was the best way of doing it. He rested into his seat, easing it back one more notch for comfort. It'd been a good day and a long one with the drive and all the walking but he loved being a granddad. Hmm, Granddad. He'd been feeling his advancing years lately. Not that he couldn't hold his own in one on one football or basketball with Finn, or shin the wrong way up the slide when necessary, but he'd found himself tired in the middle of the day. Indigestion had plagued him lately too, his food either loitering on the way down or requesting to come back up. And some of the aches in his arms and legs had got worse. Oh, listen to you Granddad!

7

The rain hadn't dampened the premier. Stars continued to glitter under the random fire of paparazzi bulbs and Aidan and Angel had taken their turn up the red carpet. In her gown of purple crushed velvet held halter style at the neck by a diamond collar, with strands of diamonds streaming down her back and from her ears and her hair twisted and pinned on her head, Angel looked the part of movie star but had played her not inconsiderable part, by marketing the film. As they stepped from the limousine, they'd been spot lit by cameras and Aidan had basked in the attention.

Angel loved to watch Aidan with the rich and famous at events like these. He made everyone around him relax and smile and she often wondered what a dangerous con artist he would make if he ever chose to pursue such an avenue. He'd also taken the opportunity at the after party to promote his landscaping business and his newest project, vertical gardens, while Angel had worn her corporate mask, relied on non-committal conversation and been grateful when the party broke up.

She stood at the mirror in the bedroom of Aidan's London apartment, boxing up her jewellery to go back to the bank and gently removing her make-up. Still wearing her gown, she unpinned her hair, causing cascades of wavy curls to tumble over her shoulders and chest.

"I couldn't believe he'd heard of me!" said Aidan, returning from the bathroom, rubbing his hair with a towel. "He's got a house in Beverly Hills!"

"Unfasten me, please," said Angel.

As the tiny clasps were loosened, Angel's dress fell from her shoulders to the floor and she turned, arms across her breasts, wearing nothing but a smile. As her fingertips brushed her nipples, a thrill of pleasure traversed her flesh, culminating between her legs. The room was soon transformed with a golden glow from the sidelights by the bed and Aidan lay her down, covering her body in sweet kisses while she, in turn, traced the muscles on his arms and chest, feeling the tautness of expectation beneath his skin. Shoulders, necks, ears were kissed and bottoms and breasts caressed in a blur of honeyed pleasure that enveloped them both.

Aidan lay on his back and Angel kissed his belly, her bottom near his shoulder demanding to be stroked. His hands obliged while his fingers sought her soft, aroused flesh and with Angel on top of him, they wallowed in topsy-turvy. Tongues, mouths, lips and teeth brought moans and sighs while skin heated and purred with pleasure. Angel gasped as Aidan pulled her to him and he watched her face betraying her pleasure as with every thrust he thrilled her. Her hands sought his face and she brought his succulent lips to hers, kissing and biting.

Aidan released his hand from her bottom and they rolled together, limbs entwining, fingers and lips seeking while all the while Aidan thrust and withdrew with slow, deep strokes. Pulse racing, Angel climbed on top, Aidan's feet off the bed almost touching the floor, as she took control of his manhood from above. With her feet on the bed by his hips, she watched the excitement on his face as she administered slow dips, followed by a few faster, almost withdrawing his length before taking him slowly and deeply again. Limbs, tongues, breasts, flesh burning, genitals screaming, Aidan lay her on her stomach, kissed her bottom one last time and then smothered her with his body.

Angel felt his arm across her belly pulling her bottom up and towards him until her sweet spot expanded and she cried out in ecstasy as he, in turn, exploded his passion and love inside her.

"Did you speak to Donnie Spellman?"

"Which one was he?"

"Small, dark, with the model on his arm in the green dress," said Aidan, overtaking a lorry in the Mercedes.

Angel shook her head. "I remember the dress but not the man."

"He's got contacts in Italy, Rome mostly. His brother and mother own hotels and a restaurant there. Donnie owns a casino or two. Monaco, I think he said, or was it Cannes?"

"Didn't Georgio Spellman date Natasha Fox for a while, the girl who was originally to star in the film?"

"You're right, though I didn't see *him* there."

"But Donnie's a good contact?"

"For sure," said Aidan, "But you know what these people are like. I'll be patient, but I'm keeping a finger on the pulse of this one. A toehold in Rome could prove both useful and lucrative."

The convertible was unconverted as they sped down the motorway in incessant drizzle and drifting fog. The queue to cross south was backed up so, they chatted easily, moving one car length at a time, discussing Aidan's networking success the previous evening.

Angel loved his excitement and enthusiasm, confidence with new people and his relaxed attitude to business. Most of all she admired his surety in the belief that he would succeed, in fact not just succeed but fly to the top of his profession. The energy he gained from working with the earth fired his passion to combine nature with structure, creating gardens for people that truly stood alone as works of art. Angel expanded her companies with less fervour. She kept to herself the conversations she'd had last evening. Nellie Van Firtel had pleaded and Carolena Morton had begged but a fashion house label and a range of perfume were not on Angel's list of priorities at the moment. The small part she'd played in Hincham's last movie had exposed her to enough celebrity and she wasn't out to pander for more and if Aidan knew the part she'd been offered by Clint Greenstone in his next movie…

The sun was forcing it's light through grey clouds as they pulled up onto the driveway and steam rose up from the car as the rain dried and the sun began to bake metal.

"Fancy a swim?" asked Aidan as he retrieved their bags from the boot.

"I was hoping for a game of tennis," said Angel, taking her handbag, "But it's too wet."

"Pool it is then," said Aidan.

The fire blasted flames up the chimney. The rain outside plunged vertically into the earth until a violent gust buffeted raindrops against the windows, drowning out the crackling of the fire.

Aidan drew the curtains while Angel lit candles on a low table to illuminate their feast. Fragrant pilau rice steamed from a central bowl dotted with shining peas and succulent sultanas while a pan of chana glistened and beckoned them, smells of coriander and tomatoes watering their mouths.

"Sorry you missed your tennis," said Aidan, poking the fire sending tinder crashing before he piled on more logs.

"Not much of an Indian summer," said Angel, spooning food into two bowls and passing one to Aidan.

"Thanks. Is that what they forecast?"

Angel nodded. "Supposed to start yesterday. Weekends due to be scorching." A moan began a crescendo that grew to a howl and culminated with a wet crash on the windows. "Can't see it myself.

"You working tomorrow?" said Aidan, "Hmm, gorgeous. Did you make this?"

"It's from a recipe Sophia gave me from Daljit. Came with hand-blended choli mix. I cheated and used tinned chickpeas to save time but yes, all my own work," said Angel. "Mmm, it is good. Yes, I'm working. Stacks of mail and emails from Fiona and I'll need to call her about next week?"

"New York?"

"Only four days but still, I was hoping to play tennis before I went. You're around at the weekend, aren't you?"

Aidan nodded, eating.

"I thought I'd invite Jed and Sophia but, with the weather as it is…"

"Well, I'm not supposed to be working tomorrow but Jed wanted a hand with a job in Kent, though the weather might have finished that off too!"

"It's a shame."

"I'll call Jed anyway, sweetheart and I can help you tomorrow, if not."

"And Sophia is staying at Maddy's house this week while she's in Edinburgh…"

"We could always set up table tennis in the ballroom."

"I hadn't thought of that."

"It's not the same, I know," said Aidan, helping himself to another spoonful of chickpeas, "I know you like your tennis."

"Good idea though," said Angel, "Much better than indoor football."

Aidan laughed. "But that was fun."

"But *you* get over excited! Football and chandeliers do *not* go well together!"

Naked and glowing, they lay on rugs and cushions before the fire, Angel eating lemon sorbet and Aidan smoking a cigarette. The wind outside had ceased its anger and the rain its velocity. A velvety evening embraced the lounge, as phrases of exquisite jazz touched their ears and Indian incense tickled their noses and it was here, like this that Angel was at her happiest. No clothes to clutter the human body energized with food and drink and warmed by the fire in the grate. No people to intrude, to demand or enquire of her to use her mind or steal her time. Just she and Aidan, together and as they held each other, an owl called outside and then again and again, until the answer came.

Aidan began to kiss her. His mouth at first soft and gentle and then, as his hands sought her breasts, firmer and more impatient. She pulled back from him and looked into eyes of vibrant jade, sparkling and glittering with desire. She felt the warmth in her feet and legs as the flames caressed her, her skin swelling and prickling with excitement.

"Am I the mistress here?" she whispered.

"No," said Aidan, pushing her onto her back. "*I* am the master."

With Finn dropped off at school and Scarlett at pre-school, Jenny hurried home as a weary autumn sun attempted to smile upon her. It was the first day of term and with two free hours before her dinner lady shift began, Jenny was determined to make the most of them.

Since talking to her mum and making her decision Jenny felt lighter. Her old determination had begun to resurface and though sleep had proved fitful these past two nights, she felt exhilarated by the ideas that were forming in her mind.

The thought of life without Scott was a scary one but one that needed to be faced and Jenny reasoned that the sooner she made the break from him, the easier it would be to begin plans for the future.

In her diary last night she had started a list but at the moment it only contained people, those she loved who would be affected by her decision. At the top were the children and then Scott. Last night as Scott snored, she played the scene over and over in her head, how she would tell him and each time, his reaction was different and each one left her cold and empty.

The engagement calendar on the kitchen table reminded Jenny that Finn and Scarlett had birthday parties to attend on Saturday and Finn again the following week so, with her heart banging in her ears, Jenny decided that Saturday was the day to tell Scott, while the children were out of the house. She marked a star against the day before clearing away the breakfast remains and filling a bowl at the sink. Relief flooded over her, calming her heart. The decision was made.

On the back of the chair, her phone rang in her handbag.

"Hi mum."

"Jenny, oh Jen. I'm sorry hun…"

"What's the matter? What's happened?"

"It's your dad. He's in hospital. He's had a heart attack."

October

8

"Thanks so much for coming with me," said Jenny, as they cruised up the impressive driveway to the house.

"It's my pleasure. It's good to see you smiling," said Tim, adjusting his grey beard on his smooth chin, "Not sure how long *this* will last though!"

Jenny laughed and suddenly shivered as the parking attendant beckoned for them to stop.

"You'll be fine," said Tim, "You look amazing."

"Angel let me choose what I wanted," said Jenny, smoothing the pale blue velvet down her arms as she got out of the car, "She had the pointy hat and everything!"

"You and me both!" laughed Tim, withdrawing his own black hat from the back seat and giving the car keys to the attendant.

Merlin, resplendent in starred hat, gold belted tunic and black cape entered the party with the Lady Guinevere, ethereal in pale blue velvet and chiffon, upon his arm. Jenny spotted Zac and they exchanged a nod and a smile.

"Friend of yours?"

"He works for, well, he's a friend of Angel's," said Jenny, as they walked up the wide steps to the arched double doors. "She'd offered any help needed for the party when she replied so when the arranged security let Vincent down, he called her. This is her friend's house too, while she's away travelling. Oh, there's Sally and someone I recognize but can't put a name to. Oh Tim, I hope you're not going to be bored."

"Will you stop worrying, sis. I'm a big boy, you know. I shall have one drink, lots of food and amaze the ladies with the tricks I can do with my wand!"

The entrance hall, marble floored and oak panelled was awash with fairy lights, while the massive central chandelier twinkled its welcome from above. A line had formed at a table by the staircase and Tim and Jenny joined it behind a six foot tall Batman and a generously endowed female Robin. Batman introduced his wife to Jenny as the line shuffled forward. Ticked off the guest list, Jenny and Tim were offered champagne or juice and given directions for the dining room, rest rooms and the garden room. The ballroom hummed with conversations and laughter, bubbling above the beat of disco music as they approached. Rob in blue tights and cape, red shorts and a blue tucked in t shirt bearing a red 'S' on a yellow background, microphone in hand, greeted them.

"Hi Jen. How ya doin'?"

"I'm good thanks. Nice costume."

"Thanks," said Rob. He grinned. "Feel a bit of a plonker in tights but you gotta go the whole hog for a party."

"Definitely!" said Jenny, mesmerized by the twenty stone Superman before her.

"Err, who've you come as? I've gotta announce you," said Rob, wielding the mic. "You someone from Hogwarts?"

"No," said Tim, "I'm Merlin and this is Guinevere."

"Oh, right," said Rob.

"Arthurian legends?"

"If you say so," said Rob, shaking his head and switching on the mic. "Merlin and Jennyvere!"

"That'll do," said Jenny, leading Tim by the arm as a queue began to form behind them.

Banqueting tables and chairs around the edge of the room were half full as they made a circuit, Jenny scanning for faces she recognized. A voice here and there of 'Jenny!" beckoned them over and Tim stood smiling happily as Jenny caught up with her old schoolmates. An SS officer stood with the DJ, surveying the room like an ironic, benevolent headmaster.

"Vanilla Ice and Charlie's Angels!" Jenny turned to see the new arrivals, Justin and Tiffany strutting into the room and Clare and Danielle keeping close behind them. Conversations ceased at the announcement but different muttered ones began upon recognition of the four. Justin greeted the SS officer with a high five and a 'Bro!' while the women sought welcoming faces and a table to share. They found none.

Jenny and Tim had taken seats with two couples, the wives of which knew Jenny from school and work and conversation bubbled about the latest arrivals.

"Can you believe the size of her? I wouldn't have recognized her on her own!" said Marilyn Monroe.

"Maybe she's got glandular problems," said Cher.

"I don't know," said Marilyn, "But what on earth possessed her to wear a red catsuit!"

"It's certainly an eyeful," said Elvis.

"Justin and Tiffany still together?"

"Looks like it," said Marilyn, "Though everyone knows their youngest isn't his."

"Really?" said Cher.

"Oh yeah!" said Marilyn. "Justin may be tanned, but he's not *that* brown!"

"Really! Does Justin know?"

"Oh yeah, but she lets him do what he wants so he doesn't care *what* she does! I was at Reds Saturday week for Rachel's 30th. 'Member Rachel? Still stay in touch from antenatal. Well, Justin…"

The gossip buzzed on and Tim lent into Jenny and nodded towards the DJ stand. "That's him, isn't it? Spring Dance?"

Jenny nodded.

"And by the conversation…," said Tim, nodding towards Marilyn.

"Trash then and trash now!" said Jenny.

"And the women?"

"All of them! Rob's okay," Jenny conceded, "Just easily led."

"And the bloke at the mic makes up the whole gang?"

Jenny nodded. "Vincent. Nasty piece of work. Was living with Elaine Holt for a while, remember her?"

"Not really," said Tim.

"They have a son," said Jenny, "He's the kid who puts worms in people's lunch boxes and pulls legs off daddy long legs. Sounds like childish mischief, I know, but when they were studying mini beasties, he got into the classroom at lunchtime and drowned the snails, spiders, everything in red paint. I heard the teachers," she continued, "And his reason for doing it? To watch them dying, he said. Bet there's 666 tattooed on his skull!"

"How old?" said Tim.

"Four!"

"Hmm, someone should nip that in the bud as soon as, or he'll only get worse. What's Elaine like?" said Tim, watching Vincent and Justin laughing at the DJ stand.

"Nice girl," said Jenny, "But not very bright and a bit soft, you know."

"Does he spend much time with his dad?" said Tim, not taking his eyes off the men, whose repartee had begun to include surreptitious glances around the room.

"King Arthur and Morgan le Fay!"

Tim's body held off breathing for a while at the sight of Angel entering the ballroom and when it started, he could feel his heart beating in his ears, resounding with expectation. He'd seen it in her all those years ago but the young, quiet Angel had rarely had the opportunity to explore her femininity then but now, as a stunning, confident woman entered the ballroom, he saw the fulfilled potential of that intelligent, humorous brown eyed girl.

"It's good to see you again," said Tim, as he and Angel sat in the garden room. Screened and partly covered, the room boasted cane tables and chairs and four outdoor heaters. Tim and Angel sat by one of them.

"You too," said Angel. They sat in warm silence.

He'd been entranced on seeing her in the doorway; her straight dark hair to her waist, shining like Japanese lacquer ware and her medieval dress of midnight blue, tied with a simple gold cord. He'd barely noticed her companion in shining livery. Just Angel, in her simple blue dress that fitted every curve to perfection. The recollection rendered him tongue tied.

"How's your dad doing?" said Angel, sipping from her champagne flute.

"Doing well," said Tim, "You know Jenny…we…all of us appreciated you coming ….and helping." He looked into her eyes now and felt himself begin to fall.

Angel dismissed his words with a gentle gesture with her fingertips. "I was glad to be there for her…all of you."

In the silence that followed, Tim revisited that night at the hospital. He saw wires and lines enwrapping the pale figure laid flat on the bed and felt the dim grey murmur of death packing the room, pushing down on him, his ears ringing in pain.

With his arms around his weeping sister, Tim watched Angel as she stood at the foot of the bed, her arms held out in front of her, palms upturned. The pain in his ears and heart heightened for an instant, but as Angel slowly turned her hands over, he felt the fog of death lifting, escaping through the ceiling and he drew a clean, fresher air into his lungs. Jenny ceased her crying and watched as Angel spread her arms wide and began to sing a song whose notes were almost flat but within the framework of the rhythm, suffused into a lilting melody. The sounds flowed through Tim's ears, touching his soul as they travelled.

He would never know the words Angel spoke to the nursing staff straight after, but the new tests showed a blood clot in his father's leg that once spotted, was easily dispersed with medication.

"Thank you," said Tim, "You mean a lot to Jenny, you know." He ran his hand over his close cropped mousy hair and relieved his chin of the beard. "You've made a real difference to her."

"Oh, I don't know," said Angel.

"No, you have. I'm getting my sister back again. My Jenny who always had a grin and a glint of mischief in her eye. It's not easy for her at the moment I know but the past ten years haven't been easy either and, at least this way she feels like she has a choice, if not an easy one."

"She said that?"

"No, not in as many words but I feel I can say it for her. Am I speaking out of turn?"

"No, not at all. It's how I see it too but so many people will settle for their lot, rather than pursue what they really want because it's too difficult."

"Nana Ward used to say 'You can't make an omelette without breaking eggs.'"

"Wise lady".

Tim nodded. "And I've broken a few eggs in my career."

"Wanna share the recipe?"

Tim looked down at the table then up into laughing eyes. "Oh, I just meant I've had to take a lot of flack as the young, keen copper, eager to learn and progress. Put a few noses out of joint with my missing rungs on the career ladder while making my way up."

"Worth it though?"

"Most definitely. I love my job, and there's not many people who can say that nowadays."

"Any downside to a perfect career?"

"Of course. I have to make the most of any time off and I learnt early on to make sure I left the job at work and didn't bring it home."

Angel remained silent but kept eye contact and nodded.

"Yeah, ruined a promising relationship by being on the job 24/7," said Tim, running his hand over his head again, "She was a lovely girl. Not her fault I was so far up my own arse about my own prospects and promotion. Twenty eight with all our lives ahead of us, but my preoccupation and lack of thought wrecked any future we could have had."

"But you've learnt your lesson?"

"Yeah but too late."

"Too late for then but not too late for now."

"True, but I lost the woman I loved."

"Then, if she's lost, she wasn't the right woman."

"Sure?"

"Of course."

"How can you be?"

"Because you learnt your lesson on her. It wasn't the right time for either of you. If she's moved on as you have, it might be the right time now but that I cannot be sure of."

Silence clung to them like a bubble wrap blanket, squeaking under the weight of unspoken thoughts. Tim looked around him at the intricate bamboo screen and abundance of foliage in terracotta and blue pots, his mind mulling over Angel's words. "I'd never looked at it like that."

"Sometimes a different point of view can help."

"And that's how you helped Jenny?"

"Maybe."

"She said you knew everything."

Angel laughed her full raucous, powerful laugh. "Oh no! Not even close but I've had the luxury of time to study and learn. Even so, knowledge itself is not enough." She continued and Tim watched her, as the eloquence and thoughts transformed her face into pure energy. "And how much time would one need to gain all knowledge? Many lifetimes I believe and even then, what of understanding? Now, if I had all the knowledge and all the understanding, then maybe I would know everything."

As the ballroom stirred at the arrival of Morgan le Fay and King Arthur, Tim wasn't the only person entranced by the vision in blue in the doorway.

Justin's heart clamoured in his chest, sweat pimpling his forehead as his eyes beheld the tall, dark elegant woman on the arm of a mythical king. His breath rasped in his throat, causing him to cough as he strained to quieten the gasp his heart strained to cry. His palms flooded with sweat and he wiped them on his baggy jeans while trying to extricate a hint of liquid from his mouth to moisten his lips.

He watched Angel and her consort as she greeted her friends and he studied the lines of her body and then her face, hopefully undetected behind his sunglasses. As his eyes visited Angel's contours, Justin remembered the girl he'd held at the Spring Dance and his palms tingled at the memory. It had all been a joke, a con at first, his flirtatious glances and lingering looks but, as he'd watched her, that quiet girl, he'd realized she wasn't dull or boring as he'd thought but merely a bud, shyly waiting to blossom in the world. They'd danced and talked and he'd been stunned by her words, so gentle and thoughtful and then he'd held her, like the delicate flower she was, as they danced close together.

Angel turned her head, her hair moving like a skein of silk and looked up at him on the DJ stand beside Vincent.

Justin's breath ceased as her eyes took his, bore deep into his soul and then spat him out like an unexpected unwanted piece of gristle. He rocked on his feet, grasped the table in front of him and gasped a hurried breath before sipping his beer again, keen to still his quaking heart.

As Angel's gaze returned to her friends, Justin saw her in the moonlight on that warm, March evening and his heart raged for the injustice he'd caused her. She'd believed him, felt she knew him enough to trust him and he'd betrayed her. He saw with clarity the pain he'd caused her, the blow to her confidence, self esteem and most importantly, her trust in humankind and he bit his lip as tears welled behind his sunglasses. And what had she left him with? The ability to chat up and bed every female he desired. He'd thought it a blessing, a useful skill at sixteen and yet, only now, only now with Angel before him, did he truly understand what he had sacrificed for all the years of lust. Justin hung his head but knew Angel saw him and he hoped she could feel the remorse that he felt.

The far end of the garden room, more out than in, had been designated the smoking area. Gliding between the milling party-goers, waitresses dispensed drinks and gathered glasses. A half laden tray hit Aidan in the stomach as the bearer turned and he caught it before it could fall.

"Allow me," he offered with a nod, "Why don't we fill it up on the way?" The teenage waitress smiled with gratitude as they stacked the tray and departed for the bar.

"Proper little knight in shining armour, ain't cha?" said Tiffany, as Aidan reappeared looking for a seat.

He bowed low. "My oath of chivalry forbids me to abandon a damsel in distress, m'lady."

"Oh, quite the poet too!" laughed Tiffany, swigging her Bacardi and coke too hard so a trickle ran from the corner of her mouth.

"Allow me," said Aidan, producing a napkin from nowhere and leaning forward to dab her mouth.

"Geroff!" said Tiffany, "Park that pretty behind down here and tell me how you know Angel."

Aidan smiled gently. The golden torque around his neck matched the coronet about his blond hair, which fell to his neck in natural, loose strands and set off his jade eyes and chiseled features. He removed his sword belt and sat down opposite Tiffany.

"And I thought I was impressing you with my gallantry while all you're interested in is Angel!" he said, producing a silver cigarette case from a pocket in his tunic.

"Oh, I dunno," said Tiffany, "I like a man to open doors for me 'n' I'm quite impressed by a man in uniform."

Aidan smiled, extracting and lighting a slim hand rolled cigarette, "You'd have loved me in my previous job then."

"Oh yeah? What was that?"

"Stripper."

"No way! You're 'avin' me on!"

"No, honest injuns," said Aidan, making a cross over his heart.

"I would have liked to have seen that," said Tiffany, undressing him with her eyes. She grabbed the arm of a passing waiter. "Get us a large Bicardi and coke, would ya?"

"Certainly madam and for you sir?" replied the young waiter, cloth on arm and tray poised.

"Thanks, yes, lime and soda, thanks," said Aidan.

"Certainly sir."

"That's not much of a drink," said Tiffany, as the waiter departed.

"Driving," replied Aidan with a grin.

"Ah, so you're the chauffeur."

"Amongst other things."

"Really? I was only joshing ya! You're really Angel's chauffeur?"

Aidan laughed, head back, relaxed, green eyes twinkling. "Angel and I are friends. Aidan," said Aidan, offering a hand.

"Tiffany," smiled Tiffany taking it. "Where's that fuckin' drink?" she said, looking over Aidan's shoulder.

"I'm sure it won't be long. Would you care for a cigarette?" said Aidan, the silver case materializing in his hand.

"Cheers, thanks." Tiffany accepted the light and inhaled. "So, if you're not the chauffeur, why're you driving?"

"I offered."

"What? You turned down the chance of a good piss up?"

Aidan laughed again and relaxed further into his cane chair, loosening his laced arm guards a little as he spoke. "I don't need alcohol to have fun."

"Well, nor do I," said Tiffany, "But it bloody well helps!" The drinks arrived. "So, how did you two meet?"

Aidan rolled his eyes to the ceiling and grinned, "Ah, Angel again. Well, we first met six, maybe seven years ago, I can't remember exactly. She helped me start up my own business."

"As a stripper?"

"No," said Aidan, "I'm a landscape gardener,"

"Oh right. So you do her garden?"

"Gardens, yes, the planning and some of the donkey work."

"She's got more than one house?" said Tiffany, bloodshot eyes wide with questions.

"Yes, she does," said Aidan, "But enough of Angel, what about you? No, let me guess." He sat upright and viewed the woman before him. The fierce blond ironed hair was not so straight now, where the rigours of alcohol and dancing had caused Tiffany to perspire. Wisps and strands curled and stuck to her face and her fringe had begun to frizz. Her thick foundation skirted her hairline like an orange mask, while her top lip pouted without help from her mouth.

"You own a chain of beauty salons," said Aidan, his face looking quizzical and absorbed, "Or maybe hairdressing salons."

"Get away wiv ya!" giggled Tiffany, "Me! Own shops! Flatterer!"

Aidan looked serious. "I'm not normally too far off the mark. A boutique then? Designer clothes?"

"No! I..well..no…I"

"Ah, a lady of leisure."

"Yeah, well, yeah, you could say that."

"And it all takes time; trips to salons and boutiques and lunch dates."

"You takin' the piss?"

"No way!" said Aidan, "I know! Can you imagine how long it takes to wax this lot before a gig?" He indicated the length of his body.

Tiffany laughed. "Oh, I'm imagining!"

"So, what do you like to do for fun?" said Aidan, sipping his drink.

Tiffany put her drink on the low table and leaned forward. Two red plastic globes defined by the Lycra cat suit filled Aidan's eye line. "Now, there's a question."

Angel bumped headlong into an officer as she left the ladies restroom. He was no gentleman.

"Sorry, didn't see you."

"Obviously. How are you Angel?"

Angel looked directly into a pair of cool grey eyes, strangely enhanced by the SS uniform. Drawing on her skill, she invoked a protective bubble around her and stood tall, calm and confident. "I'm very well, Vincent, and yourself?"

"Excellent! It's going very well. Most kind of Miss Stanton to allow us to use her home and your bouncer seems very capable."

Angel nodded at the slight compliment, amused by the term 'bouncer'. "I'm just glad I offered assistance if you needed it, with you being let down in the end."

Vincent shrugged, not taking his eyes off Angel. "Shit happens. There's always alternatives."

Despite her protection, Angel felt the skin bared to Vincent's gaze tighten, almost cringe in distaste from his scrutiny. "And how's Damien?"

Vincent frowned, looking puzzled.

"Your son?"

"Oh, Darren. He's fine."

"My mistake. Must have misheard. So how's fatherhood?"

"It's okay. Easy really. Don't know what blokes make such a fuss about. Drink?"

"I have one at the table, thank you."

"You are stunning, you know," said Vincent, leaning against the wall, an annoying barrier to Angel's departure.

"You're too kind," said Angel, returning his gaze. "Oh, that reminds me. Miss Stanton is back from her trip next Friday. I thought you might like to arrange a small 'thank you' for her arrival home. Flowers perhaps and I know from experience she has a penchant for pink champagne."

"We'll have to see what we can do then," said Vincent, unmoved and immoveable.

Angel had had enough. She looked at the wall that Vincent leant on and in her mind she visualized where its components had come from; the sand, cement and brick and the trees that had provided the panelling. She saw the process of its formation and she saw it now, solid in it's foundations, dug deep into the earth. She suggested to it, that Vincent was in her way.

"Ow!" yelled Vincent, leaping away from the wall. "That's hot!"

"What is? Sorry?"

"The wall!" cried Vincent, rubbing his arm. "Don't touch it!" he added as Angel's hand moved.

She stroked the wall and gently smiled at Vincent. "Too many JDs, Vince," she said, "Puts ideas in your head."

Angel walked through the welcome escape gap, childishly waving and saying 'bye' as she went. It was naughty of her to use magic like that she knew but sometimes...

"Having fun?"

Angel and Jenny sat in the garden room, the strains of party music filtering into their conversation.

"It's all got a bit manic for me," said Jenny, "I don't mind a conga but not surfing on tables and clambering about on the floor!"

"I know what you mean," said Angel, adjusting her hair to cover her shoulders and huddling closer to the heater. "You warm enough?"

"It has got chilly."

Angel hailed a passing waitress. "Would it be possible to have two mugs of hot chocolate, do you think?"

"I'll see what I can do," said the teenage waitress, "There's tea and coffee in the dining room now but I'm sure hot chocolate can be arranged." She hovered in front of them. "There's cakes and pastries too."

Angel leant forward. "Well then, let's go the whole nine yards. Please may we have hot chocolate with cream and extra sprinkles and double chocolate muffins for two."

The waitress giggled with delight, swinging her tray with one hand and covering her mouth with the other. "Now, that's chocolate heaven! You're with the knight, aren't you?"

"Ah, yes," said Angel, "Aidan has made his mark, I see."

"Such a gentleman," continued the waitress, "And sooo handsome! Oh, you could just melt into those gorgeous green eyes….Oo, sorry! I shouldn't have…"

"It's okay, really, don't worry," said Angel, "He has that affect on people." The waitress smiled with thanks and departed to fill the chocolate requirements.

"He is gorgeous," said Jenny, settling into her seat, "Always so kind and relaxed."

"Mmm, that's one side of him, sure," said Angel, "But he can be angry and illogical when he wants. Human nature is many faceted and the balance we keep is dictated by the integrity of ones mind at any particular moment."

"Wow, where did that come from?"

"Not sure," said Angel. They made eye contact and laughed. "You were telling me about Scott, or trying to above the noise. How's it going now?"

"Well," said Jenny, hands determinedly on her thighs, "He was angry. Very angry. Probably still is but I think he's realized that just yelling the same things at me isn't going to work."

"So, you know what you want?"

Jenny nodded. "I can't live with him any more," she continued, gaining momentum as her thoughts flowed. "Yes, I know that financially, we're going to have a lot to sort out and money's going to be tight and with Scarlett being so young, it'll be hard for me to work more but Mum said she'd help, but then I worry about her because of Dad…"

"Hey, steady on. One step at a time," said Angel.

"I know, I know! It's just that, now I've decided, I don't want to waste time!"

"But taking time to decide what you want to do and how you want to do it isn't a waste and could save you hurt in the long run. But you know that, Jen. You're smart."

"Am I?"

"Yes, and you know it."

"Do I? I'm so full of doubt most of the time."

"But you know you can't live with Scott."

"Oh yes!"

"Well then, use that as the starting point and the rest will fall into place."

"If only I could be so sure."

Danielle emerged through the crowds in the ballroom, buoyed to the front door by the force of "It's raining men." In her experience it wasn't, so she headed for the dining room, selected suitably portable savouries and was about to seek out the garden room to devour her spoils, when she spotted Zac's tall, broad figure in the front doorway.

"Err, would you like a drink or anything?"

Zac spun round and Danielle felt herself redden at the intensity of his gaze. "That's very thoughtful of you, miss," said Zac, a gentle smile softening his big dark face, "A glass of still water would be most welcome." Zac looked at the plates in Danielle's hands. "Shall I relieve you of those for a minute?"

Sweating and confused Danielle thrust her goodies towards him and wobbled backwards before turning and making for the dining room again. He'd accepted a drink. He has my food. He smiled at me. He has my food. Water, still water. He has my food. The water from the bottle slopped out of the glass and Danielle steadied herself on the table top, taking a deep breath. It's okay, it's okay. He'll give it back when you give him his drink. Why did you ask him? I don't know, I don't *know*!

With every cell in her body shrieking in fear, Danielle returned to Zac and they swapped a glass for two plates.

"You can have one, if you like" said Danielle. What? Where did that come from? Something's in my head!

"Well, thank you, miss. That's very kind," said Zac, "I rarely eat carbohydrates but it looks like it's going to be a long night so I shall join you," he added, his words deliberate and thoughtful. He indicated a door behind him, "Shall we? I can set the internal alarm for the door."

"So, it was Tiffany's idea to be Charlie's Angels," said Danielle, popping in another sausage roll, "Alright for her! I was so scared I didn't sleep a wink last night!"

"But you came," said Zac, smiling, his white teeth lighting up his face, "That was very brave of you."

Danielle blushed, vying with the colour of her catsuit, "Well, I couldn't let the others down and I know Clare was scared too." The final bite sized vol-au-vent was devoured.

"I'm glad you came," said Zac.

Danielle swallowed. "You are?"

Zac nodded. "You're the only person apart from Angel to offer me a drink."

"You know Angel?" said Danielle, pushing her grey streaked dark hair from her face and lifting it from her neck.

"You're warm," said Zac, "Let me switch on the air con. Ah, that's better," he added, as the chill air touched his forehead.

"Yes, thank you," said Danielle, "You mentioned Angel?" She licked her finger and dabbed at the final pastry crumbs on her plate.

"Yes, she got me the job tonight. Well, I come with the house in a way."

"Do you?" said Danielle, searching her plate for more food and then scanning Zac's likewise.

"This house belongs to a mutual friend. I understand the organizers were let down by their security and then their chosen venue had been double booked. It's a beautiful house, isn't it?"

"Mmm," said Danielle,

"Is there something wrong, miss? Would you rather be elsewhere?"

"Yes! No! I don't know!" Danielle looked up into Zac's kind brown eyes pleading for him to understand, begging him to take pity on her.

"I know I'm not the greatest wit where conversation is concerned," said Zac, "But I'm a good listener, Danielle. You seem confused." He reached forward and gently took the sweaty plump hands that Danielle had been wringing in her lap. "Why don't you talk to me about it?" He brushed her hair from her face with a broad, clean hand, stroking her cheek as he did so.

"Oh, I…"

"Zac, my name's Zac and you can talk to me."

The mugs of chocolate arrived, cream swirled, sprinkled and accompanied by two slices of layered chocolate cake on plates with forks and napkins. There were long handled spoons too. "No muffins, sorry," said the waitress, "But this double chocolate cake looked good so, I brought that instead."

"Very thoughtful and sensible of you," said Angel. She pulled open a small cloth bag that hung from her cord belt and secreted a note into the girl's hand. "Keep it or share it as you see fit," said Angel, "You've the makings of a successful future, child. Use your skills wisely."

The girl opened her hand and then her eyes wide as she glimpsed the scarlet note, "I can't ….I .."

"Yes you can," said Angel, smiling, "We believe you're worth it."

"Oh, miss, thank you," said the waitress, thrusting the note into her front pocket, "I really like working with people," she added, smiling shyly, "Thank you." She almost curtseyed and scuttled from the garden room.

"You're so kind," said Jenny, reaching for her cake.

"No, I'm not," said Angel, sitting back with her mug and spoon. She began lifting sprinkles and cream a teaspoon at a time and savouring them. "It's an investment."

"Investment in what?"

"The next generation."

"Okay, but why?"

"Well, I've no offspring of my own and that child showed politeness, willingness and the ability to think on her feet. She's bright and pretty, which always helps and she now knows she's a good and appreciated waitress."

"And?" said Jenny, pressing the fork into the plate, ensuring cake and chocolate cream, "Mmm this is good."

"And she'll think about what else she could do, be, become. So, I didn't just give her a well deserved tip."

"You gave her an idea, a choice…"

"Hopefully a future doing what she enjoys and is good at."

"It was still kind."

"Well now," said Angel, "Sometimes one does enjoy being the eccentric philanthropist in ones old age!" They laughed and time passed in chocolate ecstasy.

"Have you ever wanted children?" said Jenny.

"Honestly, there's been two occasions in my life when I thought I wanted a baby, but that's not the same as wanting children, just a biological body urge thing. No, I can't say I've ever wanted children."

"I don't regret having mine."

"Of course you don't! Just because you're not with their father doesn't mean you think less of them!"

"Though I do worry about the effect this will have on them."

"You're bound to, Jenny. I feel for you because I know how much you care about them and all your family but remember, you've spent two years doing it Scott's way and it doesn't work for you. You have a choice."

"I know, but I'm making a choice for the kids too."

"True, and we must all be responsible for our choices. When they're older, they will know you parted them from their father."

"Ouch! That hurts!"

"And it should. It proves you've not made your decision easily. They will know that you valued yourself, your life and your happiness just as much as theirs."

"Bloody hard though," said Jenny.

"True, but its not all down to you."

"What do you mean?"

"Scott will have the choice as to the sort of father he is and your mum, dad, Tim and all your friends and relations will have a part to play in the children's lives."

"Meaning?"

"If Scott is a reliable, loving father in the kids lives, they will be happy."

"Whereas, if he's mean and whingy and resentful or doesn't turn up or lets them down....Angel, I'm beginning to see. Everyone's happiness is everyone's responsibility and it's not just my job to make everyone happy."

"The penny drops."

"Awesome cake," said Angel, finally resigning her plate to the table, "And I don't use that word lightly. If that was made by the caterers and our delightful waitress works with them..."

"She's onto a good thing already?"

Angel nodded. "And I might have to use them for my next party."

"Any plans for one?"

"Well," said Angel, pretending shyness, "You and I do have a rather special birthday in May."

"We do, don't we," said Jenny.

The tiny door was barely visible amongst the dark panelling in the hallway. The key from Angel's pouch fitted neatly and the silent mechanism allowed her and Aidan a stealthy entrance. Stepping forward, Angel turned on the lamp and a cosy 'study-come-library' glowed into existence as the low energy bulb fired up.

Aidan discarded his sword belt, sunk into one of the huge leather chairs in front of the cold empty fireplace and patted his knee. Angel joined him, legs on either side of his and leant forward nuzzling into his chest. He stroked her hair and kissed around her hairline.

"You sorted with Tiffany?" said Angel, pushing back from his chest a little and nibbling along his jawline towards his ear.

"Absolutely. She has my card," said Aidan, before letting out a low gentle moan as Angel reached his neck.

"That Vincent is a bastard," said Angel, her kissing sinking below the folds of the neck of Aidan's tunic. "Do you think Mads can handle him?"

"For sure," said Aidan, tilting back his head as Angel continued kissing, her hands dexterously seeking the hem of his tunic, finding it and stroking the bare flesh beneath.

"Zac's been working on Danielle and has her number," said Angel, watching Aidan's face as she tweaked his erect nipples. "So, our work's about done here."

Aidan sat upright, pulling Angel's arms from under his tunic and held her in front of him, gorging on the beauty before him, lust oozing from her lips and desire firing her eyes. "I think, madam," he said, letting go her arms and tugging up the folds of her skirt until he found her bare thigh, "I deserve payment for embarking on my hideous quest with such commitment." His hands began to stroke, up and down, each time rising a little higher, then receding back until a moan from Angel ceased his wandering. She stood and he levered his breeches from under him and let them drop to his ankles.

Angel looked down at the beauty before her. Green eyes framed by blond strands held fast by the gold coronet shone with desire while he held his manhood, erect, shining and beautiful, unashamedly in both hands. She slid the neck of her gown to her shoulders and leant forward allowing her breasts to emerge in front of his eyes as she placed her knees on either side of him in the seat and lowered herself down, uniting their bodies in the pleasure they both desperately yearned for.

As the evening tried on the overcoat of night, stars yawned and winked into existence through the garden room windows. Whispered, briefer more intimate conversations filled the air and Angel, Jenny, Tim and Aidan shared a peaceful cup of tea as the grandfather clock in the hall chimed once. They'd joined in the compulsory party songs around midnight, Tim now minus hat and beard crooning magnificently to 'New York, New York' but, finding the stalwarts still keen to indulge and with only so much of 'Come on Eileen' to be borne, they'd made their retreat. The women shared renewed acquaintances, shock encounters and general gossip, while the men talked easily about the stars and the planets. A sudden burst of music interrupted all conversation and landed an excessively drunken and boisterous conga line into the garden room, led by Tiffany, mascara smudged and lipstick bleeding, closely followed by Clare, dishevelled and breasts straining from her catsuit. The oncoming line also featured Rob, sweating, grinning and intent on the shapely backside he was holding, attempting to get his feet not only to step but indulge in the occasional kick too. As they swung past the table, Tiffany made a grab for Aidan, while Rob seconded Jenny and Tim followed smartly behind. No one approached Angel. She smiled as she

watched them moving around the tables, Aidan rolling his
eyes at her, while attempting to add some semblance of
rhythm and co-ordination to the proceedings. Angel watched
as they left the room and sighed. I hope he doesn't tire
himself out before we get home, she thought. I've only had
oedhouvres.

Angel stood behind a screen in the hallway, seemingly
refreshing her lipstick, hidden from the three women talking.
     "How can you say that? He's really nice!"
     "Look, anything to do with her…leave it, okay?"
     "But I really like him!"
     "How can you, you silly cow! You've only just met 'im!"
     "So! He speaks nicely to me, I like it."
     "You fell for a smart arse last time!"
     "No, he's not like that. Not smarmy or, you know. It's like
he thinks before he speaks and…and..what he says is kind
and makes sense and he wants to help me."
     Angel smiled into her mirror.
     "Tiffany's right. Angel's bad news. Anything and anyone
to do with her is a 'no, no'," said Clare.
     "Well, you're here, aren't you? It's Angel's friend's house!
And *you*!" said Danielle, pointing a finger at Tiffany, "You
can see you'd do *anything* to get into that knight's pants!"
     Angel smiled again.
     "So what?" said Tiffany, "That's just sex. I'm not all," she
brought in her shoulders, affecting coy and added a voice an
octave higher, "'he's so kind when he speaks to me'!
Anyway, he's black. You wouldn't catch *me* with a black
man. Aidan's different. I'll get him along to do my garden
and then fuck 'im."
     Angel stifled a gasp. Tiffany's racism was one thing but
her blatant self-belief was a shock to anyone, especially
when you saw that her idea of beauty was taken from
celebrity magazines and soft porn movies.

"What? Just like that?" said Clare, a hint of envy in her voice.

"'Course," said Tiffany, "He was giving me the come on earlier. Where's the fuckin' cab?"

"I don't care what you say," said Danielle. "I like Zac and I'm going to see him again!"

"Oh, do what you like! Just don't come running to me when it all goes wrong, which it will and you will and so I don't know why I'm boverin' to talk!"

Because it stops you having to think, thought Angel.

9

The house was quiet when Tim woke up. He touched a button on the ipod next to him and gentle music flooded his pillow as he looked around the familiar room. Sadness doused his body, as he lay alone in his double bed. He felt the lump in his throat pre-empting tears and growled angrily at his weakness.

He'd come to terms with splitting up with Vanessa and moving back to his parents' house but the last five years had been a lonely existence. He wasn't ugly or unlovable, he knew that but somehow he'd got out of the habit of socializing and meeting new people. He'd maintained a close circle of friends since the split but their regular nights out had been thwarted somewhat by the arrival of girlfriends, who'd become wives and the latest spoke in the wheel of socializing, babies. The lump in his throat rose again as he viewed his own chance of fatherhood and recognized it as no more than a precious, distant hope.

He turned over, forcing back tears. With his 33rd birthday two weeks away, he'd never imagined he'd be single and still living at home. Granted, his career had progressed even faster than he'd hoped but he'd learnt the hard way that, if there was no one to share the success with, it felt far less of an achievement. So, as he'd sought the ladder and fixed his sights firmly on the rung above, he'd also chiselled out a groove for himself, safely back at home with mum and dad, a life of working, eating and sleeping.

With a mug of tea and a chunk of the Sunday papers, he returned to bed a little more cheery, his mind retracing the previous evening's antics. A fancy dress party had been different and he scanned the ballroom in his head, revisiting the range of costumes. There'd been three Elvis' he recalled and two Federers, though they could have been any tennis player at all. The invite had specified 'rich or famous' so he presumed the women with too much make up and too few clothes were from both categories. He continued to recall the costumes and the fact that the most attractive women wearing them were all accompanied by men. Strangely, he couldn't give any body a single face, except Angel. He didn't believe in 'love at first sight' and yet, the feeling that took over him when he'd seen her enter the ballroom had been immense, overpowering and all consuming.

Tim sipped his tea and snuggled deeper under the duvet, no heating being on this cold October morning with both his parents attending church. Emotions were fiery juggling balls for Tim. He knew they were there, acknowledged their tendency to go up and down but, whenever he tried to grasp one, to make sense of it, it burned him and made him throw it back in the air again but, he recognized that Angel had had an effect on him and so he tried, with fire proof gloves, to get to grips with it. Of course, the first time he'd seen her since she left for Wales all those years ago was at his dad's hospital bedside. Tim shut his eyes and tried to remember the detail. Emotions triggered his memory. He'd felt relief at her being there; calm, hopeful and he'd trusted implicitly that she could, somehow, resolve the situation. And what had she done? How had she done it? His eyes flicked open. He didn't know and yet, normally that would frustrate him as, after all, his job, his life was finding the solutions to the crimes put in front of him but, he realized, he didn't need to know. Angel had been there, worked her magic and Dad was well again.

Tim finished his tea before covering his whole body in the sweet warmth of his duvet, wriggling his toes and fingers before succumbing to its weighty comfort. Angel was beautiful. That was a start. Kind, intelligent, fascinating and beautiful, but how did he *feel* about her? Here, he was at a loss. Part of him wanted to undress her, caress her and make love to her all night but another part wanted to worship her, on his knees forever, knowing that one kind smile and a kiss on the cheek from those devastating lips would last him a lifetime. He took off the fireproof gloves and let the thought of Angel flow into his mind and she nourished him, comforted him and filled him.

The key in the lock roused him from his musings and he felt himself half empty once more.

November

10

A pop up interrupted Rob's enjoyment of the online sex show. 'Are you the man we're looking for?'

He cancelled it with a growl and resumed his beating as the girl on the screen, knees on the edge of the bed, slowly removed her knickers. 'Stuck in a rut and need a new direction?'

"Fuck off," muttered Rob, deleting again.

Still kneeling on the bed, the girl's hand appeared holding a large black dildo. 'Do you want to work for 10 years and never have to work again?'

"I'm no porn star! Fuck *off*!" yelled Rob, as the girl emerged under the pop up, covering the dildo in lube. He watched, hands fiddling, as she rubbed the black rubber all over her bottom and thighs, dwelling a little where it found a natural orifice.

'This isn't about porn; it's about you!'

"Oh, for fucks sake!" Rob hit the highlighted website and five minutes later, had forgotten all about bottoms and dildos. For the moment.

Knock. Knock. Knock. Silence.

Knock. Knock. Knock. Silence again.

Knock. Knock. Knock.

"Who is it?" called the voice from behind the door.

"My name's Eli. Wayne from the pub sent me."

"Oh, for fucks sake!" muttered Clare, wrapped in a dingy grey dressing gown. "It's not even midday. Come back later!" she called.

"Ok, that's fine. When would be convenient?"

Clare stopped scowling. A considerate client was a rarity. "Err, two o'clock and money through the letterbox first."

"That will be great! Wayne told me about the money. I'll put the envelope through now and come back at two. Sorry to have disturbed you."

A clunk of the letterbox and then retreating footsteps followed and Clare bent down to pick up the bulging envelope. She tore it open. "Hundred quid! Bloody hell! Has that fuckin' Wayne sent me a fuckin' perv!" She sighed and turning caught a glimpse of herself in the mirror screwed to the wall.

Brown eyes in watery red sockets looked back at her while her wan forehead creased and frowned with concern and then, just for a moment, a flood of new thoughts entered her mind, thoughts she'd abandoned years ago as she resigned herself to the reality of the life she'd been forced into. Could this be the one? A man to take pity on her, be kind to her, even love her? Take her away from this endless Fairground of Disappointment? Escort her from her House of Horrors, away to his Castle in the Sky? Tears prickled her eye sockets, making her nose run and the mundane act of wiping the snot with the sleeve of her gown broke the spell and she stood hopeless and forlorn, weeping.

"Justin Preston?"

"Yeah?"

"Good morning. My name's Kitty Mason. I'm ringing on behalf of the Anderson Foundation. Do you have a moment?"

"Look, if you're trying to sell me something or sign me up for some charity, you can forget it."

"No, no, not all. The complete opposite, in fact. I'm ringing on behalf of Miss Anderson to arrange a meeting about a possible contract, if you're interested. This is Preston Construction?"

"Yeah it is and I might be but I've got a lot on at the moment."

"I see. No time for a meeting then?"

"I'm sure I can fit something in but just as long as your Miss Anderson understands I'm chocka with work until the end of Feb."

"Of course, of course. The plans are at the preliminary stages at the moment but Miss Anderson is keen to select the construction team now, as she wants them in at ground level, you understand, while the plans are proceeding."

"Okay, sounds reasonable."

"The meeting is set for this Friday at 11am at her offices in East Cheap. There will be three other building firms there, just one representative from each and you are the final selection."

"Right, so, who're these other firms?"

"I'm afraid I'm not at liberty to say, Mr Preston, but they've come highly recommended as, I see from the notes, have you. Shall I book you in?"

Justin bathed in the compliment a moment before adding, "Sure, sure, big job is it?"

"Yes, Mr Preston, it is."

Rob read and reread the homepage on the website. Wrapped in his towelling gown and a chilled glass by the keyboard, he jotted down some notes and then some figures on a pad on his knee. He picked up the glass but replaced it without drinking. He chewed the biro as his eyes rescanned what he'd written and his hand flicked to another page on the website. He grabbed the glass again and sat back, looking into the space above the computer screen.

Work had slackened off. Yes, they were getting by but money was going out quicker than coming in and had been this past year. He'd have to admit that his enthusiasm to seek work had been dulled since Louise left and he'd been drinking more. He put the still full glass back on the desk and viewed it for a while. Yeah, quite a lot more and his food intake had increased in quantity but suffered in quality. And then there was Teresa. She'd stuck by him when her mother left, or was it that she felt pushed out by Rashid, her mother's new boyfriend? Anyway, she was his daughter. She may not be his own blood, but he'd brought her up as his own and she deserved better then this. Maybe this job was what he needed. There was scant information on the website but the contact details showed a London number and a City address so, it had to be kosher, didn't it? The display on the computer showed 1:04 as he closed the computer down and went to bed.

Knock. Knock. Knock,

Clare walked up the hall in a short denim skirt, pale pink v-neck jumper and four inch cork wedge sandals. She'd washed her face and hair and attempted to tidy both, settling on pink as the theme for her face and a pink floral scarf to hold back her hair. She scanned her image in the glass before opening the door.

Eli stood before her in jeans and jacket and a hamper held easily in one hand. Everything about Eli was big; hands, face, body, feet and grin. His blond freckled nose and unruly hair were more farm hand than bank manager but something in the way he stood suggested he would always command respect. "I had time to attend to some provisions," he said as he walked past Clare at the door.

He turned as Clare let out 'hey!' as he entered and his big square face looked puzzled. "You were expecting me, weren't you? And I've paid for two hours in advance, haven't I?"

Clare shut the door and lent on it. "Yeah, yeah you 'av."

Eli's grin took over his face again. "Well then, I say, let's get started! Eli," he said offering his hand, "I'm very pleased to meet you, Clare."

Disbelief crowded Clare's face as she took his hand and he lifted it to his mouth and kissed it, looking up at her with a twinkle in his eye. "Look at you, all edible in pink," he said, still smiling broadly, "I just knew!" He laughed. "I have strawberries and pink champagne to match! I'm ready to indulge if you are!"

It was gone midnight when Clare stirred and looked first in bewilderment and then remembrance at the sleeping giant beside her. Eli moaned and snuffled a little next to her and turned over draping his huge strong arm over her stomach. And here he is, thought Clare, still here, in my bed after an evening of....? She couldn't put a name to it or a label on it at all because she'd never experienced the like in all her twenty nine years. The strawberries and champagne had been accompanied by teasing and fondling and Eli had even produced two large scented candles that had filled the bedroom with mellow light and soft fragrance as they made love. They'd agreed, at 4 o'clock, on another £100 for Eli to stay for the evening and, being a Monday, they'd not been interrupted. Strokes and massages by those enormous hands had been followed by hours of sexual pleasure, ending finally in a third orgasm for Eli and a resounding, single multiple humdinger for her and then sleep, together.

Clare caressed the fingers of the hand on her belly before rolling under it, spooning into Eli and falling asleep.

"It had to be this bleedin' Friday!"

"It can't be helped. That's the day of the meeting."

"I bleedin' heard you the first time but I want to go out!"

"You probably can but we've been told to allow the whole day and evening if necessary. May even go onto the next day, but they put you up," said Justin, sitting on the end of the pine bench attached to the table, drinking from a can and smoking.

"Yeah, and *that* sounds dodgy for a start!"

"Tiffany? I'm bein' well patient about this but you're startin' to annoy me."

"Oh yeah?"

Justin's blue eyes were blazing, mouth set hard, "Yes, you stupid cow! This is a big job, do you understand?"

Tiffany stood, leant against the kitchen worktop, arms folded under her breasts, chewing and nodding. "So you keep saying, so what?"

Justin moved and had her arms behind her back and her body and head pinned to the cupboard in an instant. "Because Tiffany, because I am sick of graftin' my arse off nine hours a day on pifflin' little jobs, scraping a living that keeps you in designer clothes and fuckin' botox! Do you understand?" yelled Justin. His raised voice exhumed a dark, chubby little girl in a bright pink velour tracksuit from the lounge.

"Out!" shouted Justin. Chelsea left.

Justin's face pushed into Tiffany's and with her head against the cupboard she was forced, wide eyed with terror to look at him. "Yes, Tiffany, this is a big job. So you see, I've come home to tell my lovin' wife that after Friday, I could land us the biggest job of my life, our lives and all I've heard is fuckin' me, me, me!" Justin was bright red in the face now, snarling his words, twisting Tiffany's arms behind her as he spoke. "So I suggest you fuckin' shut up, do you hear? Because, if I don't get this job, I might just decide you ain't worth any more o' my time, get it? And you know what that means, don't ya? Don't ya?"

Tiffany nodded, tears streaming down her cheeks. Her arms felt painful and bruised but the verbal pain was the worst. Without her meal ticket, she was nothing.

At the tears and the fear, Justin's anger receded and he loosened his grip allowing her arms freedom and he stepped back from her, breathing heavily.

"I'll get you another beer," said Tiffany, rubbing her arms and opening the fridge.

"Yeah," said Justin, nodding, "Beer'll be good," he said, sitting down, "Have one yourself."

"Thanks, thanks," said Tiffany, sitting opposite him at the table and opening his can for him, "Look, Just. I'm sorry okay." She put a hand out to him but he moved from her touch. She ignored the move and continued with the verbal tack, "Just, I really am. You know I ain't bright and I don't fink fings frough sometimes but *you* do. You're the one wiv the brains, always been smart and if you fink this meeting's worf it, then I'm happy wiv that."

"You should be," said Justin, into his can.

"I know, I know, I'm really sorry."

"Just fuckin' words."

"No, it ain't, it ain't just words. You're my rock Just and I know you fink I look good just for me but, it's all for you babe. I just wanna look my best for you," said Tiffany, pouting lips in his face.

Justin regarded his wife at the table. Her inch thick foundation had crevices now from her tears and the weight of black eyeliner and false lashes filled her eye sockets like two bedraggled spiders. Her breasts sat on the table edge, looking about to roll away under their own volition and finally the mouth, the ugliest fish pout he'd ever seen. But, here they were, fourteen years on, still married, still together, the family half grown and the opportunity of a lifetime on the horizon and, despite himself, he was happy to stay with her. She was a good cook, looked after the kids well and kept a clean and tidy house. They had few cross words, few words at all really and it suited him. He enjoyed the occasional one night stand, being at the age which attracts impressionable late teenagers; he was old enough to have lived and gained money and sexual experience, but not too old. His truck had been the perfect accessory to ensure his sexual freedom and he smiled at the thought.

"We okay, Just?" said Tiffany.

"Yeah, yeah, we're ok," said Justin. Tiffany put out her hand and Justin took it. "You'd better check Chelsea's all right."

"Okay, Just," said Tiffany, letting go of his hand and getting up, "I will."

11

The walls in reception had carpet on them and Rob took this to mean it must be a high-class establishment. That and the gentle, feminine smile of the sleek, well-groomed assistant who'd offered him a seat and tea, had reiterated his hope that this was a kosher set up indeed. He'd also been given a clipboard with an application form attached, which he proceeded to complete and had just finished, when he was beckoned down the flock walled corridor to an office at the end.

"Mr Carter, this is Mr Manning," said the perfect assistant, as she opened the door.

"Ah, Mr Manning. Thank you, Penny. Do take a seat, Mr Manning."

"Rob," said Rob, taking the proffered seat.

Jed bent his head to the CV in front of him. In his made to measure dark grey Saville Row suit, he exuded quiet confidence and calm as he watched Rob out of the corner of his eye, surveying the room.

"So, what are you working on at the moment?"

"Not much, if I'm honest," said Rob, "That's why I answered the ad."

"Last job then?" said Jed.

"It's all down there. Removals last week, job in Somerset," said Rob, "And the week before a couple of my lads did security at a 21st and I think there was a house clearance."

"And what do you like to do to relax?"

"Well, I see my mates at the pub, watch the footie, you know."

Jed nodded. "Anything else?"

"Nah, not really. When my wife was still around we spent a lot of time shopping and going out but…"

"I understand," said Jed, "It's hard after a break up. Friends choosing sides."

Rob nodded. "They were mostly her friends, ya see, to be fair."

"Rob, can I be honest?"

"Sure, sure."

Jed sat back in his executive seat and surveyed the chaotic figure before him. There was no doubt Rob had made an effort. His pink shirt had ironed in creases down the front, spattered now with sweat and his suit jacket didn't meet across his chest. The Mr Blobby novelty tie did nothing to enhance his costuming and his new dark jeans straining at their limit, encased huge wobbly thighs and didn't help with any overall smartness. Jed looked into the blotchy pale face, accompanied by chins that held pale bloodshot eyes pleading in their gaze.

"What I see, is a man with a van and a few heavyweights, whose fallen off the planet after his wife left him and who has turned to drinking more and not looking after himself and has lost the drive and ambition to run his own business."

"You're about spot on," said Rob, nodding, "When you put it like that, I wouldn't employ me!"

"However," said Jed, smiling, "You're here. Why?"

Rob wriggled in his seat, extracting a none too clean handkerchief from his pocket and mopping his forehead. "Well, it was the ad, see? Made me think."

"Yes?"

"Well, I'm nearly thirty and look at me! What a bloody mess!" Jed smiled as Rob continued, "I wasn't always like this. Yeah, yeah, I've always been the big man, but not this big."

As Rob talked, Jed could see the thought processes on the blank screen of Rob's face, blatant, open and honestly displayed. "So I thought, maybe, just maybe this could be a new start, a new way of life. I'm cool wiv driving and bodyguard stuff. I'm no intellectual but I know politeness and manners. Me mum was always hot on that."

"And if you're working, you can't drink."

"Oh, yeah, that especially," said Rob, animated now, "I'd 'ave a new routine, ya know. Sort me meals out, working in the evenings and maybe even get training again."

Jed nodded and smiled. "So you used to train at the gym?"

"Yeah, boxing," grinned Rob, "Was quite good as a youf but didn't stick at it. Look, I guess what I'm sayin' is, I need a chance." His face was sad now, mouth tight and worried eyes watering. "This ain't easy," he admitted, "I ain't used to beggin', right, but, wiv a chance, a chance to do somefing new, I reckon I could turn me life round, ya know, get back on track. Might even get a taste for the business and set one up o' me own!" He laughed before adding, "And that was probably a bloody stupid thing to say!"

Jed looked hard at the wreck of a man before him, before getting up and pacing the room slowly and then perching on the front of his desk.

"I'm hearing you Rob, I'm hearing what you're saying and everyone deserves a chance but I'm a business man. I'm only here this week to interview and employ new staff as we're expanding. Usually, the team here runs smoothly without me and that's just it. I don't need any hassle but," he continued, watching Rob's face resigning itself to rejection, "I'd like you to spend an hour with Penny, who'll tell you all that's required by us to fulfil the job requirement and then we'll talk again." Jed stood up. "What do you say?"

"Really?" said Rob.

Jed nodded. "I'm not saying 'yes' yet. Find out more first and we'll speak again."

"Great! Fanks!" said Rob, getting up, "I won't let you down, Mr Carter."

"Okay, Mr Manning," said Jed, opening the door, "Penny will look after you."

It was gone 10am as Eli and Clare munched croissants and drank steaming hot coffee from cardboard cartons, side by side on Clare's sofa. They had showered upon rising and Clare's lack of provisions hadn't fazed Eli for a moment. He'd left for the shops, reassuring Clare with 'But you didn't expect guests for breakfast!'

Clare glowed. She'd cranked up the boiler and sat in her towel, hair wet and frizzing. She seemed excited and happy, like a child on a birthday treat. The lines on her face seemed less profound and the deep-set worry on her forehead had softened.

"Clare, such a pretty name, does it have a meaning?"

Clare shrugged as she tried to sip at the hole in the lid of her carton. Volcanic hot liquid burned her lip. "Dunno".

"I can check it out," said Eli, reaching for his phone. "Are you named after anyone?" he added as he accessed the internet.

"Couldn't say," said Clare, abandoning her coffee and nibbling cautiously on a croissant. As the buttery sweetness hit her palate, she ate freely and with obvious delight.

"Ah," said Eli, "It means bright, clear and shining. Like Clare de L'une, I guess. Not an easy name to live up to but a name that cries out for a fresh start!"

"Dunno," said Clare. She frowned, creases furrowing her forehead as she sought for something to say. "Eli is an unusual name."

"Ah, yes, true," said Eli, "My father was a Baptist minister. I'm named Elijah, after the prophet."

Clare looked bemused. "But you're called Eli?"

"I shortened it," said Eli, abandoning his phone, "Elijah means 'My God Yahweh', my father presuming that I would accept his religious beliefs, whereas Eli means 'My God'. I felt it allowed me to choose my own." He grinned at Clare. "I'm afraid my father was a rather forceful, uncompromising man. Didn't exactly bring the love and forgiveness of God into our family lives."

Clare looked at him and smiled, croissant crumbs in the corners of her mouth, her face a picture of blissful ignorance.

"So, what do you do for Christmas?" said Eli, abandoning his first attempt at getting Clare to open up and trying another, as he removed his cup lid and dipped a croissant.

"Nothing," said Clare, shaking her head.

Eli nodded. " Business quiet, so you take some time for yourself. You're lucky! I've four brothers and two sisters and more nephews and nieces that I can count! Christmas is manic!"

Clare smiled up at his rugged face, speckled now with soft blond prickles and easily imagined him in a big house, rough and tumbling with countless children.

"And the presents!" Eli continued. "It's a nightmare! You just think you've got the hang of Bob the Builder and

Teletubbies, then along comes Peppa Pig and Ben Ten! I
can't keep up!"

Clare sat back on the sofa and sipped her plastic cup of
orange juice. She seemed startled at first by the 'bits' but
continued sipping, enjoying the fresh sensation. "I have a
sister," she said, "And a mother, but we haven't spoken in
years."

"Well, that's sad," said Eli, "Family's important. So not
much support from your family when you were younger
either?"

Clare shook her head. "I hated school. I started a
secretarial course at college but I gave it up to get a job."

"Ever thought about studying again? You could go back to
secretarial college." said Eli, "It's amazing what you can
study part time!"

Clare shook her head. "It's all beyond me now, all new
computers and stuff."

"But everyone can learn if they want to," said Eli,
watching Clare's face beginning to set firm, "What about
something you've always wanted to learn about?"

Clare shook her head again. "Can't think of anything."

"I don't know," said Eli, "What about more creative
subjects, if you don't fancy computers or office work?
Aromatherapy, gardening, glass painting, reflexology....?"

Clare finished her juice and looked up, chewing her
bottom lip with her teeth. "They're the type of stuff you take
up with friends," she said "Wouldn't wanna do stuff on my
own."

"And I bet it's hard to see friends regularly, with the
unsociable hours of the job?"

Clare nodded and then remembered something. "I've just
met up again with some old school friends."

"Cool," said Eli, dabbing at crumbs in the carton with his
finger, "So, you'll be seeing them over Christmas?"

"I could, I suppose," said Clare.

"Well, I'd like to see you again, before then," said Eli, "I'm away for a bit but back by the 20th December."

Clare blushed and her towel fell down displaying oodles of pale freckled flesh, which she hurried to conceal, causing the bottom of the towel to flap open.

Eli watched, feeling his breathing quicken. He leant forward and stopped her hands at their frantic concealing. "I like them like that," he said, "Clare, I know it's a cheek because I've no more cash on me but, could I stay, just half an hour more?" His hands moved up from hers, up to her shoulders and round to the flesh of her breasts.

She reached out to him, pulling his head to her chest. "'Course you can, lover."

"So, there you have it, gentlemen," said Kitty Mason, "The ideas so far and the possibilities laid out before you. Any questions?"

The three other contractors began to ask questions, talk timescales and logistics while Justin sat and stared at the proposal in front of him. From time to time, he turned a page and stared again.

"Mr Preston?"

"Hmm?"

"Any questions, suggestions?"

"Yes," said Justin, "I think there should be an indoor pool and Jacuzzi baths, stuff to do in the warm, you know."

Kitty jotted shorthand on her pad. "Excellent! Well, it sounds like you're all interested."

The men nodded.

"So," continued Kitty, "You've an hour to put together a presentation to Miss Anderson. No waffle, you understand. Short and concise, please. Lunch will be served in here at 1pm and the presentations will begin at 2pm. The rooms next door are available with internet connections and, if you need anything, give me a shout."

Sophia's cool, blue eyes undressed the handsome man standing in front of her, imagining the sculptured curves of the muscles on his torso and arms and the feel of those rough hands on her skin. She saw them naked together, her slim body enwrapped in Celtic tattoos, her sensitive nipples aroused by pure muscle. She tutted at her mind's meanderings while smiling encouragement as Justin began to speak. Her smile turned to fascination with what she heard.

"I'm no public speaker or expert presenter," said Justin, "In fact, I'd rather sit, if you don't mind."

Sophia nodded her consent.

"So, to be honest, I've been sitting these few hours thinking, thinking about this whole project and trying to see it working. No, but not the build, you see, that's easy." He stopped at Sophia's raised eyebrows. "But it is, Miss Anderson, to any decent builder 'cos you work from plans see, take your time with the calculations, use good, reliable suppliers, all that stuff. No, it's the spec of exactly what you need the building for and why and, having kids myself. I've had a few thoughts."

"Let me get this straight, Mr Preston," said Miss Anderson, "You've been given time to write a presentation which will get you an enormous lucrative contract if successful but, instead, you've been sitting thinking about changing *my* original plan?"

Justin put both hands to his face, rubbed and looked up, shaking his head. "Sounds crap, doesn't it? 'Specially put like that but..."

"Say what's on your mind."

"Okay, well, may as well now, I suppose. Honestly, " said Justin, taking a deep breath, "I just couldn't sit back and watch all that money spent on such a worthwhile project when it could be even better. There. It's said. I'm sorry." He stood up. "Shall I?" He gestured to the door.

Sophia shook her head and beckoned him to sit. She smoothed her straight blond hair from her face with both hands and then rested her chin in them with her elbows balanced on the table. They were at eye level now. Her brain was computing at a phenomenal rate and it came down to three options; he was either very stupid and had been prepared to throw away the opportunity of a lifetime or he was genuinely worried about the project and its' success, which seemed unlikely so, and this was the real surprise, he was immensely intelligent and, faced with three top building contractors and all their resources, recommendations and backing, he'd realized he couldn't compete and decided on a brave, new way to stand out from the opposition and secure the deal.

"I'm surprised, Mr Preston. Surprised and impressed. Kitty told me about your idea for a pool and Jacuzzi suite and more indoor facilities and activities. I'd be honest in saying, I'm a little affronted by your nerve in questioning my plans, but, I admire your courage and sense of pride in your work, not wanting to work on a project you felt had even more potential. We need to talk more."

Relief crowded Justin's face as she spoke, rapidly replaced by boyish eagerness as Miss Anderson continued. "Now, I've two more presentations to hear, Mr Preston, and I feel I owe it to these gentlemen to hear them today. In fact," she stopped and thought for a moment, "Yes, I'd appreciate you sitting in, perhaps on the sofa there and then, we'll talk tonight over dinner about 7pm. I'll get Kitty to book Chin Chin's and a hotel for you."

Vincent stood in the ice cold shower, head tipped back, fierce jets of water bombarding his face like hail stones in a blizzard. The email had been short, terse even and yet, though the words had suggested a meeting to talk business, the few sentences had intrigued him, as if what they didn't say was shouting in his head.

He reached up, switching the shower head to cascade and began his cleansing ritual. Green gel scoured his scalp, ears and neck and he probed and scrubbed producing bubbles that cascaded down his narrow frame, puddling around his bony feet. He cleansed his face and with soapy hands, he massaged his genitals, before standing once more under the icy torrent, allowing its pressure to wash away the suds. She sounded so much younger than he'd imagined, but she was a friend of Angel's and *she* wasn't old, so why had he presumed Miss Stanton was? The décor in the house had given no clues to the occupant and yet, he'd imagined her to be a middle aged woman. The email said she might have business he would be interested in, but how was she aware of his talents? He kept his dealings to himself and never mixed business with pleasure but he had a feeling this evening would prove enjoyable. He smiled, capped regimented teeth filling his face like tombstones in a desert and nodded to himself in agreement before covering his torso and limbs in shower gel, the sharp tang hitting the back of his throat. He rubbed and massaged, seeking every inch of his body, cleaning carefully between each of his twelve toes.

Grinning like the lion that caught the wildebeest, Rob opened his front door.

"Teresa!" he called, "You home?"

Silence greeted him as he proceeded to the kitchen and opened the fridge. As his hand touched the can, the chill flicked a switch in his brain and he shut the fridge door, leaving the can in situ. He went in search of the kettle. Groceries were delivered regularly but rarely made their way to the cupboards and he waded through ripped open carrier bags until he found the appliance he was seeking. He fought to get the kettle under the tap as the sink was piled high with pans and crockery but succeeded and finally hit the switch on the wall.

Rob stood back and surveyed the kitchen. His grin drooped to sadness and his eyes lapped with tears. He leant back against the fridge, his ring weighted fingers holding his face, shoulders shaking with shame. The click of the exuberant kettle brought him back from his torpor and he stood straight, inhaling deeply. He wiped his face on his sleeve and then looked thoughtfully at the snail trails he'd produced along the arm of his only suit jacket. "Arsehole," he said, breaking into a grin. He found a clean mug at the back of the cupboard, gathered tea bags, milk and sugar and added, "But not for long."

Teresa returned from work to find her father, wearing an apron imprinted as a French maid and pink rubber gloves encrusted with suds, dancing round the kitchen, washing now clear worktops and cupboard fronts, singing Hot Chocolate's 'You sexy thing.'

Sleety rain hammered the window and the weak grey light of a winter's day tickled the bedroom walls where Clare lay on her bed, contemplating the day ahead. A bulky brown envelope sat next to her. For most, this would be a regular occurrence, making choices and decisions and organizing meetings, shopping, trips out and friends but not so for her. She rarely thought anymore, what would be the point? Her life was always the same; secure enough punters to pay the rent and bills and eat. She was lucky. She had a roof over her head and regulars who covered most outgoings, only needing her to hit the streets when her cravings overtook her income.

Wrapping her gown around her and flicking on the side lamp, she collected her tin from the bottom of the wardrobe and sat, cross-legged and eager on the bed and tipped it out. She began to fill the scruffy envelopes it contained with notes. The 'rent' envelope was full and 'bills' looked healthy and so, smiling and chuckling to herself, she ran to the bathroom, shivering as she knelt on the floor by the toilet bowl and pressed around some floorboards behind until one popped up and she retrieved the brown tobacco tin from under it. Taking her treasure to the bed, she began to count it into the remaining notes, humming softly as she did so, a warm glow spreading over her face and her pulse revving. The final total made her gasp and she fell back on to the bed, laughing as she threw the wad of notes up into the air where it fell like confetti.

Sweet and fresh from her bath, Clare wedged into the corner of her sofa and sipped her tea; black but bearable with two sugars. A used envelope and pencil lay next to her with the magic number written on the top, highlighted by asterisk stars and little hearts. Where to begin? Well, Eli had posted £200 through the letterbox. She smiled at the recollection and the message. 'Treat yourself. You deserve it. Ps I really like stockings and suspenders! See you on the 20th December.' And with the treasure money, there was even more. Money enough to start afresh? Her mind went back to Eli's message and that big, rugged handsome face. The memory was the future, a little beacon flashing before her, a reason to be and so, between now and then.....where to begin?

Against Tiffany's wishes, he'd packed an overnight bag and suit and sitting across from Miss Anderson, Justin was glad. Changed from her navy suit to a purple and gold paisley wrap over dress, cut high under her tiny bust, Miss Anderson was exquisite. Justin glowed in the reflection of her perfection. Everything was perfect. Smooth, fresh, young and perfect. An amethyst at her cleavage sang and danced, flicking light and colour into his brain until he realized he was staring and dropped his head to the menu. His mind still clattered though. He knew he looked good this evening. The elation of securing the contract, all bar the signing, had boosted him like a drowsy bee having consumed a tablespoon of sugar. The fit of his mandarin style suit jacket showed off his shoulders and the white cotton shirt beneath felt soft and sustaining. He rubbed a hand across his tanned face, highlighted now with a hint of shadow and turned his gaze to Miss Anderson.

"I'll be honest," he said.

"Aren't you always?"

Justin grinned. "Okay, I admit it. No, I was going to say, I haven't heard of half of this stuff. I apologize," he added, seriously, "if that makes me stupid or unsophisticated but, I'd rather you choose the meal than have my dinner ruined by my own inadequacies. I'm starving!"

Sophia's eyes twinkled and she laughed easily, causing Justin's stomach to tremble. "There's no shame in admitting one doesn't know something," she said, smiling, "Learning is what makes us grow and we should always strive to learn more."

A waiter hovered and Sophia ordered an array of dishes and a bottle of vintage Bollinger. "I'm sure you'll want to celebrate with your family," she said, at Justin's raised eyebrows at the final request, "But I feel this is a special occasion, the beginning of our business workings together, and should be marked as such."

Justin nodded and smiled and as the food arrived, he relaxed and talked, sat back enchanted as Sophia spoke with animation about her plans for the children's hospice and soon, they were chatting easily.

"Miss Anderson…"

"Sophia will be fine for, though this is a business matter, I hope you'll agree that it's more of an out of work celebration," smiled Sophia.

"Of course," said Justin. "But I think Miss Anderson and Mr Preston works well on a business footing."

Sophia nodded her assent.

"Sophia, I'm intrigued." Sophia raised her eyebrows, chopsticks half way to her lips, waiting for him to continue.

Justin put down his fork, chopsticks having caused more laughter than sustenance, and sat back in his chair. "You're very young and yet, you speak with such experience on so many levels, as if....I dunno, as if building a hospice on a twenty acre site, with all the logistical and financial problems that throws up, all of it is just, well, organizing a village fête!"

Sophia popped in the morsel and pointed her index finger, manicured and French polished, waggling it as she talked, "Now, no knocking village fêtes! The logistics of elderly disapproving parishioners, over enthusiastic and often vomiting children and disputes over the cake making competition can be quite testing!"

Justin laughed and carried on eating, relaxed, happy but still intrigued.

Sophia helped a little with his curiosity. "I do know what you mean though. I've been accused and berated for being too serious all my life, except by granddad. It's his company I run, and ever since I can remember, he's been there to listen to me, teach me and support me. Now he's gone, I've total responsibility for making sure I carry on his work in the way he would have wanted. Maybe that makes me even more serious sometimes." She shook her head. "Anyway, I don't know about you, but I'm ready for coffee? Shall we take the remnants of the champagne and head back to the hotel?"

Still processing the story he'd been told, while his groin shuddered with anticipation at the last sentence, Justin nodded. "Sure," he said.

Rob and Teresa sat at the glass dining table at the end of the lounge, eating Chinese takeaway from the cartons. It wouldn't have been Rob's first choice for dinner but, under the circumstances, he'd decided they deserved a treat. He grinned at Teresa and she laughed as their forks went for the same pork ball.

"Thanks for helping, Trees," he said.

Teresa shrugged and carried on eating.

"No, it's been a good evening," said Rob, shovelling chow mein and then pouring sweet and sour sauce into his bowl. "I just needed a push to get me goin', that's all and this new job did it!"

Teresa nodded as Rob talked. "I start in the New Year, see. New year, new job, new start. Fuckin' ideal. Gonna get me some new clobber, not much though 'cos I intend to lose some o' this," he patted his belly, "before I get proper togged up. I came home all excited and wasn't sure where to start, ya know but sorting the kitchen seemed a good place and then, with you helpin' 'n' all, we've done the whole house!"

Teresa nodded. "The neighbours will fink we're men'al, hooverin' at fuckin' nine o'clock at night!" she said and carried on eating, nibbling on a prawn cracker as she watched her dad.

Rob laughed. "Yeah, probably! But, feels good, don't it?"

"Yeah," said Teresa, "It does and…"

"Go on."

Teresa dropped her cracker and her head. "It's..it's nice to hear you laughing when you're not pissed."

Rob nodded to himself and put down his fork. "You're right, Teresa, yup, fuckin' spot on. Feels good too, ya know? I… I'm sorry, okay."

"It's okay," said Teresa, looking at her lap.

Silence prickled the room as echoes of rows and arguments hung in the corners. Thoughts with no voices crashed around Rob's head and he tried to make sense of unfamiliar feelings that were bubbling at the surface of his mind.

"Err…look, I'd like to give you a hug right now, Trees, but I, err, I don't wanna like, and, and…I'm not sure I wanna be kinda pushed away so, could you maybe…." But before he'd finished, Teresa had risen from her seat, landed in his lap and was crying salty tears into his neck as she hugged him.

He put his big arms gently round her. "Ah, sweetheart. Dad's here now."

December

12

Angel lay on her back on top of the soft linen bed covers, watching Aidan in the full sized mirror over the bed. The sight of his bottom cheeks, bronzed and tight quickened her pulse as he bent to his kissing and licking. Soft, lilting sounds of a flute accompanied by waves crashing on a beach filled her ears as she closed her eyes and surrendered to his caresses.

Angel knelt on the rug in front of the fireplace, piling kindling and tinder before setting a match to her 'doughnuts' of paper.

Aidan lay on his front at the bedstead, watching her. "I can do that."

"I know, but I like making fire," said Angel, smiling as each paper ball caught in succession before sizzling the kindling and firing up the tinder.

"I know," he said, "Shall I grab some pillows?"

"Mmm be nice and there's wraps under the bed. It's draughty."

"I can see," said Aidan, lobbing pillows at her, "It's rude to point."

She stuck out her tongue and grabbed a thrown wrap to go round her before turning to the fire again. Aidan joined her, first kissing the top of her head before getting comfortable. He leant into her and she responded in kind. "Wasn't sure if you needed time alone?"

Angel shook her head. "No, the opposite if anything. Yule seems a long time coming." She leant forward, grabbing the poker, stabbing into the bottom of the wood fire. As flames shot up from the increased oxygen, she piled on two logs and satisfied, snuggled into Aidan. "Thank you for not saying 'can't you wait for your presents' or something."

"Nearly did," said Aidan, with a grin, "But I could see that triteness wouldn't go down too well right now."

Angel smiled and stroked his face and jaw line, nuzzling into his neck. "I know we've spent three years getting here," she said, "But now it's all in motion, maybe I feel a little fear."

"Fair enough, but no regrets?"

"Oh no!" said Angel, pulling back and looking into the eyes of jade that she adored, "Of course not!"

"But who are we to judge these people?"

"We're not judging them, they judge themselves," she said, not taking her eyes from him.

"And who judges us? Who oversees what we do?"

"We look after each other and, if necessary, the law of the land can judge us and find us innocent."

"Even though we've tempted these people?"

"Life is full of temptations but we're not offering that and you know it. We're the benevolent ones. We offer opportunity and choices. Fuck, we're the good guys!"

They laughed and Aidan cuddled her to him. "Just playing devil's advocate."

"I know, I know and you do it so well."

"I shall take that as a compliment, in every way it was intended."

"You should, husband," said Angel, rising to her knees before him and letting go her wrap.

Their eyes met and Aidan saw the red glow in the depths of Angel's eyes, old, deep and dangerous. "Lilith?" he said, licking his lips and swallowing hard as he gazed at her naked body wearing its fiery halo, excited and voluptuous before him.

Angel nodded. "Come to me, Asmodeous, my husband."

Jenny sat on her lounge floor, back to the sofa, papers spread on the rug all around her. The house was silent except for the occasional crackle of a warmed up bauble on the tree and the rhythmic soothing growl behind her, which served Bagpuss as a purr.

Wrapping the fleece closer around her track-suited frame, she reached for a sheet of paper and tipped the gold-framed glasses off her head to her nose to read it. She perused the rows of figures before picking up a second sheet to compare and then reached for her pencil. Cross legged, she made amendments and rewrote, leaning on the TV guide as a desk until finally, sitting back and reaching for the ruby filled wineglass on the coffee table next to her.

She saw the tree, bound round with tinsel and dripping with home-made glitter stars and cotton wool snowmen from years of preschool and school activities. She looked up to the star on the top, at the intricate filigree silver wire work, pronouncing her successful completion of an evening class in jewellery making and she smiled with pride. Not the earrings and pendants as produced by the rest of the class but a five pointed beauty to adorn the family tree. The children adored it. Only Scott had dampened her achievement by insisting it should be a Star of David and therefore, have six points. Jenny slugged a mouthful of wine and sighed. Another reason for the mental list; he never supported anything I wanted to learn or achieve. She looked round the shadowy lounge, the tree and her angle poise, the only illumination, and allowed her thoughts to go back, back to the day they'd bought the house. Together, excited, plans spilling from their lips and fingertips, they'd traced the walls with love and future promise. And they'd created a home for themselves then and now for the children so, it would be best to stay if she could, wouldn't it? Surely stability at this time was what they needed, wasn't it? And yet, what she craved was a new start, a new beginning.

She scrabbled through the papers and selected a hand written letter and read it while sipping more wine. She rubbed her cold nose with the back of her hand and silently cursed laminate flooring. The thin rug was an ineffectual barrier to the cold this winter's night and she shivered as she read. In her hand she held one solution to her problems, she knew that, but however hard she tried, she couldn't picture herself, the new Jenny, the old Jenny with the new bits, she smiled as she recalled, just couldn't see herself living her life here.

She shook her head and sighed, until a shooting star of an idea exploded in her mind and she abandoned the lounge, first making piles of paper and switching off the lights, before settling at the dressing table in her bedroom. She swept the bottles and jars into the laundry basket and opened the bottom left hand drawer.

"Mumma! Mum! What doin'?"

Jenny found her arm shaking.

"What doin' Mumma?"

Bleary, ears ringing, Jenny's head rose from the surface of the dressing table. "Mmm?"

"What doin' Mumma? You was asleep."

"Were asleep," said Jenny, coming to with a jolt. She blinked and rubbed her eyes before sweeping Scarlett, in pink pyjamas, onto her knee and holding up her night's work.

Scarlett clapped her hands and bounced with delight. "Star! Star! Star!"

"Yes it is," said Jenny, laughing "For Auntie Angel's Christmas present."

Already seated at the table were a petite dark haired young woman, Zac, the bouncer from the party and a big blond man that Vincent didn't recognize. He knew he was struggling not to show his disappointment.

Miss Stanton introduced herself, her 'friends' and civilities over and food ordered, Vincent heard the words he'd been hoping for. "I do hope you're hungry, Mr Rogers. We're famished! In fact, that's part reason my friends have joined us and the other is, I hate sitting in a restaurant by myself!" She laughed as the wine waiter filled her glass with pink champagne. "So they won't be staying, just eating and leaving so we can have a chat. I hope you don't mind."

Vincent shook his head. "Not at all." He surveyed the diminutive figure in front of him, imagining her feet not touching the ground under the table and her legs swinging. Miss Stanton wore her fine brown tresses pinned on top of her head, strands and ringlets loose and dangling on her face and at her neck. At her throat, a red agate glowed in the brightly lit restaurant. Her soft brown eyes and tiny rose bud lips were accompanied by round pink cheeks, giving her an even more doll like quality.

Vincent was impressed. He admired her nerve. No way could she own that big house, no way and here she was on the pretext of a business meeting! But why him? How did she know him? Had she been at the party in disguise? Now, there's an idea. No one would have noticed another guest in fancy dress, but Angel had said Miss Stanton was away. He'd find out the truth. He always did.

The food arrived and they ate in silence.

"So, the party went well?"

"Yeah, mmm," said Vincent, putting down his knife and reaching for his wine glass. "I was pleased with the response. Seems most people are curious to find out how their school friends turn out."

Miss Stanton nodded. "And the house was satisfactory?"

"Absolutely, ideal. I'm very grateful to your family for the use of it." He continued eating.

"Mr Rogers, you're mistaken. It's my house, my home actually and you hired the house from me," said Miss Stanton as she, Zac and Eli stared at Vincent.

"Forgive me," said Vincent, "I just presumed.."

"Well don't!" said Miss Stanton, "Presumption can lead to all sorts of problems!" Then her button nose scrunched up and she laughed, turning back to her plate.

Zac and Eli continued to watch Vincent, who moved his head awkwardly, trying to shift the prickles of sweat gathering around his collar. He tried a relaxed smile towards the two men but they continued their observance, occasionally eating a forkful of food. Vincent shifted his fork around his own plate. He felt annoyed and confused under such ferocious looks and his brain sought for an angle to undermine the men. "So, have you always been bouncers, err, security?" he said.

The looks from the men ceased this line of questioning. Not that they were viewing him like something that had crawled out from under a stone but rather the most heinous, vile slime to slither out from the primordial soup. Vincent returned to his plate and the meal continued in silence until Zac and Eli rose from the table and left, with a nod to Miss Stanton.

"Such sweet boys," she said, watching them go, before turning her smile to Vincent, "Shall we order dessert and then I'll tell you why I asked for a meeting?"

Vincent was angry. He felt out on a limb, as if everyone knew the rules of the game except him. "I don't want dessert," he said, "But I *would* like to know what's going on!"

Miss Stanton's smile faded and her eyes chilled in their sockets, her look boring into his brain like an aluminium woodpecker. "I'm not sure I can be bothered to tell you now, Mr Rogers. I'm surprised at you. I thought you were smarter than that."

"What do you mean?" cried Vincent.

Diners around them looked up and Miss Stanton smiled demurely at them until they refocused on their eating. She leaned forward. "And now you're making a scene. Very stupid," she said, shaking her head and folding her napkin, preparing to leave.

"You can't just leave!" Vincent leant forward and put his hand on her wrist.

As if he'd pressed the button on a magic box, Zac and Eli appeared instantly on either side of Miss Stanton, who continued once her wrist was freed to fold her napkin, shaking her head, muttering, "Stupid, stupid."

She looked into Vincent's eyes. "I thought you were smart, Mr Rogers and yet, you've worn your arrogance and prejudice like a banner at this table! Yes, Mr Rogers, Andraste House is *my* house and I own it and what's more, I also own two successful companies and, after hearing the way you co-coordinated your reunion party, I thought I might be able to offer you a role in that success. However, I don't want a man who can't control his emotions, can't demur to a little intimidation when necessary. You blew it, Mr Rogers. Well done!" Miss Stanton delivered the final words as she rose from the table and left the restaurant, closely followed by Zac and Eli.

"I call upon the Dweller on the Threshold!
    Thoth, Lord of Books and Learning
    Judge of the gods, Director of the planets and seasons
    Lord of Holy Words
    The Elder!
    All is prepared for you!
    Show yourself, Great God
    My companions wish to behold you!"

The basement was in darkness except for one huge floor mounted candlestick in which nine candles glowed. Ivy was strewn across the floor, all around the sandalled feet of the seven figures in the circle. The altar was also decorated with ivy and branches of juniper while the smell of myrrh permeated the air from the incense burner.

At Angel's summons, from behind the altar, a figure all in white unfolded, it's wings unfurling to touch the side walls while it's haloed head towered above them.

"Who calls upon the Dweller on the Threshold?"

"I, Angel, Tzaphkiel[14], Dark Angel of the Soul of Man. Why stand you in my way?"

Angel felt a searing pain in her head and spread her feet wider to take the force of the energy, strengthening her bond with the grounding earth. The pain probed and niggled like a serrated tongue on a sensitive tooth then ceased abruptly.

"Why are you here, Angel?"

"My reasons are no concern of yours, Tzaphkiel. Saturn rules us here in the black of black and that has awakened you to us. We thank you for your presence, Tzaphkiel but seek you not. The Dweller on the Threshold is whom we seek."

The earth shook like the demolition of a block of flats and, in the aftermath of dust rose The Dweller on the Threshold, head of an ibis, a lunar disc and crescent upon it.

"Who calls upon the Dweller on the Threshold?"

"I, Angel, Great God, The Elder,

I, Angel, with the power of Lilith within me!

Show us the door to our next Path!"

"You must all be tested first," said the Great God, Thoth.

He opened his arms and before them they saw the wide sparkling Nile, fringed with trees and plants, verdant and glistening under a blazing sun. They boarded a waiting boat and began to float. They watched the banks as they passed where children splashed and frolicked with their playmates

---

[14] See Glossary

and women sang as they whitened their laundry upon the rocks.

The boat turned on an eddy and the waters lulled as they ran aground and then they saw her. Her crying clanged in their ears and her grief tore into their hearts. Her howls of pain ripped into their flesh and her anguish rose in their throats. As Isis filled the world with sorrow for the loss of her beloved Osiris, the friends wept. They held each other and supported each other, soothing away the grief, empathetic and sympathetic, yet determined and resolute in their desire to move forward, repair and overcome.

Exhausted, they dried their eyes and the young queen stood before them. They knew the gesture from her heart to her lips and then to them, was one of acceptance and Thoth, The Dweller on the Threshold became the Doorkeeper who opened the door to the next Path before them and they understood.

13

Rob surveyed himself in the department store mirror as all around him, shoppers rushed to tick off the presents on their lists.

"Best so far," said Teresa, from behind him.

"I dunno," said Rob, "Didn't realize it'd be so hard to find a suit to fit."

"That ones fine, Dad. The dry-cleaners at the top of the road does alterations. I can pin up the trousers and jacket sleeves for ya."

"Can ya?" Rob turned round, looking gratefully at his daughter.

Teresa nodded. "Look, this is just for now, 'member. You're gonna lose weight, ain't cha? No point spending loads and this is in the sale and looks okay. Lose the jewellery, especially the rings, two white shirts and two plain ties and this will cut it, okay."

"Do ya think?"

Teresa sighed. "Like I said, it's the best so far. We've been here hours Dad, I'm bored."

"You're right, yup," said Rob, nodding, "I'm just used to something a bit bolder, you know and my bright ties make me smile."

Teresa took his arm. "Think about it Dad. You're the driver and security, out in the dead of night. Do you *really* wanna stand out?"

That same night, Rob sat up in bed with another new purchase on his lap, biro poised, and blankness filling his head as he surveyed the empty pages before him. Teresa had made him buy a diary. She said if he wrote down his eating, drinking, exercising and work, he'd feel a sense of achievement as the weeks went by and all he felt was lonely and scared.

Rob glanced at the bedside table next to him. Teresa had showed him how to make cocoa and had allowed him two biscuits for a bedtime snack. Rob's stomach rumbled and he yearned for a kebab, a lager and a few shots but he shook his head to disperse those unwanted former playmates. Also on his cabinet was a photo of all three of them, all snuggled together in the arms of Mickey and Tigger. The smiles caught his throat and he yelped a dejected gasp. Teresa had come into his life at four years of age, a product of an earlier relationship of her mother's, but he'd loved her as his own and she'd stuck by him. He couldn't let her or himself down again. They had been happy but he knew, deep down, if he hadn't been such a tosser, they could still be and so, putting aside his self-pity, he began to make a plan. He couldn't finish it, of course, until the work came in but at least if it was down on paper, he'd have some sort of path to follow on this lonely search for a new and better life, but Teresa was there with him and he owed it to her, to be the best Dad he could. Cocoa and biscuits consumed, he closed the book and at 10.25pm turned out the light and softly cried tears of pride and trepidation into his pillow before falling asleep.

Angel and Aidan lay spooning under the covers as the embers of the fire glistened treasure up the chimney.

Aidan kissed her neck and nuzzled into her hairline.

"Mmm, you insatiable man," murmured Angel, backing closer.

"Didn't say a word," said Aidan, sighing at the pressure on his groin, "I'm quite sleepy actually."

Angel didn't speak but turned over, pushing him on his back and fitting perfectly into the crook of his arm. She smiled and a purred sigh betrayed her contentment.

Aidan looked at her and stroked her hair. "So, you looking forward to Yule?"

"You know I am," said Angel, "I love us all being together."

"And Jenny this time," said Aidan.

Angel opened her eyes. "Yes, I think she'll enjoy it, don't you?"

"Maybe."

"Oh, you're not sure!" Angel raised herself on her elbow, "Why didn't you say?"

"Well, it's just that her parents are Christian and she's close to them. I'm not sure how a pagan festival and ritual will sit with her."

"I hadn't thought of that," said Angel, lying back down, "I just thought, well, it's a special happy time and I wanted to include her, but now…But she did say yes."

"Angel, don't worry," said Aidan, "You like her a lot, don't you?"

"Yes, I do. In all this pain of resurrecting and dealing with the past, she's the one part I remember as kind and happy, you know, and now, when I'm with her, I feel happy. You're not jealous are you?"

"No!" said Aidan.

Angel rolled on top of him pinning his arms above his head in one swift movement. "No?" She squeezed her thighs tight around his torso and dug her fingernails into his palms.

"Okay, maybe a bit."

Angel relaxed and sat up on his belly. "Tell me, truly."

"Well, I'm a bit jealous but I always am when you have fun without me. That's not the issue. I just don't want you to expect her to be 'into' the ritual like we are. Maybe tread a little softly then she won't feel awkward and you won't be disappointed."

Angel sat for a moment, digesting Aidan's words, sorting truth, purpose and intent in her mind, twisting a long dark tendril of hair around her finger as she thought. "That is very wise," she said. "And I can see I'm not always thinking wisely about Jenny."

Aidan pulled her to him and they rolled side by side, facing each other on the bed.

"It would be wise to sleep now," said Angel.

"Ah but I'm only good for so much wisdom in one night," said Aidan, his head disappearing below the covers.

Justin switched off the mobile call without leaving a message, his mouth set in a teeth-grinding grimace. No, nothing was going to dampen his mood. He'd get a cab.

An empty house greeted Justin's key in the lock, or so he thought until he entered the bedroom and noises from the en suite hit his ears. He unzipped his holdall, taking out his wash bag and grabbed his robe from the back of the door, before locking himself in the family bathroom. He put in the plug and began running hot water, scooping up toys, ducks and dolls from all surfaces and dumping them in a large plastic crate, before locating the bath oil from his bag and pouring it under the running tap. Within moments the room filled with citrus smells of bergamot and he was soon lying back in the oily water, sighing as the succulent warmth encased his skin.

What an evening! What a day! He couldn't remember such an exciting day and this morning, the euphoria was still with him. Alive, he felt so alive! His decision for honesty had been the best one he could have made and though he knew Sophia was no fool, she'd been impressed with his sincerity, and he knew it. And the faces of the other contractors! He shut his eyes and dipped below the water, grinning and recollecting the faces of the angry men that he'd been encouraged to cross-examine. His experienced eye had spotted potential 'money pits' in their plans and pitfalls in their preparations and schedules and he'd felt obliged to point them out. Resurfacing, he dried his face on the cold flannel from his bag. Ah, Sophia. He couldn't remember having such fun without sex. She was enchanting. Maybe that was it, her unattainableness. He'd felt shy about exerting his charms on her. Shy and rather foolish. So, he hadn't been charming, just himself. Yeah, they'd both flirted and enjoyed it but somehow for him, he didn't want to take it further, as if doing so would break the spell. He loved being around her, feeding off her passion, her commitment and her integrity and, once the contract was finalized and signed, he'd be working with her, maybe in a few weeks. And not just on any old build! The project of a lifetime! The dream project, the one he'd been waiting for!

"That you, Just?"

Justin didn't answer.

"Just? 'S that you?"

Justin still didn't answer.

"Look, I'm sorry, okay? I just needed to go out, ya know? The kids are at your mums 'til tomorrow so, we can talk, can't we? Just, I'm really sorry."

Justin grinned in his bath of oily musings. "I won't be long," he said, "Meeting went on 'til the small hours and I'm shattered. Why don't you make us some lunch?"

"Okay, Just. 'Course I will. You relax. I'll call you when it's ready."

Bacon sandwiches consumed, Justin and Tiffany sat in their dressing gowns on the sofa in the lounge, nursing mugs of coffee and cigarettes. Pink plastic toys had been hidden in a corner, part covered by a cream throw but leads and empty game boxes still exuded from the television, trailing across the room to the sofa.

"Sorry 'bout the mess, Just," said Tiffany, "I'll get it cleared up. Had a late one meself."

"Whatever," said Justin, keeping his gaze on his mug, "I've more important things on my mind."

"So, you're sure you've got the contract?" said Tiffany, sipping tentatively at her steaming mug.

"Have you been listening to anythin'?" said Justin, anger nibbling at his words.

"Yeah, Just," said Tiffany, "but you always say 'wait 'til its signed on the dotted line' so…"

"Yeah, but that's to stop you spending the money before I've earned it," said Justin. "Look, Tiff, Miss Anderson has shared her hopes and wishes for this project with me, ok? We're not just talking about a building here, alright? She wants to make a difference, carry on her granddads work and its *me* she wants to run this thing, understand?"

"Yes, Just, of course. So, when do you start?"

"Much sooner than I'd first thought. I've a meeting on the 27th with her lawyer. She said to bring my own but I don't need one. In the meantime, I've to put my final paperwork together and courier it over by the 24th. Now, I know I've two jobs planned for January but, I reckon Lewis can oversee them if necessary so, we could be up and running straight away, if needs be."

"It's all so quick," said Tiffany.

Justin looked at the woman beside him. For once, Tiffany wore no make-up and Justin could see the woman he'd married blemishes and all. Her eyes wore grey hoods above them and carried grey bags below, so her bloodshot eyes looked like the centres of hard boiled eggs not plunged immediately into cold water. Her brow was tight and smooth while the skin on the sides of her face fell from it like a ragged curtain and her filled lips stood out while the skin around her mouth drooped to her chin. Into his mind came an image of Sophia, soft, natural, serene and perfect and, not for the first time, Justin wondered why he stayed with Tiffany.

"It's been years in the planning, don't you see? It's not quick at all! A lot depends on the weather, of course, frost and such but we can certainly clear the site and get materials ordered. Windows are to be handmade locally so, that part of the spec alone needs to be finalized so the carpenters can begin!"

"Where is it again?"

"Sussex, near Battle."

"Where's that?"

"South coast," said Justin, irritation beginning to seep into his tired head.

"Oh."

"Near Hastings!"

"Oh right. Hey, ain't that funny?"

"What is?" said Justin, through gritted teeth.

"A town called Battle, right near Hastings! Well, who'd 'ave fought!"

Clare leapt from the sofa at the rap at the door, only just remembering to ask who it was, before flinging the door open to the beaming countenance of Eli, heavily muffled in scarf and overcoat.

"Freezing up out there," he said as Clare helped him with bags and layers of clothing. "Mmm, smells lovely in here."

Clare turned and blushed, on her way to the bedroom, "I've made us dinner," she said "I.. I thought you'd be hungry."

Eli smiled, barging her and the bags into the bedroom, hitting his head on the decorations as he went and then landing them all on the bed in a tangle. "Hungry for you," he said, pulling at the neck of her top until two white breasts were revealed. His face fell forward while his hands traced the outline of stockings and suspenders on her thighs. "Ravenous, in fact."

With the duvet around them both, they picked at the food on the plates on their laps.

"Got a bit overcooked," said Clare, "I'm sorry."

"Now, how can it be your fault?" said Eli, "I should be the one to apologize, making demands on the spot as I did."

"Oh no!" said Clare, "You didn't know the food was ready when you arrived. I should have turned the oven off. I wasn't thinking."

"Good," said Eli, "Means your thoughts were on me!" He put his plate on the coffee table. "Hey, no more apologies. Looks lovely in here. You've been busy!"

Clare glowed with pleasure at the compliment as she too abandoned her plate. She'd cleaned every surface of her sparse lounge and bought a tiny tree, which she'd stood on a crate in the window, around which she'd affixed a set of coloured fairy lights with drawing pins into the frame. Tiny red baubles and tinsel adorned the tree and she'd wrapped silver tinsel around her pictures and light fittings. The

scented candles from Eli's previous visit were alight on the
table and the room felt warm and cosy, almost homelike. She
nuzzled into Eli.

"Given any more thought to what you might like to do?"
said Eli.

"What?"

"We were talking last time, remember, about courses and
classes to give you different options for the future."

"I don't do studyin'" said Clare, snuggling closer.

"But it would be a means to an end, an opportunity to do
something else with your life, give you a choice," said Eli,
"Give you more to your life."

"I'm happy like this," said Clare, stroking his chest.

Eli sighed. "I have a gift for you," he said, emerging
naked from the covers and striding to the hallway, "Wasn't
sure what you'd buy with your money, but I hope you'll like
these." He placed two large parcels wrapped in jolly
snowmen paper on her lap and flapped the duvet over his
legs.

Clare sat up, excitement seeping from every pore as she
ripped into the festive wrappings. A soft, blue towelling robe
with a hood emerged first, swiftly followed by a satin nightie
and matching robe in cream with tiny rosebuds on. She
smiled and chuckled as she brought the smooth material to
her cheek. "They're beautiful, Eli, thank you so much."

"Blue to match your eyes and a little number to feel pretty
and special in," said Eli.

Clare blushed coyly and then remembered. "I've a gift for
you!" She emerged from the covers, still in her stockings
and put on the blue gown, still sporting tags, as she giggled
her way to the bedroom, while Eli protested that she
shouldn't have spent her money on him. She returned with a
parcel wrapped in holly paper and a bottle of cheap
champagne.

Eli backed into the corner of the sofa a little as she removed her robe and pressed in next to him. She watched wide-eyed as he unwrapped his gift. A jewellers box emerged and produced a heavy silver ID bracelet with 'Eli' engraved on the front.

"Turn it over," she said. 'Love from Clare' covered the reverse.

"You shouldn't have. That money was for you."

"Oh, but I wanted to! Wanted to say 'thank you', you know and for making this the best Christmas ever!"

"Do you reckon?"

"Of course, " said Clare, laughing "'N we can drink this and I've another in the fridge! Make a proper night of it!"

"I'd love to, Clare," said Eli, making to emerge from the duvet, "But I'm due somewhere else tonight."

Clare clung to him. "That's okay," she said, "We can just open one and you can leave later."

"Clare, I'm sorry, but I never drink and drive. Just how I am."

She looked up into his face, still soft and gentle but determined now. Joy began its long journey to despair but she waylaid it, determined to finish the evening her way. Her hands reached down under the covers and she nibbled at his bare nipples. "But you can stay a bit longer, can't you?"

"I'm really sorry, Clare but I really do have to go." Eli gently pushed her away and went into the bedroom.

Clare stood at the door in her new blue gown, untied and revealing the stockings beneath. She arranged herself against the door jam, holding her breasts out to him, bringing them to her mouth to lick and then tweaking at her nipples with one hand, the other between her legs. Eli didn't look up from his dressing. Once wrapped up again in outdoor attire, he turned to the door and witnessed Clare's final attempt to get him to stay, fingers working frantically between her legs, head back in forced ecstasy. Eli produced his wallet and counted seven twenty-pound notes onto the bed before facing her at the door. He wrapped the robe around her. "I have to go, Clare. Enjoy your Christmas."

"No!" she screamed, flinging her arms round his neck, "No! Don't go! Please stay! I want you to stay!"

Eli said nothing, his face unreadable, a blank sheet of paper as he unwrapped her from him and made his way down the hall.

"Don't go!" cried Clare, "Don't spoil it!" She grabbed his arm as he tried to open the door.

"Enough!" yelled Eli, pushing her aside like a cardboard cut out. Clare hit the wall and slid down it, sobbing. "Ah, now you've made me cross," said Eli, shaking his head as he watched her. "There was no need for all that. We had an appointment made for tonight and I kept it, as I said I would. Why spoil it? I've left money for two hours and a bit extra for you. Goodbye Clare."

"No!" yelled Clare, trying to get up, "When will I see you again? Eli! No!" The door slammed in her face.

Angel smiled at the family scene before her. Aidan and Jed, in robes of dark green, stood by the window, laughing and teasing each other as they always did. Aidan's jade eyes flashed with mischief as Maddy, robed in red, approached and threw back her head, laughing at whatever he'd said to her. Jed walked over to the sofa opposite Angel, where Sophia sat, radiant in the firelight, her red robes cuffed with gold bells. He sat on the floor in front of her engaging her in conversation. Eli and Zac sat closest to the fire on Sophia's sofa, dressed in identical black robes, exchanging an occasional word, comfortable in their own companionable silence.

Ancient carols hummed in Angel's ears as the room buzzed in time, candles dancing on every surface. She'd hoped Jenny could have arrived earlier when they'd set off in search of foliage in the grounds, but she'd messaged to say she'd been held up. The greenery shone and glistened in the swathe over the mantelpiece, glossy green holly leaves and brilliant berries intertwined with intricate ivy and milky mistletoe.

Angel gathered her gleaming white shift around her as she drew her knees up to her chin, bells tinkling on her cuffs, and thought about Jenny. The time they'd spent together as young girls had made a much bigger impression on her than she'd first thought. In the past, she'd sifted through her childhood memories and abandoned them as painful but she'd forgotten about Jenny. At ten years of age, Jenny had appeared in her life and coaxed her out of her loneliness. Smiling and non judgmental, Jenny spent time with Angel, never seeking to change her. Angel's then lack of social skills hadn't been a problem and Jenny had defended her friend, even losing other friends because of her, some not caring for the strange, quiet company of Angel. And Jenny had showed her family, where love and support were given with no thought of return. And home, a house full of love. Jenny had warmed her, driven off the chill of isolation and offered her safety and friendship. Then the universe had taken Angel's parents and uprooted her and she'd found herself alone once more but Jenny, or at least the spirit of Jenny, had unconsciously remained with her. While Angel learned and grew in knowledge and experience, she'd sought out that which Jenny had showed her and here they all were. Abandoned children from dysfunctional homes, misfits, brought together and loved as family. Those early years together had made a profound effect on Angel and she hadn't realized until she met Jenny again and with memories stirred from deep within her, Angel had taken the step to welcome Jenny back into her life.

But now, Jenny needed her and Angel wanted to give back the love she'd been shown but would Jenny understand? Would she accept Angel now as readily as she had when they'd first met nearly twenty years ago? Aidan's words of caution still quavered her resolve. How far should she go? The Yule ritual was only the beginning, an easy start to pagan understanding, but would Jenny accept even that?

A bell ringing in the hallway and Jed rising from the floor to attend to it disturbed Angel's contemplations.

"I'll get the mulled wine," said Sophia.

"Thanks," said Angel, smiling and unwinding her legs.

Aidan came over and bent to kiss her. "It'll be fine," he said, "She'll love it."

Voices filtered in from the hallway, announcing Jed and Jenny's arrival to the gathering. Angel witnessed the childlike awe and delight on Jenny's face as she entered the lounge, as she rose to greet her. Blushing and giggling a little, Jenny accepted Angel's hug and then pushed her back and inspected her.

"Wow! You look…you're like a snow queen! And..all of you! I.."

"Welcome, Jenny to our Yuletide celebration," said Aidan, opening his arms. She accepted his embrace and soon, they had all hugged her and welcomed her to their gathering. On the sofas or on the floor before the fire, they sipped the wine, laughing, smiling and talking.

Jenny sat with Angel on one side and Maddy on the other, chattering excitedly. "So, hang on, this is like your Christmas day?" said Jenny.

"In a way," said Angel, "But the Christian Christingle has more of the same root. The idea of celebrating and ensuring the Sun's light is strengthened and continues to bring us light and warmth, I think is similar to the Christian idea, though I think it's more centred on Jesus being the light of the world."

"That's daft," said Maddy, "How can a person be brighter than the Sun?"

"It's a metaphor, sweetie," said Jed, "Jesus' teachings, goodness and kindness were to light a path to being better people, a light in a world of darkness."

"Oh, I see," said Maddy, "He was a good person then?"

"Yes, he was," said Angel, "A prophet, before his time as they generally are, a communist and a philosopher."

"Really?" said Jenny.

"Well, I believe so."

"It's just…"

Everyone's attention focused on the conversation between Jenny and Angel and Angel saw Jenny's doubts and worries bubbling at the surface. For the first time in a very long time, Angel was scared.

"Jen, we were both indoctrinated with the fact that Jesus was the Son of God, born on 25th December, dying on Good Friday and rising on Easter Sunday but I can't accept that as fact. I've studied more, learned more and have a different view now but..." Angel took Jenny's hands and looked into her eyes. "That was religion. This isn't. This is a way of life, an acceptance and understanding of this planet, the universe and the diverse and wonderful ways it behaves and our own intrinsic part in it. I hope you'll enjoy being part of the celebration, Jen and won't be offended."

To Angel's surprise, Jenny threw back her head and laughed, squeezing Angel's hands in hers. "Oh, Angel! I'm so glad you invited me. Thank you." Jenny looked at the slightly bemused faces, "Thank you all. You see, I've been talking to the Moon ever since I can remember!"

Cloaked like the others, Jenny held Maddy's hand and followed behind Jed as they climbed down the stairs to the basement. She couldn't stifle a gasp as they entered the dimly lit chamber, it's walls towering up to the darkness. She held tight to Maddy as they fanned out around the room, while Aidan and Angel lit the wide, cream candles that were waiting in the candlesticks and sconces in the walls. As each came alive, it added it's light to the golden glow in the chamber. They also lit two prepared braziers and soon, the room was crackling and dancing with fire and heat and smoke swirled up to the darkness of the roof, skipping and buffeting the participants as it went.

A massive stone block, draped in a rich red cloth stood in the middle of the room, abundant with glossy green leaves, ivy, Scarlett holly berries and silver crystals. Evergreen boughs, mistletoe and pine cones jostled for space. Golden cones of candlelight spread a gentle radiance that hovered above the stone, strangely powerful and luminous. Jenny noted the candles, black, white, red, green, silver and gold and objects she didn't recognize, as well as a chalice and a dagger.

Angel and Aidan stood before the altar, both in red cloaks, and placed a crown upon the head of the other. Angel's was ivy, with glowing gems of silver and gold, while Aidan wore a circlet of oak leaves and holly. A smiling Sophia who indicated to loose her hood took Jenny's hand and she stood with the five friends, hand in hand as the ritual began.

Candles charged, lit and anointed sent tantalizing smells to Jenny's nostrils. The words, the circle, the air filled with fragrant incense and the crackling of the wood in the braziers, sent Jenny drifting back in time. She saw herself amidst other companions, ivy wound in circlets about their heads, standing in front of a wooden altar upon which cream, fatty candles glowed among the greenery.

Aidan placed a gold ring upon Angel's finger and they all began to sing. Fragments of song stuck in Jenny's mind as the vibrant voices washed over her; 'Queen of the stars, Queen of the Moon,' 'Lord of life, seed of light,' 'The Holly

King's ending is now' and 'Mother Earth, Father Sun, We are one.'

Angel and Aidan, hands held, arms aloft began to chant, "Our home, the Earth is decked with fir and green holly….the God and the Goddess renew the circle of life, passion and love.." and as they continued, tears fell from Jenny's eyes, though her smile remained and she raised her head to the sky as the words washed over her. She stood beside a river. In her hands she held a wheel of ivy, dotted with fat and a wick alight in each and as the singing bounced around her, she skimmed the wheel into the water where it caught the current and floated away. Jenny watched it spinning flecks of gold light into the distance.

"Queen of life and light, we thank you for bringing the newborn Sun" and Jenny understood it all. She knew who she was and she felt welcome, whole, a part of but not apart from and she shut her eyes and sent her message to Arianrhod, the Goddess of the Full Moon.

While Zac and Aidan rearranged the lounge, everyone helped prepare the plates of seasonal food. Slices of turkey and beef, stuffing balls, crispy parsnips and shiny carrots as well as rice, nut loaf and steaming green vegetables adorned the low tables. Upon cushions and bolsters they sat or lay to eat their meal. Crystal goblets held ruby luxury to accompany the food and, though they'd supped and nibbled on spring water and spicy biscuits after the ritual, they all tucked into the feast. Forks and fingers were in abundance and Jenny watched her fellow diners, frequently using the finger bowls and thick linen napkins and did the same.

"Jenny?"

"Mmm?"

Zac sprawled next to her, offering a piece of turkey from his fork and she smiled and opened her mouth, like a baby bird, for him to feed her. The succulent juices engulfed her taste buds and she nodded, eyes wide and then smiled even more, when Zac's huge gentle face beamed down on her. Jenny watched Angel, who had changed her white gown for red before helping in the kitchen, as she and Aidan shared their food, sometimes exchanging a word, a smile or a kiss. Maddy sat in Eli's lap, biting off a morsel of food for herself, her little nose screwing up as if deciphering the components of what she was eating and then, if satisfied, she would feed the rest to him. Eli sat, as if protecting her, one hand holding his goblet, patiently waiting to be fed by Maddy. He smiled at Jenny and raised his glass. She smiled back, reaching for her goblet and did the same, warm and safe amongst the companionship that surrounded her. She ate the tenderest asparagus, butter running down her knuckles and the sweetest stuffing balls, soft in the middle with apple and cinnamon and, as the feasting lessened, her head filled with questions. She knew it wasn't the time to ask them but she also knew that she would find the answers very soon.

Aidan rose from the floor and lit candles set in a log on the table, before taking two huge logs from the basket, one new and the other partly burned. He turned to his attentive audience. "And as the Wheel turns, let last year be consumed by the all cleansing fire and let the New Year of life, hope and love begin!" They all cheered and clapped as he shoved the logs deep into the hearth.

"It's my job to take this year's log out before it gets too burned," whispered Zac in Jenny's ear, "Don't let me drink too much of this and forget."

Jenny turned and smiled into the dark, serious face. She took his cheeks in her hands and kissed him gently on the forehead. "I won't," she said.

The music changed, joyful and clanging, voices raised and parcels appeared and were passed around, navigating food and candles. Jenny found her bag behind her and worried for a second whether her gifts would be welcome and then, the worry was gone and the unwrapping began. Zac beside her had a pair of soft black leather gloves from Aidan and Maddy on the other side, squealed with delight at a china mug covered in fairies. Jenny's own pile produced a chocolate orange and a hand embroidered needle case before she unwrapped a book entitled, "The Wheel of the Year", a gift from Aidan. She stifled the urge to start reading and continued ripping paper until a cry from Angel silenced the assembly. With tears streaming down her face, Angel stood up mouthing 'thank you' to Jenny and held aloft Jenny's present; an intricate silver five pointed star, set in a knotted golden circle.

Swathes of indigo, violet and purple back-dropped the altar and against it hung a silver, crescent moon. Lilies and iris flowed over the altar entwined with cucumber and watercress. A silver pentagram vibrated and shone in the light of the circle of candles. A wand of new willow lay across it.

Seven figures stood in the circle, identical in pure white shifts and new flat leather sandals. Each wore a moonstone on a leather thong about their necks bar one, who wore a citrine flecked with azure, as the sweet scent of jasmine and exhilarating ginseng invaded their senses. A single voice and then the joined chorus protected their work and raised the power.

Seven figures stood on fine white sand, the depth of night around them dappled by a host of glittering stars. A crescent moon appeared and they hailed and greeted the goddess Levanah.

She descended to the horizon where she spoke to them. "Welcome worthy travellers to the sphere of Yesod[15], the Treasure House of Images. Here, everything that is to

---

[15] See Glossary

manifest on earth must first emerge and gain strength. Every dream, every wish and desire must first become an image and be given form here with me. I am the Force before the Form, the Divine Source of all being, who succours humankind and takes care of its needs."

Levanah paused, smiling down, her pure white hair glistening with stars as it enfolded her naked body and her eyes, the bluest cerulean, twinkling like planets. "As individuals, you've been brought together and lead to this point. You've been strengthened and tutored within a family unit, relying on each other for nurture and support. From this point on, whilst travelling the astral planes beyond this realm, you return to your individual status. Guidance and learning will be different for each one of you. Within you exists a special image, now in your unconscious but soon to be made conscious. Be aware of your dreams and you will know. No longer will you view the earth as you once saw it, all things separate and disconnected from each other. You'll see not just the Form but the Force that inspired it and, as you strive on the plane of Malkuth to make sense of these wonders in the face of criticism, disbelief and unkindness remember, you have seen Yesod."

Dark and murky water crashed and flowed all around and above the circle, smashing and mixing and wallowing in a mass of uncertainty. Above the thunderous waves they heard anguished moans, screams and cries and they held each other's hands tighter, seeking comfort from the touch. Levanah rose out of the chaos aboard her crescent train. Silver and glistening in the midst of the darkness, whispering her purity over the bedlam, she calmed and cleansed the waters and they quietened and stilled.

Angel lay in the centre, on the hub, as the wheel began to turn and she rose up into the sky, past the earth and the universe, on into space. There she lay with all that is around her. She saw planets and stars and, as she watched, silver threads began to join one to another and then, each and everyone to her and as each thread attached, she felt a tingle or a buzz and on and on, the threads crossed and joined and soon, space was dark no more, as every planet and star she could see and all the dark matter between were connected.

14

"Now! Now! Do it now!"

Vincent looked into the red indignant face of his son and smiled as he undid the new box that had been slammed into his lap. They sat together on the rug as the gas fire burned their faces and behind them, an artificial Christmas tree lurched into a frantic break dance sequence.

Stickers attached, aerial fitted, batteries installed, the remote control was snatched from Vincent's hand. "Mine!" said Darren, turning his back on his father.

"And *I* will show you how to work it," said Vincent, snatching it back.

"Noooo!"

"But you don't know how to use it!" shouted Vincent, trying to keep possession of the controls as Darren grasped for them. "I can show you!"

"I *want* it!" snarled Darren.

"And you shall have it when I've showed you how it works," said Vincent, smiling at the angry snot ridden, tear stained face. "You want to be the best at it, don't you? I can show you the best way. You can battle with your friends and win."

Darren's face subdued a little and he knelt on the floor. "It's mine though," he said.

"Yes, it's yours, don't worry. Come and sit on my lap and I'll show you."

Father and son played together, manoeuvring the tank around the lounge, even setting up obstacles for it to overcome, until Elaine stood in the doorway, nervously watching them. Dark roots showed through her straightened blond hair and no amount of make-up could cover the strained, tired face as she spoke. "We'll have to get over to Nana and Granddads soon."

"No!" yelled Darren, not taking his eyes from the game. "Don't wanna go!"

"I'm sorry, sweetheart but we have to. You can take your new car with you."

Darren turned his green brown eyes on his mother and stared at her. "It ain't a car. It's a tank and it's gonna beat everyone."

"Okay, well…" Elaine shuffled in the doorway. "You can take your tank with you then and Daddy's coming to get you tomorrow to spend the day with him then, okay?"

"No fuckin' way!"

Elaine gasped. "Darren! That's very rude! You don't speak to people like that! Apologize at once!"

Darren turned his eyes to his mother again and was about to retort when Vincent, his eyes on Elaine, whispered in his son's ear. "Okay, I'll come." Darren stood up. "But there'd better be presents when I get there."

"Of course there will now, say sorry for being so rude," said Elaine, coming into the room with coat, gloves, scarf and hat.

"No," said Darren, "and you can't make me."

Vincent smiled as he drove back to his flat. The car throbbed with American heavy rock and Vincent nodded along as his mind retraced the morning's events. Darren was a bright boy, clever in fact, if channelled the right way. He'd already got the measure of his mother, stupid cow, and far exceeded the potential of his peers. The school had said he was unruly and rude but he just needed to be occupied, that was the way with very bright kids. He'd learn when to speak and when to store the information for later, for more effective use. That was part of growing up and he'd learn to keep his true feelings close, not wearing them and displaying them all the time. He'd learn. Giving yourself away left room for enemies to get to you. Don't give them an inkling that was the answer. No chink in the armour where they might detect a weakness. He'd teach him that.

A break between songs, stuck in roadworks on the motorway, an unwelcome memory pushed to the forefront of Vincent's mind. He'd not hidden his feelings with Miss Stanton. The reflection caused his cheeks to heat but his irritation and anger soon turned to annoyance at the stupid woman who'd tried to play games with him. He didn't need her and her business opportunities!

The traffic edged forward and a bleary winter sun came out from the dirty white sky. So she owned two successful companies. So what? She'd probably been born with a silver spoon in her mouth and a knife and fork as well! Bet she didn't know about grafting from nothing! Vincent dismissed the incident from his mind and began looking forward to getting home and spending the afternoon and evening alone. No interruptions, no worries. His freezer was full, his wine rack stocked and he'd bought himself all the latest combat games and movies. Life was sweet. He didn't need Miss Stanton!

Clare didn't know what time it was or what day it was and she didn't care. There'd been two punters last night, both a bit drunk, but she hadn't cared, just painted on her Scarlett smile and done the job.

The curtains were closed and the only light was from the remains of the scented candle on the table. Next to it sat the jewellers box. Clare wrapped the grubby quilt around her, shivering as she watched the flickering flame.

So, he was just another punter. Not a friend, a lover or a future. How could she have been so stupid?

She recalled his telephone call the previous day. 'I'm so sorry we parted with unkind words, Clare. It wasn't what I wanted. You seem to have misread the situation, that's all, and I'm sorry about that. I was ringing to book for New Year's Eve but I'll understand if you don't want to.'

She didn't. She'd shouted and screamed at him to leave her alone, leave her to her own miserable life. He'd tried to talk to her about choices but she wouldn't listen and now, she sat alone, cold and bereft of all human contact, as even her regular punters had lives to live over Christmas and New Year.

From down in her stomach, down in her being, from the deepest reaches of her soul, the green-eyed monster assembled and formed. It rose and gained power, swelling and expanding until her every pore exuded vicious, acidic slime. She hated them all! All the wives and girlfriends, all the women and families that took her lovers away from her! She pictured Eli at Christmas, nieces and nephews bouncing around him, the table heaving with food, wine and gifts and women at his feet.

He sat on a throne surrounded by naked women and he lifted each chin, stroked and caressed each breast and they smiled lovingly at him, hoping to be chosen. She saw him on a huge bed, entwined with one woman, stroked by another and all the while, they were smiling and then she saw her, Angel, amongst the sweating bodies. Dark hair, brown eyes and perfect teeth smiling up at her and then, Clare was in the room, consumed with jealousy. She pointed the gun and began firing into the bodies, laughing as their smiles turned to screams and she shot them, killed them all for taking her men from her. The blood didn't move her or disgust her; it was necessary to rid her of her pain. She felt happy and fulfilled, rid of all those who'd wronged her and then, a body moved on the bed and Angel sat up. A gaping hole in her forehead and two in her chest hadn't killed her so, Clare fired again but Angel ignored the new wounds and pointed at Clare.

Angel's words spoke in her head. "You're angry at the wrong person, Clare. I didn't take Justin from you. He never loved you, you were just for sex."

"You shouldn't be angry with me, Clare," said Eli, rising from the bed, the left side of his face, flesh hanging and blood dripping. "I didn't do anything wrong. I was a good client who showed you choices, a different way of life you could choose."

All the women began to stir and Clare stepped back as they rose and came towards her, skin and limbs Scarlett and broken and their voices joined in a communal song in her head. "You've wasted your life dreaming of a man that was never yours. You've hated and damned, when you could have loved and shared. You've sought love from men incapable of giving it and now, you've lost Eli, a good man who gave you the chance to respect yourself."

Clare backed away, holding her head, willing the voices to stop but they kept coming. "Is this what you really want? Revenge on people who've never hurt you, so you can carry this imaginary burden for the rest of your life? Look at yourself! Look at yourself!"

Clare stepped back off the edge of the cliff and woke up.

"Clare? Is that you? It's Danielle."

"Hi."

"Clare, you okay?"

"Yeah, just nodded off, that's all."

"Okay, right, well, I was ringing to see how you were and to wish you a Merry Christmas."

"I'm good thanks."

"Right, okay, it's just, well, we haven't spoken since the party and we said we'd keep in touch and, I thought, today.."

"Yeah, well, I'm fine, been busy and…I lost your number."

"Okay, but Tiffany gave you hers."

"I've been busy, I said," said Clare, staring at the candle in front of her.

"Are you really okay? Clare?"

"Look, I'm not a great one for keeping in touch."

"Sorry, I was just concerned about you, that's all."

"That's nice."

"I'm not being nice, I've been worried."

"Well, there's no need. I'm happy doing my own thing," said Clare, ringing the grubby telephone cord with her spare hand.

"Whatever you say," said Danielle. "Well, anyway, Tiffany and Justin are having a New Year's Eve party. Tiffany's not said much but, it seems Just's landed a big new contract for next year and they're celebrating. Why don't you join us?"

Clare stared at the lessening flame, drowning now in the sea of wax around it.

"Clare?"

"I heard. Maybe."

"Look, since we got together last year things are looking up for Tiffany and Justin and, well, I've been seeing Zac and I'm feeling so much better. Look, we were there for each other at school and.."

"I'm fine on my own."

"Okay, look, I'm independent too, ya know but sometimes, its good to lean on your mates…"

"I have to go, Danni, sorry," said Clare, watching as the flame guttered and choked.

"Okay, okay, but the offers there, Clare. Shall I give you Tiffany's address? Clare? Clare?"

Clare hung up the phone as, swamped by the abundance of fiery liquid, the flame went out.

15

In her all in one sleep suit and thick fleecy dressing gown, Jenny shivered around her mug of coffee. A wintry, runny dawn began to break through the patio doors as she snuggled deeper into the sofa and drew a blanket around her, causing a growl from Bagpuss as he tried to hang onto it.

"Sorry, old man," said Jenny as she stroked the disgruntled cat. A rhythmic roar was her reward.

Jenny rubbed her tired eyes and yawned as a hardy bird began to welcome in the day. Sleep had avoided her since the winter solstice but ideas and plans had filled the void and though weary, she smiled to herself as the decisions of last night flooded her brain. She touched the moonstone on the cord around her neck, her gift from Angel and remembered the wonderful Yule ritual, until the key in the lock wiped her mind clean and she leapt off the sofa as the opened door hit the safety chain.

"Can't even get in my own house," said Scott as she let him in.

"It's for safety," said Jenny, "Sorry, I should have told you. Dad put it on. You're very early."

"I told you I would be here before they woke up," said Scott, "Did you think I'd let them down? Something else to hold against me?" He headed for the kitchen, "It's fuckin' freezing in here!"

Jenny let out all her breath, let her shoulders relax before breathing again and adding a cheerful smile before setting off to placate her almost ex-husband. She knew it looked like her old smile to him, but it wasn't. This time, behind her mouth, her eyes and mind shone with life. Life and hopes for the future, her future and that of her children. As the kettle hummed, footsteps and squeals could be heard overhead.

Familiar smells of Christmas flooded Jenny's senses as she stepped into the hall with Finn and Scarlett.

"Dandad!" squealed Scarlett, breaking into a tottering run before Colin scooped her off her feet. She giggled with delight.

"Merry Christmas!" said Colin.

"Merry Christmas!" said Jenny, smiling as Finn spotted Uncle Tim in the kitchen and headed that way, the ideal person to help him with his new space Lego.

Maureen wiped her hands on her apron and greeted her daughter with a big hug. "Merry Christmas, darling. You okay?"

"Mmm, yes, thanks mum," said Jenny.

"You look tired," said Maureen.

"Busy time, this Christmas lark!"

Maureen raised her eyebrows.

"Yes, have had a lot on my mind, no, I'm not sleeping well, happy now?"

"I worry," said Maureen, shaking her head and putting her arm around Jenny to guide her into the kitchen.

"I know," said Jenny, leaning into her, "I love you for it but I'm getting there and I'm happy."

"Good," said Maureen.

Dinner was immense and Jenny felt stuffed and sleepy as they entered the front room to begin the present opening. A tray of tea sustained the adults as Scarlett and Finn set about their task of distributing the gifts from beneath the tree, as Nana Mo read out the labels. In the background, familiar carols and Christmas songs were crooned, while Uncle Tim lit the fire and the candles on the mantelpiece. As the pile of presents grew for Finn and Scarlett, they found their postman tasks harder so, with a shared nod between Nana Mo and Jenny, the time was given over to the children. Finn's new jumper, socks and scarf were soon discarded when a large Lego box emerged from Santa Claus wrapping and he sat with Granddad Colin, unopened presents next to them, constructing his very own Space Station for his Lego craft. Scarlett opened one present at a time, carefully piling up the gifts as they emerged, the height of the tower seeming somehow critical. Books, DVDs, CDs, even a jumper piled well but when an enormous Bagpuss emerged and sent the tower crashing, Scarlett began to cry. Jenny scooped her and Bagpuss onto her lap in Granddad's big chair by the fire, soothing her with whispers and stroking the wispy blond curls. Within minutes, they were both asleep.

Jenny stirred and felt a soft blanket on her shoulder. She smelled the scent of home and breathed in its safety. She sensed her lap felt lighter and then voices began to filter into her head. She heard her name and she listened.

"She'll be fine, mum. She's just tired."

"I know, I know, but I want to help."

"You do, mum, by being you. Jenny knows you're there if she needs you and me and dad. Scott has the kids tomorrow so she can get some sleep then."

"I know, but she's trying to do it all, you know and with all the upheaval and finances and she's lost weight!"

"She did pretty well at dinner!"

Jenny struggled not to smile.

"Yes but that's put in front of her! Goodness knows what she's eating at home!"

"She's fine mum. She's got a family who love her and good friends."

"Yes but everyone's so busy at Christmas, I just worry she's lonely!"

"Mum, listen, I don't think I'm speaking out of turn by repeating this…"

Jenny strained to hear, her face reddening with the effort.

"…But Jenny once said that she felt more alone living *with* Scott than without him and, since she's met up with Angel again, she's beginning to find herself, her old confident self. She'll be fine."

"Yes, yes, you're right I'm sure. It's just, with Dad last year and now this with Jenny…"

"I know mum, but she's fine. She can decide what she confides in us. She's her own person."

I am, thought Jenny, I really am.

"Scott not happy?" said Maureen as Jenny came back into the lounge.

Jenny shook her head. "Is he ever, but it makes sense so stuff him! Thanks for letting us stay, Mum."

"No problem, love."

"And, thanks for sharing your room with Finn."

"No worries, sis. You okay?"

"Yeah, bit weary I guess."

"Been a long day," said Tim, "And once Scarlett had her nap, it got even longer!"

Jenny smiled. "She's a live wire, I know. Up before 5am!"

"But so good," said Colin, "No trouble at all, either of them."

"Thanks Dad."

"No problem, Juney, you relax now."

"I did say to Scott I could drop them to his for 10am but he's insisting on picking them up from here at 9am. Sorry."

"Shush, no more," said Colin, "They're both sound asleep after a happy day with their family. That's all that matters. Rest now."

"I will. Actually, I'd love a glass of brandy, if there is any," said Jenny.

"You sit, I'll get," said Tim. "Think I'll join you. Anyone else?"

"Sherry for me, love," said Maureen.

"I'm fine with my tea, son, but you and Jenny help yourselves."

Jenny stoked the fire, using the gnarled tongs to fish out lumps from the coal scuttle before topping off with a large log. She settled on the rug, leaning back on her Dad's legs, feeling five years old again, before taking her glass and proposing a toast.

"Thank you for a wonderful Christmas Day everyone and let's drink to a Happy New Year for us all!"

"Cheers!"

Maureen retrieved her knitting from the magazine rack next to her chair and a regular 'click, click' merged with the song of the roars, gusts and crackles from the fire.

"I have some news," said Jenny.

The knitting stopped and Jenny felt her dad's hand on her shoulder.

"I've been thinking a lot about what I'm going to do and how I'm going to do it and, I've made a decision. I'm going to sell the house."

"Oh, Jen! Are you sure?"

"Yes, mum," said Jenny. She reached by the fireplace for her bag. "So, I'm returning your cheque. No, please," she added, as her mum and dad made to speak. "I want to tell you my ideas."

Maureen, Colin and Tim sat back and gave her all their attention.

"Mum, dad, I know it's all your savings and that's partly why I can't take it. Hang on, please. If we sell the house, Scott thinks he'll get half, but he won't. I've spoken to a solicitor and me and the kids get the biggest share plus, Scott will have his money and he can get on with his life."

"But if you take the cheque, love, you can pay him and not move," said Colin.

"But I want to move dad, need to in fact. Let's just say the hopes and dreams I had when I bought the house still linger there, a constant reminder of how unhappy and disappointed I've been."

"Oh, love..."

"But not all the time, mum. There's been a lot of joy in that house but the sad memories remain. I need to start afresh and, as long as Finn has a room of his own that he likes and Scarlett her teddies and me there to love them, we'll be fine."

Tim nodded. "And you've been in the house a while and have the new kitchen..."

"...and bathroom and en suite," said Jenny, "It'll sell easily and I can buy something for me and the children together. Something to make our mark on."

"But what about mortgage?" said Maureen, "You'll still need one?"

"I've spoken to the mortgage company. I can transfer the one I have to another property and cut it down a bit with some of the profits from the house."

Maureen's needles started up again.

"You'll stay local though?" said Colin.

"Yes, but I'm thinking about another area. Finn's okay at juniors, I don't mind a bit of a drive, but our local senior school is going down the pan..."

Coffee was made and brought on a tray with Christmas cake that no one had room for but they all managed a small piece anyway.

"Sounds like you've thought about this a lot, Juney," said Colin.

"I have dad but there's more. The school job's been useful but it's not what I want. It's deadly boring and doesn't pay enough."

"But if you go back to the City, you'll have child minding and nursery costs, especially if you're further from us," said Maureen.

"Mum? When I was little, when was I at my happiest?" said Jenny, clutching her knees to her chin.

Maureen looked at her daughter and smiled. "When you were making something. Fairy cakes, collages, paintings, stuff out of cardboard boxes...do you remember the show jumping course you built in the garden?"

"And you made us all gallop round it?" said Tim, "I had a mate round. Right plonker I felt!"

They all laughed.

"Well, I'm going to be making again. I'm going to go back to what I'm good at and makes me happy. I'm going to work with silver."

A fresh pot of tea and hot milk for Maureen and Colin, announced the final part of the evenings deliberations before bedtime.

"So, you'll accept Angel's money but not ours?"

"Mum, please, it's not like that and you know it. This is a business arrangement. Everything I borrow, I'll pay back and, with Angel's contacts and help, I know I can do this. I *really* appreciate your help and, if it's alright, I'll need to borrow a little for up front moving costs..."

"Solicitors and stuff?"

"Yes dad and estate agents and stamp duty, all sorts. I can pay you back when the house is sold and we sort out the savings accounts."

"And moving is what you really want, Juney?" Her father's quiet voice, worried but full of love and respect for his precious Jennifer Juniper, made Jenny smile.

"Yes dad. I need a fresh start."

"Then we'll help any way we can." Her father's tired face brought tears of relief, joy and exhaustion to Jenny and they flooded her face as her dad scooped her into his lap.

16

Vincent hated the days between Christmas and New Year and was glad he had work to do, though the rest of the world seemed incapable of any. He'd made one or two new contacts at the reunion and one in particular he'd felt worth a follow up. He absently flicked a business card with his thumbnail. This guy was small fry though, importing two campers a month for resale, plus any others he got hold of. Hardly big business, but part of that was the fear of risking too much. His mind pondered and quantified and he occasionally noted down some figures but the face that stared in his mind, the voice that called in his head was Miss Stanton's.

Vincent flicked the card across the desk and pushed back his chair, anger rising on his temples. He clenched his fists, striding to the kitchen and returning with a bottle of beer. He scowled as he turned on the pc, sat down and logged on to his mailbox.

Tim waited in the wine bar. Considering its proximity to Canary Wharf, it wasn't too busy this lunchtime, many of the financial employees having taken the time off between Christmas and New Year. He'd spent longer than usual getting dressed but still arrived half an hour earlier than the pre-arranged time, all the while convinced that she would cancel. He waited.

The air in the basement stirred with subtle perfume as a figure approached and roused him from his reverie. "Can I get you a drink?"

Angel stood before him, tall, elegant and cloaked in a coat of fur. He declined a drink and went to stand but she beckoned him to stay seated and soon returned from the bar with two large glasses and a bottle.

"They had a favourite, Bourgogne Aligote," she said, removing her coat, "I hope you'll join me."

Tim pushed away his house white and gratefully accepted the glass she poured for him. "Amazing coat," was all he could say.

Angel laughed. "I receive many outraged looks and comments when I wear it, attitudes to fur having changed so much." She removed the coat and gently laid it on the chair beside her as she spoke. "I bought it, what, must be ten years ago from a little shop in Chelsea, you know, a kind of eclectic mix of new and old, east and west." Her eyes held his as the story unfolded. "The coat belonged to an elderly lady who'd lived nearby. It was at least seventy years old when I bought it and the lady in question lived to 102. In her last years, she gave away many of her possessions. She'd been a bit of a bohemian, a free thinker, a staunch believer in magic and reincarnation and the coat cried out to me. So, considering the souls lost to make it, the least I could do was buy it, have it relined and cleaned and wear it to keep me warm!"

"A noble sentiment," said Tim, "But you've more balls than me!"

Angel laughed again, her soft brown eyes soothing his worries and relaxing him. "I bought a statue as well, if I remember, of Anubis and I still have it now. Do you ever do that?" she said, sipping her wine.

"What's that?"

"Feel drawn to a shop or a place and what one finds there stays with you and changes you?" said Angel.

Tim's mouth made a grimace, "Can't say I do."

"It's alright, Tim, relax. It's not a test." She put a hand on his arm as she spoke and he looked at the perfect long fingers and manicured nails. "I just wondered."

Tim smiled. "Sorry, just a bit tense. It's always an odd week between Christmas and New Year."

"How so?"

"Well, there's the big Christmas build up then the day is over and I've always felt I just want to get back to the routine again, you know," he said, running a hand through his mousy cropped hair and seizing her eyes in his, "But there's this delay, almost another build up before New Year's Eve, which is always a disappointment."

"It is?"

Tim nodded and then laughed. "It is for a sad single bloke like me!"

"Nonsense! You just don't go to the right parties," said Angel, "I know women who'd be queuing up to kiss you at midnight!"

Tim blushed at her words and then dismissed them just as quickly. He knew she was just being kind. His serious face returned. "So do you have plans for New Year?"

"Is that an offer?"

"No!"

Angel smiled.

"You're teasing me, aren't you?" said Tim.

"Just a little," said Angel, "I'm away. Fly Saturday. It's just for a week."

"Nice," said Tim. He looked gloomily at the glass he'd been twisting and took a swig, "Nice wine."

"Tim, what's the matter? You said you'd like meet up to talk about Jenny but…"

Tim rallied from his misery at the sound of Jenny's name. Gone was the self pity and the yearning and, in its place he carried his love for his sister. "Yes, I did Angel. A few things really but first, I wanted to say 'thank you'."

"For what exactly?" said Angel. She sat on the seat beside him, so close their thighs almost touching, her breath warming his face and soul.

"For everything really. Jenny and I had a good chat on Boxing Day and she spoke a lot about you and your friends and the welcome she'd received at Yule."

Angel nodded but remained silent, waiting for Tim to continue, which he did. "You've given her a focus now."

"And before?"

"Before, you showed her she had choices. I guess pagan rituals are a personal choice too but the focus has turned to herself, her life, her career."

"Isn't that everyone's focus?"

"Maybe but not recently for Jenny. Scott made sure of that. He was selfish when I first met him but, since embracing and indulging his bi-sexual self, he's become even worse and with Jenny taking her parental duties so seriously…"

"There's been little time to think about herself."

"Absolutely!" said Tim.

They continued talking about Jenny, pouring more wine and ordering home-made scotch eggs and salad. Relaxed, Tim talked about his work and Angel shared a little of her business dealings.

"In a corporate environment, I'm afraid there are certain criteria that must be adhered to, qualifying oneself to be part of the pack. I even put my name to corporate Christmas cards! What a hypocrite I am!" Angel laughed.

Tim laughed too. "We all follow the rules to fit in."

"Oh, generally, I make a *point* of disobeying them but, my accountant is a wise woman and sometimes even *I* have to tow the line!"

They finished the wine discussing Jenny's decision to move and the possibilities of her starting her own company and Tim bought them lattés.

"So, how about you, Tim? What plans have you got for this year?"

"Do I need some?"

"No, not necessarily, but isn't this the time of year to put resolutions and goals in place?"

Tim shook his head. "The job takes most of my time," he said, "And then mum and dad and Jenny and the kids the rest. I've friends of course but my plans for this year are tied up in the job."

"So DCI Parkes never has time to dream?"

Tim stood on the platform, hopefully scanning the departure boards. It seemed a Sunday service was in operation, ludicrous he felt, as the station was rammed with travellers for the festive season. A prospective train clicked up for platform 14 and he was drawn along in the throng towards it.

He'd vacated his seat for a young mum with a toddler in a pushchair and a tiny baby strapped to her chest, just visible beneath her mum's padded coat so, he stood, crammed in the doorway with an armpit as his main view.

What did Angel know of his dreams? Of course, he wished and wanted like everyone else, but he'd made his choice and picked his focus in the same way that Jenny had and his had come out as the Force. There was nothing wrong in that. He could be himself there. Calm, reliable, solid DCI Parkes. That's why he'd earned his stripes so rapidly. His total dedication to the job made him organized, thorough and precise.

The heat was oppressive as the train moved out of the station and suggestions of opening a window by the standing passengers were met with growls of indignation by those seated. The toddler in the pushchair caught Tim's eye. Her tiny blond head had been relieved of it's hat and she sat patiently looking up at the towering range of humanity around her. The train stopped. Her mother was trying to calm the fractious baby, surreptitiously pulling layers aside beneath her coat to find the breast her child so needed, while talking gently to the little blond cherub beside her.

Tim witnessed the frowns, rustled newspapers and disgust on the faces of his fellow travellers but he felt strangely peaceful as he watched the perfect domestic scene unfold on the crowded train. The train began to move. Once attached, the baby ceased it's mewling and the mother turned her full attention to the mite in the pushchair. A cup of juice, a tub of carrot sticks and a marmite sandwich appeared, followed by a storybook that Tim recognized immediately.

The train stopped again and the lights went out. A few gasps and squeals were followed by moaning as newspapers were folded and dark silence fell on the carriage, only interrupted by the occasional grumpy muttering until a tiny light appeared and he heard the familiar words followed by a giggle from the pushchair, 'he ate four strawberries, but he was *still* hungry!' and, in that moment, Tim knew what he wanted. Maybe it *was* a dream but, if he wanted to make it a reality, *he* was the one who would have to change. He'd been sitting around waiting for too long. Happiness wasn't going to seek him out.

The lights came on to a half-hearted cheer from the carriage but Tim didn't need further illumination. As the train trundled its way east, he brought his dream to the forefront of his mind, playing out the contented scene in his head. Arriving home, his key turning in the lock, greeted by a beautiful wife, a stunning brunette, carrying their baby son on her hip while a toddler with blond curls pulled at his leg to be picked up and, once in his arms, he saw the four of them in the hall mirror. A wife and children in a home of their own.

January

17

Lazy waves shuffled up the beach, cleansing the fine white sand before sauntering back to the ocean. The day shone clean and bright. Palm fronds swayed beneath a cerulean sky and the hot sun melted into it like a pat of organic butter. The verandah of the cabin stretched out to the sand, a side extension of which became a private pier into the water.

Angel and Aidan lay naked on their futons on the verandah, a cotton canopy spread above them, just their toes nudged and tickled by the sunshine. The silence was like an exfoliating massage, stripping away all cares and worries, relieving the muscles of tension and filling the mind with a warm, soporific peace. The sun too and the occasional whisper of a wave, lulled the body into child's sleep, free of responsibilities and pure of thought.

Minutes went by, but no one counted them. Time was only visible by the movement of the sun and when it hit its peak, two figures walked up the beach. One was a man, pulling a kind of sand raft and the other, a woman, with a basket on her head. Lunch had arrived.

Aidan and Angel sat cross-legged, reaching for the luscious fruits spread on a woven grass mat between them, ripe mangoes and pineapple setting their mouths drooling. They fed themselves and each other, laughing as the juice ran down their arms. Parcels of fish, steamed in banana leaves were devoured, the soft flakes melting on their tongues. They finished with fresh figs and pomegranates, eager fingers scooping at the flesh. Satisfied but sticky, they walked to the sea to wash but the warm, clear water propositioned them and soon, they swam and splashed contentedly in the ocean. They emerged and stood together, lips locked, allowing the sun to meld them together.

"Good idea of yours this," said Aidan, propping himself up on the futon and reaching for a bottle of water.

"I thought so," said Angel.

"Handy your mate owns a private jet as well as an island."

"Ah, material possessions making you jealous again?"

"No, just saying it's handy, that's all."

Angel, her long hair a single plaited coil down her neck and naked bar a sarong skirt, turned her knowing eyes to her lover.

Aidan laughed. "You know me too well! Not complaining though. This is heaven."

"Is it?"

"Ah, a theological discussion," said Aidan, turning onto his right side as Angel settled on her left.

"Not necessarily. You know I think heaven is a personal concept."

"And not a reality?"

"But then you have to define heaven first," said Angel, "And here and now, that's only possible against an earthly perspective."

"So?"

"Well, if you believe those who've written about heaven, it's beyond any earthly understanding so…"

They continued, back and forth, until the sun began to lose its heat and the ocean brought forth a cool breeze.

"So, if you believe a place is heaven, wherever it is, then you have a right to include it in your chosen reality?" said Aidan.

Angel turned her head to the ocean. The gentle lapping had changed to a rolling rumble and flecks of surf glistened orange as the setting sun spread out across the sky. "I believe so," said Angel, "But to choose a heaven suggests an affiliation to a certain belief system." She turned to Aidan, sitting up on her haunches as she continued. "As me, I have the right to choose. I have no affiliation. I made my choice when I settled on this Path, but I understand your point." She smiled and nodded.

Aidan sat up, scooping her off her feet and laying her on the futon. He straddled her easily and looked down into the face he loved beyond any other and at the naked, dark tipped breasts caressed by tendrils of glossy mahogany curls that had escaped their moorings.

"And you, my Angel, made the right choice and chose the right Path, and I, in your wake, did too, as did the others," said Aidan, his eyes shining, growing brighter in the oncoming dusk, "To change situations, events and people by ones own will is within everyone, but only *we* believe it possible. It's our destiny to seize the opportunity." His eyes shone white and Angel breathed in his power.

"The Deadly Sins were named by Christianity, named to oppress and terrify the people, to bring them to God, humble and pliant, yet you, my love, through both selflessness and selfishness, can offer to wipe their slate clean because, which ever Path they choose, you give them themselves!"

Angel sat up into his arms, their legs wrapped around each other, locked in their embrace. White pulsing light shone from Aidan's eyes while Angel burned with a fiery red aura, her skin shining with vitality and desire.

As the sun dipped below the horizon, Aidan cried out. "Those who have wronged us will be shown both compassion and revenge and they will choose their own destiny!"

"No, I'm really sorry," said Vincent, nursing a glass of red wine, "I let personal matters interfere with business. Inexcusable, I know, but I'm most grateful for this invitation and it won't happen again."

"How old is your son?" said Miss Stanton, leaning back into the broad, high backed settle that gave them some privacy in the wine bar.

"Four," said Vincent, "Such an important age. Forced to conform to school and rules and yet, not that long ago, just a toddler."

"But you *did* get to see him though?"

"Yes," smiled Vincent, the joy of fatherhood blazoned across his face. "Only a couple of hours on Christmas day but we spent all Boxing Day together. Thank you. Thank you Miss Stanton for asking. I really appreciate that."

Maddy viewed the penitent face in front of her and didn't believe a word of it. Angel had told her Vincent's desire to know what he'd missed, propelled by greed, would make him contact her again and the pretence of domestic squabbles over Christmas access was a simple excuse, also as Angel had predicted. Maddy sighed and wished for the millionth time she was as clever as Angel before smiling in her knowing way reaffirming that, she was her own person and could be as clever as Angel if she liked.

She pulled her camel coat from her neck and loosened her scarf. "Nevertheless, how do I know I can trust you?"

Vincent had obviously been waiting for that one as he replied promptly. "You can't but I'm sure you and your heavy weight friends could soon track me down!" He laughed, hoping to lighten the mood.

"You see, there you go again!" said Miss Stanton, slamming her glass on the table. "Now you're making assumptions that I would do business using a background of menace! No," she shook her head, "You may be good at what you do but I'm not risking you near my business!"

"I'm sorry," said Vincent, his head lowered, hands rubbing hard on his knees, "I don't know how you can trust me or anyone! I just hoped, I guess."

"Look," said Miss Stanton, leaning forward, "I'm not even sure what I have to offer would even suit you but, if you're seriously looking for leads to get in at grass roots, work hard and make big bucks, I guess I could provide those."

"Really?" said Vincent.

Miss Stanton laughed. "In my business dealings I've met all sorts. My companies are all clean, scrupulously so, I wouldn't want it any other way but, I know people, who know people, who know people and there lie people who I won't work with, don't even socialize with, to be honest. Just my way." She took a sip from her glass before continuing, "Yachts on the Med dripping with champagne and hot guys are all very nice but, for me, knowing that lifestyle has been achieved at the expense of others, isn't my style."

"Guns?" whispered Vincent.

"And drugs and....people," said Miss Stanton. "Like I said, I don't *know* these businessmen but, I could give you a few names of people who could point you in the right direction but, I'd think long and hard before getting in too deep, Mr Rogers. I'll give you two contacts. The first can help you think bigger in your own field and the second could lead you out of your depth. Your choice, Mr Rogers."

"I wanted to talk to you, Scott. Just the two of us. Try and get as much sorted as we can before we hand it over to the solicitors," said Jenny.

"Why?"

"Well, it'll save money for a start."

"Yeah, I suppose, but I'm not agreeing to anything without my solicitor being here," said Scott.

"I'm not asking you to agree. I just think we should discuss matters. Look at what's best for everyone and see it from all sides."

"I suppose."

"Well, the most important thing is your regular access to the children and you having your money to get on with your life," said Jenny.

"Oh right, so you know what's best for me and what I want, all of a sudden!"

"I've always known what you want, Scott! Your own way!"

"And this is discussing, is it?"

Jenny shut her eyes and bowed her head. Opposite her at the kitchen table, Scott continued grumbling. "You think you know it all, don't you? Got your piece of paper with all your demands on it and I've got to agree! Well, I don't call that…"

Jenny's eyes flicked open and she ceased his flow of drivel. "Scott, I'm selling the house."

"What?"

"I'm selling the house. You'll get your share and the children and I will…"

"You can't!"

"But I can and I will!"

"Right, this is you discussing again, is it?"

"And that's the problem."

"What?"

"You'll never discuss," said Jenny.

"Right, while you, of course…"

"No, we're talking about *you*, Scott," said Jenny, eyes blazing, "Why can't…"

"Me! Oh right, its all my fault…"

"Yes! It is!"

"While you…"

"No! Not me!" shouted Jenny, willing her anger to recede. "Look at yourself, Scott and stop blaming me!"

"So, it wasn't your idea to split up?" said Scott, running a finger across his eyebrows before folding his arms.

"But who made it inevitable?"

"There was no inevitable! You decided for everyone," said Scott, "Changing everyone's life at a whim and…"

Jenny sat, her eyes fixed on the fake tan and manicured nails. Her stomach churned with anger and helplessness fell on her shoulders, weighing her down. Every word she spoke turned against her, every effort turned on its head. There was no point to this.

"I'm sorry, Scott," she said, quietly.

He smiled with satisfaction. "Of course you are so, there'll be no more talk about…"

"No, I'm sorry I tried to discuss this with you. You ended our marriage, Scott, when you told me you were bi-sexual and taking a male lover…"

"Look, we've talked about this…"

"No we haven't! You decided and told *me* how it was going to be!"

"Do you know how difficult it's been for me?" shouted Scott, hands spread flat on the table, face reddening beneath the tan.

Jenny adopted the same position and yelled back, "Do you know how hard it's been for *me*? To be told by the person you love, who you have children with, that you're not enough, no longer attractive, that you've been usurped by a man!"

"But *I* had to keep my feelings secret for years!"

The anger left her, draining from her body, a burning agony filling the vacuum. The pain of deceit and the terrible knowing that she'd never been what he wanted seeped through every artery and vein. He'd said it, right here and now. Their marriage had been a sham for years, many more than she'd realized. She'd tried not to believe it but there was no hiding now. The truth gave her courage. "Go, Scott, just go. You'll be hearing from my solicitors."

"So, how much you lost?"

"Twelve pounds in five weeks," said Danielle, smiling, "And that's with Christmas and New Year!"

"'Course, you can't really tell yet," said Tiffany, sipping her diet drink as they sat at her kitchen table.

Danielle didn't stop smiling. She felt different, as if all the fat were loosening from her frame, getting ready to be shed. She was proud of herself. "It'll take time but Zac says that losing it slowly and steadily while changing my habits, it's more likely to stay off."

"Well, I suppose he knows best," said Tiffany, "But I've lost a stone in two weeks before now…"

"But I'm happy doing it gradually, honest. Zac says it's like a journey to discover myself again."

"'Zac says'" mimicked Tiffany, "Don't you ever think for yourself?"

"Yeah, all the time," said Danielle, "But Zac's the expert."

"No he's not! He's a fitness instructor and they're two a penny!"

"Fitness instructor, masseuse and life coach," said Danielle, "And, as he used to weigh twenty five stone, I reckon he's an expert!"

"Whatever," said Tiffany, "Seemed nice enough at New Year but remember, he's a friend of Angels."

"So?" said Danielle, smiling, "She's been a good friend, by all accounts."

"Well, he would say that."

"Tiff, she's alright. Look, you might have felt at school she had some sort of influence…"

"She did! Justin told me!"

"And you believe everything Justin says now?"

Tiffany thought a moment, her forehead desperately trying to move with no success. Her tan was particularly bright today and her thick false lashes clung to her face like two hairy caterpillars on an orange. "Whatever," she said, "But she got her come-uppance at the Spring Dance."

"Yeah, I know and I've never been happy about that."

"What?"

"You heard. It was cruel, really harsh. I remember at the time thinking how glad I was it wasn't me."

"Oh, come on! It was just a prank."

"But she trusted Justin and believed he liked her and we both know what that feels like."

"Well, she shouldn't have thought she had a chance with him."

"Why? We three did, and there were plenty of others."

"But you went along with it!"

"We all did, Tiff. Vincent's plan to get his own back on Angel because she wouldn't look twice at him," said Danielle.

Tiffany nodded and sipped her drink. "I'm sure she put a spell on Justin though."

Danielle rolled her eyes to the ceiling and sighed. Some things you couldn't change and Tiffany's mind about Justin was one of them. And Clare too. All these years on and *she* still believed that Justin had loved her and that somehow, Angel had taken him away from her.

The phone in the hall began to trill and Tiffany got up to answer it while Danielle looked out of the kitchen window. It was only two o'clock but the weather outside resembled dusk. Grey clouds filled the sky and buffeted around the garden in the gloom of a sunless day. Damp and cheerless, they hassled the leafless shrubs and bare trees, coating them with icy spit. Danielle shivered and headed for the kettle. It had boiled and she had made her black coffee with a sweetener when Tiffany returned to join her. Beneath the scoured skin on her face, Tiffany looked nauseous and she grabbed Danielle's arm as she sat.

"What's the matter? What's happened?" said Danielle, her heart thumping in her ears.

"Clare's dead."

Angel stood on the beach, a simple circle scuffed on the sand around her and before her the rolling waves of the sea were made mercurial by the full moon. Four oil lamps, mere bowls of simple clay, lit the quarters as the breeze off the ocean caught the cloth of a dark vivid blue sarong encasing Angel's body, flying it like a flag. As the moon sprinkled silver on the beach, it shone on a rugged brown zircon, hung on a cord of plaited reeds, nestled in the curve of Angel's breasts. Though she stood bare shouldered in the darkest point of night before the strength of the ocean, the air in the circle warmed her, as if the light of the moon had turned to sun.

"Oh Great Goddess of the Moon
Patroness of Witches!
Protector of pregnant women, mothers and children!
Oh Wise Goddess!
Dark as night
Illuminator of our dreams!
First of all women – Lilith!
Welcome to this circle
Queen of the Magic!
KI-SI-KIL-LIL-LA-KE!"

Angel felt the presence of Lilith in the circle, her fire and passion, her desire and lust but Angel stood beside her and looked upon her for the first time. Lilith was a tall, elegant figure whose eyes gleamed in the moonlight as tendrils of fire and flame snaked and swirled about her legs. Her long red hair fanned out from her head, a vibrant halo of power, caressing her luxurious features as the depths of all womanhood were blazoned across her face. Full lush lips, a long aquiline nose and huge almond eyes sat proudly below

a high forehead, queenly, regal and powerful as the Dark
Goddess truly was.

Angel looked to the ocean once more as she fought to
stand alone in the presence of Lilith and she raised her arms
to the stars as she spoke.

"Uriel above me
Michael beneath me
Raphael to my left
Gabriel to my right!
By the Power of these Great Angels
Surround me with light!"

Four Angels stood in the shadows of the oil lamps, their
perfect muscled bodies glistening in the moonlight. They
wore simple, undecorated breastplates over their flesh, a
sword belt at their waist over a dark kilt and each, a plain
coloured cloak. Arms wide and wings furled, they embraced
their Invoker, filling Angel's limbs with sizzling white
energy and her heart with courage. Lilith breathed flames
into Angel's breast, filling her head with power and her body
with desire but Angel's spirit was strong and she stood alone
at the entrance to the Path.

"Oh Gabriel, Prince of Change!
Great Angel of mercy and vengeance
Bringer of truth and hope!
Guide me as I set upon this Path!
Wrap your cloak of blue around me
So I may see!"

With the cloak of Gabriel upon her shoulders, the heat of
the flames left Angel and she knew she was herself.

"I stand before the portal ready to learn,
A child and yet not a child,
A babe and yet full grown,
Years of man have aged me,
Yet my spirit burns eternal!
Show me the clarity I seek upon this Path."

The air in the circle buzzed in Angel's ears as before her stood the Angel of the Path, Raphael, Prince of Brightness, Beauty and Life. He spoke to her.

"Though the Universe is in constant flux,
Wending and winding through chaos to harmony,
Life force, your spirit, your true self remains constant,
Heal the past and you will be well."

Raphael raised his arms and his wings unfurled touching the stars and the light that emanated from his being was golden and warm, sending honey through Angel's blood. She felt all the knowledge within her rising to the surface, slowly and tentatively, playing peek-a-boo as the healing yellow light filled her soul.

The sand beneath her feet became rich verdant grass and the smell of the earth and the sounds of nature came to her on a woody, sunny path. The air chuckled with spring as bees busied and birds twittered freely as they flitted to and fro, finishing their nests. Angel followed the path as the trees became less dense until she came upon a clearing and saw a Hebrew letter hanging in the air before her and she cried the name aloud. "Samekh!"

An explosion of light and heat burst in front of her and all the trees, plants, everything was incinerated, turning the landscape to grey, inanimate ash. Silence oppressed her and tears fell from her eyes but, as she listened she heard a pulse, a flicker of a heartbeat and as she watched, the ground at her feet began to tremble and swirl. A column of grey dust began to form, growing as it rose, gathering momentum until it too exploded and there, filling the world was the Phoenix, the bringer of life and Angel gazed at its artistry. She didn't just see a wondrous bird with feathers of red, orange and yellow but a fiery beauty, blazing with light and life, love and hope, a positive, resurrected life from the nothingness all around it.

The Phoenix raised its majestic head revealing feathers of vibrant purple at its neck and looked up into the sky and

Angel saw the constellation of Sagittarius, standing out in the dense dark blue. From the dull, grey wasteland the fire bird had emerged and he rose into the sky on flaming wings, roaring with life as he ascended and with a flick of his glossy comet tail, he crossed in front of Sagittarius like an arrow. Angel watched him transcend the arc of the sky and was gone.

Angel sat at her desk in the familiar classroom in front of the blackboard, watching the teacher's back as he wrote on the board. She felt the synthetic bottle green fabric of her skirt heating her thighs, the tightness of the top button of her shirt digging into her throat and the pain across her calves of thick elastic bands holding up her lifeless off white nylon socks.

She panicked, while frantically scribbling the words from the board, when the ink ran out of her fountain pen, and she knocked her textbook off her desk as she wrestled to find a cartridge in her pencil case. As she bent to retrieve the book a classmate bent down to it too and their hands met.

"What's the rush?" said Lilith, handing Angel the book, her red hair and amber eyes glistening as she spoke.

"I have to get the words on the paper," said Angel, still wrestling with her pen.

"But why?"

"I need to know the answers," said Angel.

"To what?"

"Everything!"

"But *why* can't I have a friend to tea?" asked Angel, her brown eyes brimming with tears and her bottom lip trembling as she spoke.

"Because I said so," said Mother.

"But you *know* the answer and won't *tell* me!" cried Angel, stamping her little foot in its brown sensible sandal as her mother wiped a grey flannel over her face and then her hands.

"Your father and I know best," said Mother, taking her to the table and beckoning Angel to sit.

"But *why* do you know best?"

Father sat at the head of the table. "Enough questions, Angel."

"But…"

"No! I said no! Life's journey is about seeking the answers. Your Mother and I are your elders and therefore know best."

"But, father…"

"*I am speaking!*"

Angel's head fell and so did the silence. From that moment on, she heard the world around her, the trees creaking as the wind blew, the rain teaming down her bedroom window and she felt the world too, the sun coaxing the plants from the soil and snowflakes falling on her lids and tongue but she took upon herself the silence, the less to offend or be berated. She heard her father's words as she grasped her grubby knees beneath her cotton dress with her hands and screwed up her chubby face to stop the tears.

"In September, you will go to school and your life of gaining knowledge will begin. When you have learned everything, *then* you can make your own decisions but until then, *we* will decide for you!"

"And you believe that?" laughed Lilith, ringlets quivering at her neck.

"Of course," said Angel, "When I know everything, my life will be my own."

She knew he liked her. Though the hall thronged with pubescent life, his blue eyes caught hers every time she

looked and when they met, her body reacted; her skin
prickled with warmth, her mouth dried and her womanhood
moistened. She knew he liked her. And then they'd danced.
Not a slow, smoochy, groping dance but a dance where they
heard the same notes and translated them in synchronicity so
they danced as one. They didn't stare longingly into each
other eyes but Angel felt his glances on her neck, her
shoulders, her breasts and her face. She knew he liked her.
He'd smiled and brought her a drink and they'd stood
against the panelled wall and he'd whispered in her long
dark hair. They'd danced again and she'd draped her arms
around his neck, all the better to survey the chiselled tanned
jaw line and sparkling blue eyes set in ebony lashes. She
knew he liked her.

He'd held her gently on the hips, occasionally brushing a
hand up her back, sending shivers to her knees and then he'd
asked her to meet him outside by the pond, to be alone in the
moonlight for their first kiss. She *knew* he liked her.

She'd stood and waited as he asked, her eyes shut, heart
beating, lips trembling, awaiting the kiss, the kiss that said 'I
like you', because she knew, she *knew* he liked her but
instead...

Angel sat sobbing on the wall by the pond.

"So, *did* you know?" said Lilith, next to her, loosening the
knot on her bottle green tie.

Angel shook her head.

"So what of all the knowledge now?"

"But he said...but..."

"He lied," said Lilith, "People do that."

"But everything I thought I knew..."

"...means nothing without understanding. Justin
pretended to like you. He filled your head with the
knowledge that it was so but you failed to understand the
situation. It was a joke, a prank, lift you up, smash you

down," said Lilith, lighting a cigarette as her legs swung on the wall.

Angel shook her head and resumed her crying.

Lilith put an arm around her. "You *do* know stuff, you're clever but, to understand, you need to understand people. You've always been alone, except for Jenny, so you cannot understand what makes them tick."

"But why, why would he do that?" said Angel, blowing her nose.

"Because Vincent told him to, no, bet him he couldn't actually."

"What?"

"Vincent made a bet with Justin; Justin had to get you to believe he liked you and get you to come outside for a kiss. Vincent wanted Justin to fail because you told Vincent to get stuffed when he asked you out," said Lilith, offering the cigarette to Angel.

Angel took it and inhaled. "So, when Justin succeeded…"

"…Vincent thought up the cruel and final blow," said Lilith.

Angel shook her head. "Don't say it."

"You say it then."

"No, no, it's…it's too…no…"

"Then I'll say it for you," said Lilith, "Vincent tortured a fish to death with a cigarette and then stuffed it, burned and bloody into your mouth. But did you see Justin's face right at the end?"

Angel sat, tears streaming down her face, gulping for air between sobs. She shook her head.

Lilith took the cigarette from Angel, inhaled and grinned. "You *did* know!"

The sun was high in the sky but the Welsh mountains had conspired together and produced banks of rolling grey clouds to conceal it. Angel stepped off the school bus in

jeans and jumper and hastened her steps as an ominous
rumble issued from over head. She'd no lessons at college
this afternoon so she'd planned to take her art bag to the
woods and sketch the landscape as autumn approached.

She smiled as she turned onto the track to the house. She
was only three weeks into college and yet, she'd already
made friends. Students had approached her, offered her
company and she'd enjoyed the attention. Today, Owen and
Gareth had almost fought for the seat next to her in Classics
and the memory made Angel smile. She passed a shiny black
car, parked in the hedge as the double track narrowed on the
approach to the house but gave it little thought as she
ascended the short climb and then, as the ground levelled,
ran off the front driveway to enter the house through the
kitchen.

Angel hoped Mrs Jones would be baking today but no
fresh smells rose from the oven and there was no sign of the
housekeeper at all. Brigit was also absent, Mrs Jones'
daughter who helped in the house so Angel took biscuits
from the tin, an apple from the bowl and filled a flask with
water, leaving them on the big oak table before climbing the
back stairs to her room.

She had the key in the lock when her peace was disturbed
forever by the shrill voice of Aunt Alice. "Angel! Come here
now! I saw you on the drive, child. The drawing room this
instant!"

The man from the black car was small and mousy, dressed
all in black with a high white clerical collar and he bowed
his head between his words, as if he hadn't the strength to
hold his head up for a whole sentence. He grasped a large
brimmed black hat in his hands before him, turning it $12°$
every time he bowed.

"Such a tragedy…to become someone…so very
young…Of course your parents…left everything to

you…upon your coming of age…Until then your aunt…will be in charge…of your inheritance."

Aunt Alice stood at his shoulder as he delivered his speech, unblinking and unmoved. Though more diminutive than Mr Brunswick, Aunt Alice' presence filled the cold, grey drawing room that smelt of crumbling gravestones and forgotten catacombs. Her hair parted in the middle, smearing her small scalp with sparse grey hair while her brown eyes were piercing and leered at Angel, above her severe grey dress, adding no comfort to the devastating news.

Mrs Jones and Brigit had held her as she cried the tears of loss, but they weren't for her parents but for herself. Tears for the end of her childhood, naivety and innocence. Tears for the end of family.

Angel sat at the window seat in her room as the rain thundered on the sills, silently watching as the heavens unloaded their tears. Minutes and then hours passed before her and soon, as the sun dipped below the horizon somewhere in the wet outside, the grey light of dusk descended on the scene through Angel's window, turning the trees to gallows and the mountains to fortresses. In her heart, the agony of fear twisted the words from her lips and she cried out her pain to the night and, in reply, a breeze took up that soon became a wind and blew the clouds from the sky revealing a multitude of stars and, just peering from behind a peak, the full moon.

The Moon smiled a gentle silver wish upon Angel as it rose and Angel's heart breathed with happiness. They spent the night conversing in this way until, as the birds broke free of their silent sleep and the sun yawned and stretched upon the horizon, Angel understood what she must do.

Angel felt the damp grass between her toes and the breath of a breeze upon her shoulders as she stood in the woodland glade. She knelt to pick daisies and began making a chain.

"You've learned much, sister," said Lilith, joining a daisy to the string.

Angel nodded and smiled, running her hands over the grass, her face glowing in the warmth and freedom of nature. "I have," she said. "Knowledge for its own sake is worthless without the experience of understanding and to understand, one must be amongst others, others who understand, who see the Universe as I do."

"And you found them?" asked Lilith.

"I did."

Back on the beach in the moonlight, Angel thanked her invited guests and closed the circle before creeping into bed next to the snoring Aidan, blissfully unaware of her absence, and fell asleep.

18

It was just before 5am as Rob turned his key in the lock. In the kitchen he smiled at the counter where laid out for him by Teresa were two ham salad sandwiches wrapped in film, a small teapot with the bag enclosed and a thermos flask of hot water, so he wouldn't need to boil the kettle. He made his tea and took his mug and plate into the lounge where a small side lamp glowed in the murky light of dawn.

Rob unwrapped his supper, or was it his breakfast? He chuckled to himself and let his mind wander over his first evening at his new job. Teresa had insisted on a thermal vest and he'd been glad of it as there had been a lot of standing outside. He'd got on well with the bouncer at the first club and the two dancers were friendly. The second club had been

a bit of a dive and he'd been happy to sit in the car, awaiting
a text from Shirana to meet them at the stage door. The last
place had been far more up market. He took another bite and
chewed and then stopped, and then two more chews. A hot
flush of knowing seeped down from the top of his head and
flowed over him. He could taste what he was eating; the
saltiness of the ham, the crisp greenness of lettuce, sharp
pungent spring onions, soft sweet juicy tomatoes and a hint
of pickle. Tears welled in his tired eyes and he cuffed them
away with a laugh and carried on eating. The girls had
emerged with two men and he'd driven them to the hotel.
Keeping awake in the underground car park had been a bit of
a struggle but he had his thermos of coffee and emergency
granola bar and had only needed the former before the
message came to bring the car to the front entrance. He'd
done well and he knew it. Proud as a Coldstream
Guardsman, Rob went to bed.

Sticky dirty snow clung to the feet of the mourners as they
stood outside the crematorium. Danielle viewed the sad,
grey faces, so very few beside Clare's flowers, though the
centre was busy on the third Monday of January. The harsh
spell of weather since Christmas had tolled the end for many
frail old people, but Clare was one of the young ones.
    Danielle looked at Clare's mother and sister, clinging like
a koala and baby, faces empty and blind, as they stared at the
main floral tribute, oblivious to the people around them.
Anonymous men wiped an eye and walked away. Clare's
sister, Kathleen, accepted sympathies and acknowledged the
benefactors need to leave while her mother stood alone,
wringing her hands in holey knitted gloves, her saggy face
pinking in the freezing air. Beneath the matted coat, she
wore plimsolls and no tights, her pudgy ankles swollen like
pink blancmange escaping their mould. There were no other
women there except Tiffany, tear-stained and bereft standing

with Justin, leaning against him. Danielle saw him look at his watch. She would have liked Zac with her but he didn't know Clare and anyway, he'd booked to take part in a Triathlon in South Africa with Eli months ago. Rob and Vincent hadn't come.

Danielle felt sad. Not sad for the mother. Mrs Maloney's opinions, relayed by Tiffany, had been voiced on the telephone. "They're calling it an accidental overdose, it bein' New Years Eve, 'n' al' but I can tell ya, plain 'n' simple, she did it on purpose to spite me! She knew what she was a doin'! The trouble she's caused! A suicide in a good Catholic family! Well, it didn't work, ya see, 'cos my priest, now my priest he says 'Mrs Maloney, you *are* a good Catholic and though you may lead, you *cannot* make others follow. You've done everythin' you can for a wayward child. There'll be no reprisals for you on this earth or in heaven while you continue to repent o' your own sins.' And *how* I tried with that girl! And Kathleen tried too! How blessed am I to have one good Catholic daughter."

Danielle watched Kathleen, pinch faced like her older sister, but larger and saggier like her mother. No more than twenty-seven, she looked thirty years older. Her pale blue eyes held a future of resignation, probably a past too, agreeing and pandering to a spiteful zealot rather than cutting herself off as Clare had done.

Tiffany was still crying and though she wept for Clare, Danielle knew she was crying for the past, the teen years shared and not for the confused, unloved body in its cheap pine coffin that had disappeared behind the curtains to 'Ave Maria.'

Danielle was saddened by the waste of it all. A mother who didn't love her daughter, who even now could feel no love towards the child she'd lost, a sister who couldn't help or love her sister and friends who'd appeared too late to make a difference to a desperate thirty year old woman's life. She'd been the first of the gang to turn thirty on the 28th December and nobody had known. The phrase 'Life's too short' sprang into Danielle's mind and she felt her own mortality hanging over her.

"Probably one lonely Christmas too many," said Tiffany from the front of the car, trying to tidy her make-up in the sun visor mirror as Justin negotiated the ice rutted road.

"Wish we'd got in touch again with her sooner, maybe helped in some way," said Danielle from the back of the car.

"You can't blame us!" said Tiffany, turning indignantly, "I've tried before and we included her at the reunion. We tried."

"I know, I know," said Danielle, rubbing condensation from the side window. "So few people."

"Well, she said she wasn't good at keeping in touch. You have to make an effort to see your friends."

And get pissed with them every Friday night, thought Justin. While the women continued talking, Justin's eyes were on the road while his mind was elsewhere. He'd signed the contracts on Friday morning. He had the deal, the project of a lifetime ready to begin. He hadn't told Tiffany. He would but for now, he enjoyed the feeling of pleasure and pride in his own success. Lewis had overseen a build at the beginning of January but construction had ceased with the onset of the freezing weather. Justin wasn't bothered. He had plenty to occupy him for the next month without the need to step onto the site. Windows, doors, heating systems, drainage; the list was endless but he was looking forward to getting home and making a start.

Justin, Tiffany, Harry, Chloe and Chelsea sat at the table eating fish and chips from the paper. Tiffany eased the batter off her fish and gave it to Chelsea. Justin raised an eyebrow.

"She's a growin' girl 'n' anyways, she likes the crunchy bit, don't ya poppet?"

The chubby girl grinned and nodded.

"Well, I'm glad you're all here," said Justin, smiling, "Your clever dad has landed a big contract so, I'm gonna be working more for the next six months but," he turned his head, looking at them all as they looked up from their food, except Chelsea who kept eating. "Let's just say, we may well be moving to a bigger house next year and Florida isn't out of the question!"

Harry and Chloe cheered as Chelsea looked up. "What's Flowida?"

"It's a town in America," said Tiffany, "Where Mickey Mouse lives."

Chelsea thought a moment then her eyes began to widen, "Disneyland?"

Tiffany nodded and smiled and they all laughed and chatted over their meal.

Justin sat propped up in bed in his dressing gown, an open notebook in his lap and his pencil scribbling within it.

"You sure you should've told the kids?" said Tiffany's muffled voice from the en suite.

"What? Tell them what?" said Justin, irritated by the interruption to his flow. He put the pencil and pad on the ledge of the bedside cabinet, removed his gown and got in.

"About the contract and the money. You said 'Wait until its signed' ya know."

"It is," said Justin from his pillow.

"What is?" said Tiffany, her head appearing in the door, her face white with cream.

"Contracts signed," said Justin.

"When? What happened? You didn't tell me!" said Tiffany coming towards the bed.

"Friday, done, sorted, now shut up and let me sleep."

"Well, I'm happy to come and have a look, if you like, but realistically, I couldn't start for a month at least."

"That's alright," said Tiffany, "I want the measurements and plans done and we can work on them in any wever!"

"Well, I'm out of the country until the second week of February…"

"Oh, really?" said Tiffany.

"Yes, I'm flying to Rome on Tuesday, if the airports are open."

"What about Monday? I'm free Monday."

"Err, well, I suppose I could drop over but…"

"Good, that's good. The address is…"

"So, what's so exciting about Rome?"

"Sorry?"

"You said you were flying to Rome tomorrow," said Tiffany.

Aidan laughed and his face relaxed into his bright easy smile. "Ah, yes but its business, I'm afraid. Hoteliers interested in my vertical gardens. Quite a feat of engineering getting the irrigation to flow and keep the soil moist and then the heating system and optional solar panels." He stopped at Tiffany's blank face.

"You know, gardens on walls or free-standing. Ideal with developments where floor space needs to be utilized…" he stopped and changed tack, "Anyway, its business not pleasure but let's concentrate on you."

Tiffany broke into a huge smile, dropped her eyelids and squeezed her breasts together like two huge netballs in a sock, "Yes, let's," she said.

The temperature in the lounge was rising thirty and Aidan had stripped down to an olive green t-shirt while Tiffany sat in a mini skirt and vest top. Sketches on A3 paper lay on the coffee table.

"So, with such major landscaping, you've got to be thinking 5k for the basics, you know, machinery, soil removal, manpower and then the foundations, cabling, irrigation…Forgive me but, are you sure this house warrants the expenditure?"

"What?" said Tiffany, stopping her edging closer on the sofa.

Aidan was already pressed into the corner and was relieved at the opportunity to escape. He eased himself out and balanced his butt cheeks on the edge of the sofa and turned to face Tiffany. "Look, I'm happy to do whatever a customer wants but, it's a huge amount of money. Will you get it back if you sell? I can't help thinking…"

"Well, don't!" said Tiffany, leaning forward, eyes and breasts staring, "You said you do whatever the customer wants."

"Of course, well, I'm happy to go away and put these ideas into some sort of plan for you…"

"But now, you'll do whatever the customer wants," said Tiffany, grinning as she stripped her vest top over her head revealing two orange spheres, ridden with purple veins, adhered to her frame.

Aidan leapt up, "Mrs Preston!"

"Oh, come on," said Tiffany, getting up and stroking his arm "You knew this was gonna happen."

"What!" cried Aidan, backing away. He turned his back. "Please, please put your top on."

Tiffany approached from behind and flattened herself to his back. "Oh, come now, you know you want them. Have a feel."

Aidan unpeeled her arms from his waist and spun her round facing away from him. He held her upper arms firmly but with no aggression.

"I'm shocked, Mrs Preston. Shocked and hurt. I gave up my day before my trip as a favour to you. Now get dressed."

Tiffany picked up her vest top and put it on.

"Mrs Preston, I came to plan your garden."

"Yeah, but you was all over me at the party!" said Tiffany. "Look, there's no big deal okay. I'm not askin' for love or nuffin. You're a bloke and all blokes want sex. What's the problem?"

"The problem, Mrs Preston, is that I came over in good faith to talk about landscaping your garden. I was not expecting to be seduced by a married woman!" Aidan worked hard not to smile. His tone of indignation was almost too much to bear. Angel would have been proud of him. However, it made no dent in the armour of Tiffany's morals.

Week after week, Justin had been working, sometimes at home, sometimes in London. She'd tried everything to get him to have sex with her but he insisted he was too tired. It was probably some assistant of the wonderful Miss Anderson who'd succumbed to his charms. She didn't care who, but she did care when he wouldn't shag her as well. All this frustration had come to the fore and now, so close to her goal, her plan had been thwarted. "So, that's it then?" said Tiffany, folding her arms.

"It's up to you," said Aidan, running a hand through his sweaty hair, "I can put this episode behind me if you want me to do the garden but I will perfectly understand if you don't want me to."

"And you don't want sex?"

"No, Mrs Preston, I don't."

"Then fuck off!" shouted Tiffany, "You fuckin' tosser! You're just a player you, a tease, a fuckin'…fuckin' vag teaser!"

Aidan was glad to gather the papers and turn his head from the raging woman so he could hide his grin.

"Fuck off and don't come back, do ya hear!" She followed him to the door, still swearing at him as he piled on the layers before braving the outdoors. As he stepped out, the front door was slammed with anger at his heels.

"So how did it go in South Africa?" said Angel.

"Not bad," said Eli, bringing coffee through to the lounge. "Made up twenty two places with the swim and maintained it on the bike, but it was my road race that let me down."

"Thanks," said Angel, accepting her cup and tucking her fluffy socked feet under her on the sofa, "What do you mean, 'let you down'?"

Eli shook his head as he sat in the opposite corner of the sofa. "Just didn't have the legs left but that's okay. I'm continuing my winter training here, a few European triathlons in September and October and then I'll see where I'm at." He grinned. "It's pounding the roads for me for the next few months!"

"How many triathlons have you competed in?"

Eli leaned back and sipped his coffee. "About fifty but that's over ten years or so. Got really keen in my youth but then the distractions of the fairer sex kept me from my training."

Angel smiled. "I can imagine," she said, "But you and Zac have been training together these past two years?"

"Nearly three and Zac's helped me no end! He's very disciplined and focused while me, you know I'm easily distracted. The plan is still for us both to compete in the Iron Man African Cup in Port Elizabeth next year, April I think it is."

"And Zac?"

Eli grinned, his whole face beaming as his blue eyes flirted with Angel. "Well, you know we were talking about distractions…?"

"Of course. Danielle."

"And he has another disadvantage."

"Yes?"

Eli scratched the blond bristles on his chin with thumb and forefinger as he spoke. "Zac's not a great swimmer. He won't mind me saying that. Cycle times, running times, no problem but his swim puts him at a real disadvantage. We were talking on the way home about fitting in more swimming but he's the gym to run and personal fitness training and now Danielle. It's going to be tough."

Angel sighed. "There's always so much one wants to do. Do you mind that Danielle's gate crashed your training partner?"

Eli laughed a raucous belly laugh. "Not at all, lucky bugger! No, I say, good luck to him and it's Zac's training it affects, you know, not mine."

Angel nodded and snuggled deeper into the brown velour sofa that took up most of the lounge of Eli's tiny London flat. She felt chilly even in her cashmere jumper, leggings and socks. As Eli was always warm and didn't believe in heating, he'd provided her with a blanket that she'd wrapped around her shoulders while he sat at his end of the sofa in t-shirt and shorts. "So how did you feel when you got the news about Clare?"

Eli sat for a moment and took a swig of his coffee before he spoke. "Shocked at first, I suppose but in retrospect, I'm not surprised. I mean, I don't think she did it on purpose. She didn't have it in her."

"Just over did it?"

Eli nodded. "I did wonder if I was the reason at first but Angel, that girl lived in a different world. She couldn't focus on reality for a second."

"How do you mean?"

Eli took a deep breath and let it out slowly before speaking. "I've thought back over our meetings and while it was fun and when we were out of our heads on alcohol and sex, you know, she seemed happy, but she couldn't face reality, the real now and I know from what you've said that she lived in the past. It was like," he paused, organizing the phrases before he spoke them, "she blamed everyone for her situation but herself and so, offering to help her change, wasn't what she wanted."

"She would have had to accept that she was wrong in the past."

"Absolutely!" said Eli, sitting upright, "She couldn't do that."

"It was easier to stay the same," said Angel.

"But more than that," said Eli, "She was waiting for the perfect man to come along and make life right for her."

"I'm glad you've got your head round it. I knew you would but it is sad."

"It is, Angel, but we've all been there, haven't we?" said Eli, his broad face open, honest and sincere. "Us friends have all had childhoods in this life that could have sent *any* of us on a course of self destruction remember, but we took the opportunity of a new family that you gave us. With true family comes love and support and we've been there for each other but one has to be willing to accept the past, deal with it and embrace today."

"Wise words, Eli, wise words."

19

As the E class Mercedes Benz sped towards the city from Leonardo da Vinci airport, Aidan tapped at his laptop. The business class flight had been a pleasant one and he'd enjoyed the fussing of the attentive cabin crew so, relaxed and happy, he organised his appointments for his stay in Rome.

It was cold in Italy but nothing like the freezing conditions he'd left in England. He'd been lucky his flight had only been delayed half an hour, as a fine dusting of new snow fell at Gatwick. He'd chosen a hotel near the river, south of the city near the parks, hoping to draw on the natural elements of Rome as well as the architecture and history when planning his pitch to the hotels. Paris was easy. He and Angel often frequented its cafés, restaurants and nightlife but they'd only spent one weekend in Rome in the early days of their relationship and only left their suite for a brief stroll.

As they neared the city outskirts, the chauffeur gliding through the traffic, Aidan remembered that first visit. He relaxed into the soft leather upholstery with a smile while the delights of Angel filtered through his brain and awakened his groin. As the city rose around them Aidan looked out of the window. They passed under a massive arch and the Colliseum stood before him, curving against the skyline, impressive even in the weak winter sunlight. They drove on until the Mercedes slowed down over wide cobbled roads and pulled up at the hotel, its cream rendered frontage ice cream bright in the frosty air.

Aidan loved the simple fresh lines of the lobby décor and was equally impressed by his small suite of rooms; clean, airy and comfortable with a view out over the River Tiber.

It was mid afternoon once he'd showered, made calls and finished planning his business so, wrapped in a scarf and overcoat and his bag on his shoulder, Aidan set off in search of a café. The Palatino Bridge took him over the river, the wind picking up as he crossed, making his eyes water, where he admired the narrow streets and rendered fronted dwellings as he moved from piazza to piazza. A palette of creams, rusts and stone had been used to colour the buildings, some wearing shutters, others entered by a broad front door. The pavements were sparse of people until he reached the Piazza Trilussa where a small covered market lured in humanity, tempting it with its refreshments and wares. The smell of sweet cake and coffee caught Aidan's palate and his mouth watered as he rubbed his cold nose and joined his hosts huddled in the market.

At a table near the river, Aidan made friends. His Italian was non-existent but proved not a hindrance as he opened his sketchbook, a tin of charcoal and pastels and began to draw. With his bright blond hair and vibrant green eyes, Aidan was a novelty and soon, an excited crowd gathered round him, many bringing their chairs to sit and gaze at the stranger as he drew. Conversations, cigarette smoke and gauzy breath floated up from the crowd. The bridge and then the river emerged first on the paper, with the buildings on the other side mere glimpses of outline. Another sheet produced the market, snuck in its niche as the buildings around the piazza caressed and sheltered it from the elements.

Aidan unbuttoned his coat and took a bite of cake, eyes rolling skyward as honey and chocolate melted in his mouth. The chattering crowd cheered at his obvious pleasure and a little girl laughed with delight as he emerged from his mouthful of coffee with a frothy moustache. Ripping off another sheet of paper, Aidan drew a face framed by tiny corkscrew curls which he smudged in with brown as he did the eyes and, with a few strokes of blue that were shoulders and scarf, he turned the paper to the girl and her mother. Gasping, clapping and laughing they beseeched everyone to look as Aidan signed the picture 'AQ' and presented it to the mother with a nod and a smile. As news spread through the market, Aidan spent his first afternoon in Rome sketching portraits, giving out business cards and drinking coffee.

"Sounds like you're having fun," said Angel.

"Don't I always?"

"Yes darling, you do."

Aidan lay naked on the sofa in his hotel suite while Angel, in a white satin wrap, sat in his lap on the computer screen.

"How's Eli?"

"Fine," said Angel, "Time away did him good. He's thought carefully and put everything into perspective."

"Did the triathlon go well?"

"He was pleased with his placing and Zac too and they're both looking forward to a big event next year."

"In South Africa?"

"Yes, Port Elizabeth," said Angel.

"But no problems with Clare?"

"No, I'm sure he's fine. He feels the sadness we all do Aidan but he's convinced that nothing could have changed her."

Aidan nodded as Angel continued. "It seems she was waiting for Prince Charming to make the world right for her."

"But how could anyone do that when she wouldn't let go of the past?"

"Exactly, and even if there was such a man, a man who met up to the standards she required, how long before a smile at a waitress or a friendly glance at a shop assistant threw her world back into chaos?"

"You're right," said Aidan, "So, it was suicide?"

Angel shook her head. "Eli agrees with the police. 'Accidental death'."

Aidan nodded. "Perhaps we could go out there for the race next year?"

"The triathlon?"

"Yes, do you fancy a trip to South Africa?"

"Maybe," said Angel, "We'll have to sort out planning when you get back. We've been invited to a wedding in Scotland in August and Fiona mentioned something about a film festival. When's Cannes?"

"June I think. Who's the invite from?"

"Pierre, Pierre Laconte, owns that wonderful restaurant in Paris with the aluminium sculpture, remember?"

"Pierre whose mother looks younger than he does?"

Angel sighed and smiled gently from the screen. "Yes, Aidan, that's the one. Anyway, we can deal with our diaries when you're home. Did you manage to confirm all your appointments?"

"Yes, but they've shunted around. I'm not seeing Georgio Spellman until Friday as he's in the states but I'm having lunch with his mother tomorrow and the meeting with Caldieri has been changed to Thursday afternoon."

"You're still coming home Friday night though?"

"Why? Do you miss me?"

Angel smiled gently into the camera as she untied the ribbon that fastened her gown and held the glossy material open, exposing her voluptuous breasts, tipped with pointed brown nipples. "Why, do you miss *me*?"

Aidan arrived early for his lunch appointment and sat sketching in a small notebook as waiters scurried around the tables. He ordered a vodka martini to sip as he drew, watching the top echelon of Roman society. Gems were in abundance even at lunchtime and he greeted the enquiring glances and whispers behind jewelled hands with a smile and a slightly subservient nod. He drew the flower sculptures, trailing ivy upon their pedestals, the ornate architecture and ceiling roses and he sketched glimpses of customers at their tables; a jaw line framed by a glossy black bob, a nose accentuated by its owners high forehead and long neck and a strong jaw line neither softened nor enhanced by the pearls that grouped beneath and either side of it. As he drank the final sip of his drink, Aidan's soft pencil sketched a familiar face and within seconds, Angel looked back at him, far superior in glamour, elegance and style to any other woman in the room.

"Mr Quinn?" said a voice behind him.

Aidan stood as a short wiry lady with jet-black coiffured curls was ushered to the table. Her simple navy blue suit was cut with exquisite lines that lengthened and curved her in all the right places while the single turquoise jewel, clasped in gold at her throat, brought the eye to the commanding face. Aidan smiled and extended a hand. "Aidan," he said.

"Charlotte Spellman," said the lady, taking it. Her small dark eyes set deep in her face and large nose, gave her a bird like profile but the twinkle in the eyes and the brief but mischievous smile confirmed that the eagle persona was mere subterfuge and that beneath the surface purred a kitten. "I'm sorry to have kept you."

The waiter pulled back her chair and, once seated, laid the vast white linen napkin across her lap.

"Not at all," said Aidan, seated and smiling. "I've been admiring your beautiful hotel." He tapped the notebook.

"May I see?" said Mrs Spellman. Aidan handed her the book. "Vodka martini," she said to the hovering waiter, as she opened it. She looked up at Aidan. "Another?"

"Yes, thank you," said Aidan. He hadn't intended a second drink but he'd finished his first and didn't wish to offend by not joining his potential new client.

"So, what are you then, an artist or a gardener?"

"Both," said Aidan, "There's no reason why any garden can't be a work of art."

"And you use the setting to influence your designs?"

"Yes, though a garden doesn't always have to blend in with what's around it, as long as the underlying structure, the base components have a link to what's there."

Mrs Spellman nodded. "And this?" She handed over the book, the page open with the figures at the tables roughly drawn.

"A hotel isn't just bricks and mortar, Mrs Spellman. The clientele are as much a part of it, don't you think?"

"Now that's interesting," said Mrs Spellman, "Because the hotel *does* change depending who's in it." She smiled and beckoned for the notebook back. "When I'm in Rome, I live on the top floor and often wander about when there's only the night porter on duty."

Aidan said nothing, nodded, sipped his drink and waited.

"My husband passed away last year and since then, I've found sleep elusive," confided Mrs Spellman. She held a hand up to Aidan's mumbled condolences and shook her head. "But the hotel holds special memories for me. I adore being here. Sometimes," she leaned forward, "I wish they'd all go away and stop cluttering up the place!" She winked at Aidan who smiled back.

Salad, chicken, olives, tomatoes and bread arrived at the table and three bottles of flavoured olive oil. Mrs Spellman talked him through the oils and olives that she insisted he tried. Fresh herbs and garlic filled Aidan's mouth with flavour as they shared bruschetta and savoured their lunch.

"So, who's the last sketch?" said Mrs Spellman, dipping foccacia in a tomatoey oily puddle on her plate.

"Sorry?"

"In your notebook." Mrs Spellman pointed.

"Oh, Angel," said Aidan, looking up at Mrs Spellman.

She held his gaze. "Your wife? No, Mr Quinn, your companion, your lover, your everything. Am I right?"

"You are, Mrs Spellman."

"Good, that's got one problem out the way," she said, finishing wiping her plate.

"I'm sorry," said Aidan, "I don't follow you."

Mrs Spellman sat back in her seat as the waiter took her plate and issued him instructions in fluent Italian. He nodded, bowed and left. "Let's get coffee and talk business," she said, standing up.

Aidan abandoned his plate and slipped his notebook in his bag and, as he stood, he found his arm taken and guided from the restaurant and they strolled this way to the lift.

"Gold diggers," said Mrs Spellman, "Get them all the time. I'm glad you've a special lady back home, Mr Quinn, makes it all so much easier. Now, not that you're not a handsome young thing that my mind insists would be fun to play with but I've no heart for these things, you understand."

"You miss your husband, Mrs Spellman. I can sense the rawness of your pain and the loneliness and sadness it has brought," said Aidan, gently, "I'm a good listener and, as a potential client, my time is at your disposal and, if I could help, I would be honoured to but I would never do anything to hurt Angel, Mrs Spellman, you can be assured of that."

As the lift doors opened at the penthouse floor, Mrs Spellman squeezed Aidan's arm and led him to her Italian home. "Most gallantly put, young man. Now, let's forget this 'Mrs Spellman' nonsense while we're in private. I was Lottie Cowan, bookkeeper and part time stripper when I met my Donald so no need to stand on ceremony with me."

"So, how did your meeting go?"

"Lottie's an extraordinary woman, Angel. You'd really like her."

"Lottie?"

"Mrs Charlotte Spellman. She's thrown herself into work since her husband died and is determined to continue his business from where he left off, improve it and expand what he started with fresh ideas of her own. Seems Mr Spellman was an unsung hero in the States, encouraging young talent and supporting youth projects. She's persuaded her son Donnie to sponsor a film making competition for the under 21s and is setting up an acting school of her own, and rather than sponsor the ballet or the opera, she's keen to fund more local performing arts projects for those who rarely get a chance in that field."

"Any talk of gardens at all?"

"Angel," said Aidan, his green eyes glistening with mischief, "I do believe you're jealous!"

"I don't know," said Angel, her eyes looking down from the camera as he watched the screen. "I guess I'm like you." She looked up. "I hate you having fun without me."

"Angel, we did talk gardens," said Aidan, smiling, "And it was fun to meet such a lovely motivated very rich lady but, you're never far from my thoughts." He opened his bag and held his notebook to the camera. "I drew this at lunch."

Thursday morning dawned brighter than Wednesday and Aidan decided to walk up the river to the St Angelo Bridge and have breakfast along the way. He was tempted to return to the Piazza Trilussa, so warm had been his welcome but he was meeting Caldieri near St Peter's Basilica and didn't want to rush. He was directed to a café near the Mazzini Bridge as mopeds with pillion passengers and painted tourist carriages sped past him. He feasted on chocolate pastries and two cups of espresso, awakening and warming him, before setting off again along the path with the river as his guide.

Though the traffic flowed, horns beeped and voices hollered while the grey ribbon of the river wound noiselessly on. As he neared the bridge, the sun forced through the cloud so the angels on their plinth were partly glowing and partly in shadow with water and sky as their backdrop.

Aidan approached as the pilgrims had on their way to St Peter's Basilica and, even on this chilly January morning, the bridge and its surrounds were abundant with camera snapping tourists. As Aidan looked up at the winged figures on their plinths, he felt disappointed. He wasn't sure how he expected to feel, in Rome, on a Roman bridge first constructed by Hadrian and topped with Angels of the

Passion. Maybe moved somehow, but he wasn't. He crossed over to the castle and turned back to view the bridge from the other bank of the Tiber, leaning on the imposing stone walls, allowing time to melt and merge in his mind.

With each expelled breath, first the traffic and then the tourists were dispelled and Aidan concentrated his mind on how the bridge had looked when originally constructed. The angels on the plinths disappeared before him and he saw Roman legionnaires marching across the river, lances pointing skyward, a mass of shiny armour and red plumes. The marble fascia of the bridge glistened and shone as the troops marched towards him to Hadrian's mausoleum. He felt a presence high above him, over the castle, a mass of energy and light and the soldiers disappeared. A brilliant angel sparkled and glistened above the bridge and Aidan felt relief and joy at its presence but then the crowds began to push and shove, cramming onto the bridge, intent upon their pilgrimage until the balustrades yielded and screams filled the air as the fallen pilgrims drowned.

Aidan shivered and drew his scarf closer, lighting a cigarette as he watched the bridge repair and the entrance to it widen. He breathed deeply, confident that the angel's blessing and message of peace, health and hope would be heard but then he saw the bodies strung along the bridge, grizzly and decaying, in the name of justice. He shuddered at the monstrous images and saw the greed that paid for the original holy statues, the tolls charged by the Vatican to all pilgrims crossing the bridge. Maybe the sight of their revered holy fathers upon the bridge were to instil a sense of piety as the pilgrims made their way to St Peter's, as were the present angels, but Aidan felt no joy, just the pain of persecution by the governing body over the poor ignorant populace. He let the images leave and cleared his mind, strengthening his tie to the earth with each inhaled breath. He felt the angel's presence above him again, energy reverberating through the walls on which he leaned and his breath rose from his mouth to the sky above. Weak sunlight filtered down as he sketched in his notebook while all around him tourists smiled for cameras, lovers kissed and pilgrims crossed the St Angelo Bridge on their way to St Peter's.

The sun had gone and grey clouds jostled overhead as Aidan set off for his hotel after his meeting with Caldieri. Talking through an interpreter hadn't been ideal and Aidan wasn't convinced that his skill and passion for his vertical gardens had been properly represented. The large shiny-faced hotelier didn't smile but cracked lobster claws and issued words between chewing throughout the meeting while Aidan toyed with a salad. He'd been shown the area in the lobby to be planted though and plans had been requested but Aidan felt no enthusiasm for the job and so, he walked along the riverbank, his head bent to the increasing breeze and let his thoughts wander. The wind picked up again by the Mazzini Bridge and he hurried on, intent on cappuccino at the Piazza Trilussa. As he neared the Sisto Bridge, music reached his ears and he joined the throng heading towards it.

"Francis has a son," said a rich dark voice by his shoulder.
    Aidan turned.
    "Four daughters and finally a son," said the beautiful woman in the seat behind him.
    Aidan smiled and let the energy of the face before him ease away the pains of the day. "Congratulations," said Aidan, raising his coffee cup.
    The woman nodded. Her sleek brown hair covered the shoulders of her cream woollen coat edged with fur and while she spoke, she fiddled with the button at her throat. "He is my uncle. There is my brother, my sister and my

aunt," she said, pointing out the people, "We all thank god for this miracle of life."

"I didn't mean to intrude," said Aidan.

"Not at all," smiled the woman, "Francis would want the whole world to hear his news! I am Valentina."

"Aidan," said Aidan.

"I don't know this name," said Valentina, frowning, "Like the garden of Eden in the Bible?"

"No," said Aidan, smiling, "Ai-dan but, strangely enough, I am a gardener."

Valentina's eyes shone as she laughed and all around them the music and chatter was mixed with cigarette smoke and joy. Wine bottles gathered on tables, glasses chinked, children ran squealing through the crowds but Aidan only had eyes for Valentina. Heat rose to the surface of his skin as he watched the full red lips mouth around her words, flashes of glossy white teeth stabbing him with desire and he felt his body pulsing, gorging on her beauty. She spoke of family, her life as a student in England and her love of architecture, especially work commissioned by the church while Aidan spoke of gardens, his new projects and his love of nature. In a bubble of power, their words resonated and gleamed and Aidan's body tensed and purred, energy building in his muscles and lust thundering between his thighs.

As the light began to fade, candles were lit and strings of coloured bulbs softened the dusk and still, the music and celebrations continued. Valentina laughed at Aidan's love of cappuccino, a child's drink she called it and he smiled at her unerring faith in the catholic church but, as she sat closer to him, her leg against his, her eyes melting into his being, Aidan's phone began to ring and, as he retrieved it from the front of his bag, frozen fingers fumbling at the zip, the familiar ring tone broke the magic and he turned to Valentina as Aidan, himself again.

Disappointment pleaded in Valentina's eyes as Aidan made ready to leave. She grasped his hand and stood with him as he rose from the table, turning him towards her, her other hand at his waist. She tried to pull him closer, her parted lips trembling as she looked up into his face, but Aidan stood firm and brought her hand from his waist to his lips. He repeated the congratulations to her uncle and bid her good evening. Turning, unsmiling, he made his way across the Sisto Bridge without looking back.

"So, you don't think he'll go for it?"

"Who knows," said Aidan, "But I don't know if I want the job anyway?"

"No?"

"I feel no passion for it, Angel."

"Well, you know what you want. So, a disappointing day?"

Aidan's mind flashed with images; stone angels, Roman soldiers, rotting corpses and the entrancing brown eyes of the devout Valentina. "Yes," said Aidan, "and a confusing one. I miss you, Angel."

"I miss you too, Aidan."

Georgio Spellman was an even larger copy of his film producing brother Donnie. "So you met my mother?" said Georgio, chewing on a fat cigar. "That must have been a pleasure for you."

"We had a most agreeable lunch," said Aidan, choosing his words with care.

"Really?" said Georgio, removing the cigar, "Didn't accuse you of trying to steal her fortune?"

Aidan shook his head. "We talked of her plans for the hotel."

"*You*," said Georgio, pointing the cigar, "Got off lightly! That mean mouth old bitch even accused *me* of thieving, her own son! Tight fisted old hag .You better watch her! She's always after something for nothing."

"I wouldn't know," said Aidan, "She seemed interested in a garden for the hotel."

"Well, you mark my words," continued Georgio, as the food arrived beneath silver covers, "Make sure you've a watertight contract before you start." A tiny, dark haired waitress uncovered his dish. "And what the fuck is this? Eggs over easy, I said! Take it back! For fucks sake!"

Aidan viewed his plate. Eggs, bacon, pancakes and French fries were in abundance, glistening from their recent contact with the frying pan. "Thank you," said Aidan, smiling up at his waitress.

Aidan wandered through the park, south of his hotel as a watery sun attempted to warm his mood. Yesterday, he'd met a sullen, rude Italian and today, a loud mouthed, ignorant Yank. What a waste of time. Agreed, both men had paid for plans to be drawn for their hotel's vertical gardens but Aidan hated the thought of working for either of them. He knew the phrase 'beggars can't be choosers' and tried to convince himself that sometimes, ones clients might not be ones choice but that their connections would establish the company and provide him with a more amiable clientele for the future but, he began to see now why Angel was so selective in her business.

Two policewomen went past him with a nod, their ponytails bouncing as they walked and Aidan was struck with a thought that required further explanation. Was it Rome or was it everywhere?

Aidan sat cross-legged, his back to a leafless slim tree trunk and shut his eyes. With traffic no more than a hum and an odd beep, Aidan let his mind drift as he connected to the earth and sought the clarity he needed from nature. Everything felt wrong, out of sync in this place. He saw female policemen, guns at their sides, shapely curves under their sleek uniforms, families together, sharing and loving while angel faces of stone hid the greed and tyranny of the men who commissioned them. His trip to Rome confirmed the feelings growing inside him. There was no good and evil. No black and white. The world was grey, a mixture of both, sometimes shining through in favour of one but generally lurking on the side of the other and all the while, the outside sugar coating hid the seedy, vicious world beneath. He saw a benevolent, kind hearted mother berated and gibed at by a rich, greedy son, a stupid silicone enhanced blond holding her breasts out to him, a beautiful niece, naked in the arms of her uncle and two policewomen ripping at their uniforms, mouths and fingers seeking the other and the energy rose in him tingling his skin and firing his groin.

"No!" Aidan opened his eyes and sprang up, leaning on the tree as dizziness over came him, his mouth dry and breath heaving.

Balance regained he turned for the hotel and, as he walked briskly through the park, he knew what he had to do.

February

20

With the circle around her, Lilith by her side and the Angels protecting her, Angel stood at the portal to the Path once more, displaying her conscious mind, asking for healing for this is what she sought. The air in the circle thickened around her, warm and syrupy and tasting of tin. The power increased and she saw in the darkness beyond the altar the beginning of everything, as out of the nothing came light, energy, earth, water, air and fire and from this chaotic mix, the Earth was formed and, like a wheel turning, momentum increased and from the Earth, creatures grew and died and new ones took their place and Angel saw it and knew this physical life but, she'd noticed something. Before it all began, there'd been something else. She'd felt it, seen it, no, she just knew it had existed, a tiny glimpse, a faint whisper, a mere pinprick of the Before.

The Hebrew letter hung in the air and she cried out, "Samekh!"

Angel floated through the Universe as flame and dust spiralled and spun and all the planets and stars began to form and settle into their orbit against the blue velvet darkness.

She climbed upon a silver white stallion, its wild mane and tail streaming as they rode across the sky. They sped through reeds and bulrushes, splashing mud on Angel's feet and they galloped through showers of meteors like an arrow, flying with purpose across the sky. As she gripped the warm, strong body of the horse between her thighs, the stars and constellations showed themselves to Angel and she felt pure emotion in her heart, emotion without thought, the Force before the Form, the root substance of manifestation, that which she'd been seeking.

Angel rode on over the Welsh mountains and through the valleys, sprinkling moon dust on each pagan circle and magical gathering she saw, as the people met and embraced their Nature. Upon the horse there was no time so back she rode to the Celtic villages and on she galloped to the Dwellers in the Mountains, after The Flood.

She pulled up the mighty stallion before a sign she did not recognize and was greeted at the Temple by the Angel Raphael, the healer, who bid her enter.

Golden light bounced off the walls as she alighted from her steed and, when she next laid eyes on him, he was a centaur. Tall and proud, the handsome blond beast bowed to Angel and she took the brown zircon from her throat and bound it to an arrow. The Arrow passed to the Centaur and with his bow he let it fly and Angel knew it was the Arrow for the Swiftness of Willed Force.

The walls of the basement returned and Angel shivered as she thanked her guests, closed the circle and scampered upstairs to her room to the warmth of a welcoming fire.

Miss Stanton had been true to her word. He'd met with Mr Roman, who'd spoken with him at length before agreeing to ask Mr Kennedy to speak to him. He had, within a few days, and they'd both been impressed with his event organizational work, the company he'd established that was run so competently by Sabrina and Dale but even more, by the distribution company and its import and export dealings. A further week later, he'd finally been given access to the presence of Mr Aloroso and talk of money changed from tens of k, to hundreds and thousands. Mr Aloroso had left, leaving behind a folder and his son, a small dark, slight man, about his own age, with a scar running under one cheekbone.

Vincent sat in the chair across the wide, green leather topped desk and felt the sweat gathering in his groin. His palms pulsed as young Mr Aloroso opened the folder.

Vincent saw his photo clipped on the top sheet and his heart thumped a few beats but he quelled it. They'd checked him out, of course they had. What had he expected?

Young Mr Aloroso read through the papers before him while Vincent fought his impatience and frustration and anger at being kept waiting. Instead, he thought about that which he loved most. Numbers filled the void; tens, hundreds and ks. How he loved to count in ks!

"You're unproven," said young Mr Aloroso, his fingers locked in front of his chin, "So you must prove yourself."

"What do I have to do?" said Vincent.

"We're going to take you on a small job, as an extra hand, see how you pan out, okay?"

Vincent nodded, failing to hide his disappointment.

"It's the same for everyone," said young Mr Aloroso, "Prove yourself as one of the men, a handyman if you like and you'll be trusted further."

"Someone set a warehouse alight at the docks last night," said Tiffany, behind the newspaper, "Nearly caught the one next door too. Police think its more than arson though, 'cos the place seems to have been emptied first."

"Right," said Justin, eating toast and scribbling on a pad next to him.

"They found a body too, but they haven't iden…idenif…found out who it is yet."

"Fine," said Justin, swigging from his mug.

"It ain't fine!" said Tiffany, closing the paper and glaring at him, "Someone's dead!"

"I'm not interested!"

"You're never interesting in anyfink!" yelled Tiffany, slamming the paper and her fist on the table.

Silence hovered over the kitchen, stretched and grew like an over inflated Zeppelin, and burst.

"Four weeks! Four fuckin' weeks!" yelled Justin, "That's all! Four weeks to concentrate on getting this job right, that's all! And you want me to be interested in a fuckin' warehouse fire? For fucks sake!" He grabbed his coffee and pad and crashed up the stairs.

Tiffany sat at the table, her fingers flexing on the edge, her heart clamouring in her ears. Four weeks? Was that all? Four weeks since signing but eight weeks in total. Eight weeks with no sex and before that was Christmas and...the last time was after the Fancy Dress Party in October. October! She'd felt less frustrated pregnant when her sheer size had dissuaded Justin's sexual advances. Now, if Aidan hadn't spoiled it...

She filled the kettle and set it in motion. Ah, Aidan. She shut her eyes and green elfin ones appeared before her, twinkling with mischief and headed by a shock of blond hair. She followed the face down; neck, shoulders, chest, waist. She could remember the feel of the muscles under her hands as she'd held him in the conga line, the curve of his buttocks as she'd let one hand stray. The kettle clicked off and she opened her eyes, breathing faster and wiping sweat from her top lip. She made two teas. But laughing boy was refusing to play his part, hey? Preferring to take the moral high ground rather than sleep with a married woman? What did he know about marriage? What could he possibly know?

She knocked lightly on the door. "Just? It's me. I made you tea. I'm sorry, okay."

"I thought Vince was coming," said Justin, rubbing his hands over his face before reaching for his pint.

"Said he was, Just," said Rob. "You okay?"

"Yeah, fine mate," said Justin, "Got an early start in the morning that's all."

"Don't you always?" said Rob.

"Yeah, true," said Justin, laughing. "I've a drive to the south coast for a site meeting at 8.30am and was hoping to get an hour in before I left."

"Sounds full on," said Rob, sipping his cola.

"It is!" said Justin, "But I'm lovin' it!"

"This the job you mentioned at New Year?"

Justin nodded. "Yeah, 'n' its gonna be awesome, the beginning of the good times!"

Rob smiled and nodded. Less chins joined in the agreement and his face looked clear and bright. The pale blue and grey checked shirt he wore with the top two buttons open, sat comfortably on his shoulders, adding to his relaxed and happy countenance. Sipping cola in a pub wasn't easy but he'd done it at Christmas and New Year so, he could do it again. "Can't say I've ever seen you exactly strapped, Just."

"No, but that was all local, hands on, hard graft. This is different. This is…the big time, ya know. This is supervising, site managing and construction. The works. The only job I haven't done was by the architect and I even had a hand in the amendments on that!"

Rob nodded. "Sounds brilliant, Just. Good for you mate! I've…"

"Not that I haven't earned this," said Justin, index finger waggling to enforce his point, "I've worked hard for a lot of years to earn my good reputation."

"'Course you have, Just. No one'd say you don't deserve it. I started…"

"And, of course," said Justin, barely drawing breath, "With this type of responsibility comes the money but also the pressure. Ain't easy with the wife and kids making demands on my time."

"I can imagine," said Rob. "How are they?"

"Who?"

"Tiffany and the kids?"

"Oh, they're fine. Already trying to get me to book fuckin' Disneyworld for next February! I can't be pinned down to *anythin'* at the moment. Can't even think about it!" Justin stopped talking and drained the remains of his pint. "Another?"

"No, I'm good thanks."

Rob watched as Justin stood waiting to be served at the bar, waving his money and fidgeting from foot to foot.

"You've lost weight," said Rob, as Justin sat down.

"Yeah, probably. Runnin' on adrenaline at the moment."

"Yeah, I've…"

"And when there's work to be done," said Justin, "Who wants to spend time eatin'! Where *is* Vince?"

Rob shook his head. He too hoped Vincent would arrive soon.

Justin was on his third pint when Vincent arrived and Rob was ready for another drink.

"Big Man, you're joking! I never thought I'd see the day!" said Vincent, handing over the glass of cola. "How long's this been going on?"

"Not touched a drop since I got my new job," said Rob, "The weight's dropped off too, ya know. Seems the drink was as much to blame as the food!"

"Of course it was," said Vincent. "How's business, Just?"

"Excellent!" said Justin, "Contracts signed and I'm up to my neck in work!"

"So long as you negotiated a good deal…" said Vincent.

"Of course! What do you take me for? Was just tellin' Rob, this is it now, plain sailin' all the way. This new client has big ideas and I'm the one she trusts to put them into practice."

"Good for you, Just," said Vincent. "Looks like the New Year has started well for both of us."

"Yeah?" said Justin.

Vincent nodded and sipped his beer. "Been taken on by a new client myself. Really looking forward to it. Completed a small job for them first and now, they can't wait to put more business my way."

Justin nodded. "Cool, well of course, you've the experience while I'm on new territory with some of this. But that's the joy!" He slapped the table. "I've finally got the opportunity to show what I can *really* do!"

Vincent nodded in reply. "Of course it's good to be pushed, move into new fields, but it can take time to generate the profit with something like that. I'm sticking to what I'm good at, have experience in, as you quite rightly pointed out and that's why, the money's already coming in." Vincent sat back, smoothing the ginger stubble on his chin.

"But you're bound to have a faster turn around and get your hands on the money sooner!" said Justin. "While I'll receive half my money at the end of the build stage, a quarter once the fixtures are in and the final instalment on completion but," he leaned closer across the table to Vincent, "When there's that many noughts involved, I don't mind waiting!"

"Sounds a cushy number," said Vincent.

"Cushy! You're fuckin' kiddin'! This job…"

Rob sat and listened as the conversation batted from one side to the other like a tennis match, though he'd never felt watching Wimbledon that the players had ever showed such pride in a great shot or any indication whatsoever, that they were only in it for the prize money. He felt a bit disappointed in his friends, going on and on, not asking about Rob's new year or his evident weight loss but it was good to see them again and he knew his year had started well so, he smiled to himself, took a sip of cola and drunk to his own achievements.

As soon as Justin's car sped off the drive, Tiffany removed the laptop from her wardrobe and snuck back into bed. Naked she began trawling the dating sites.

"But you *can't* go away!"

"Yes Scott, I can."

"What about the children?"

"Mum and Dad are staying. You can still do Wednesday. They'll make themselves scarce or you can take the kids out."

"What, in this fuckin' weather?"

"Well, stay in then."

"With your parents watching me!"

"I just said..."

"Who do you think you are, eh? Fuckin' swanning off all over the place! When did *I* last go to Paris?"

"It's work, Scott. Five days and four nights."

"Work? What are you talking about? What about the school job?"

"I packed it in."

"What? Well, don't expect a penny more from me, do you hear? I pay more than my share for those kids! Yeah, right, I get it, now I know why your solicitor wants me to pay *you* maintenance! No way, no fuckin' way! You gave up your job, your choice!"

"Maintenance for me has nothing..."

"No way! I'm not paying you money so you can go off to Paris with your new man!"

"Sorry?"

"I knew all along!"

"Knew what?"

"Of course, Paris! How romantic! You and your new love!"

"I'm going to Paris with Angel."

"Yeah, right. I know you Jenny, can't do anything without a man there to hold your hand! Jenny? Jenny?"

They arrived on time at the station and were met by a smart, older man, with greying temples and a sparkle in his eye. In his chauffeur's uniform he looked handsome and dashing and bowed to Angel, taking her hand to kiss.

"Jean-Luc, it's wonderful to see you," said Angel, smiling, "This is Jenny."

Jean-Luc took Jenny's hand and performed the same manoeuvre, holding her hand a little longer, murmuring and looking into her eyes.

Jenny felt herself blushing despite the blatant charm.

"C'est ça, Jean-Luc. Allez vite, si vous plait," said Angel and with more sweeping gestures by their driver, the women were seated in the elderly Bentley while Jean-Luc dealt with the luggage.

Jenny relaxed back into the soft leather and gazed wide eyed through the window as Angel and Jean-Luc conversed in French. Sunshine had deserted them as they left England but the dull cold day couldn't dampen Jenny's excitement as her mind immersed itself in the images that sped past the window.

"We'll freshen up at the hotel first," said Angel, "I'll introduce you to Serge this evening at dinner. He manages 'La Maison de la Lune' with his wife Simone. You'll like them and, once we've established a few possible boutiques to showcase your work, Serge and Simone will be your Paris contacts for new and continued business."

"Okay," said Jenny.

"It's so you won't need me chaperoning you all the time, Jen. You'll be able to pop over for meetings and shows and Serge can be your translator and support while you're here."

Jenny nodded and smiled. "Sounds good," she said.

The hotel was bright and chic and full of new design and technology but its modern interior gently complimented the lines of the old building. Jenny and Angel shared the three-bedroom suite on the top floor, high above the town which promised to bestow a wonderful panoramic view that Angel agreed they could indulge in the next day.

Jenny wore black trousers and jacket and a revered white blouse. She put a hair band on and some lipstick before stepping into the lounge clasping her latest purchase in England, a black patent clutch bag to match her shoes. She felt nervous but smart, until she saw Angel. In vintage Chanel, her hair straight and sleek to her waist, tiny pearls at her throat and ears and killer heels in navy to match her outfit, Angel looked like she'd sauntered off the catwalk. They faced each other for a second and Jenny tried to hide the tears pricking her eyes.

"I tell you what," said Angel, taking her arm, "Let's shop today and tomorrow we will do business."

Jenny woke with the sun peeping through the skylights. She grabbed the luscious white robe from the end of the bed and wrapped it around her as she climbed the stairs to the roof terrace.

Feelings and sensations buffeted her body and brain as she stood in the freezing air, looking out over the city. It smelled different, more European somehow, a kind of coffee and brioche combination and, even this early, the streets below were crowded with cars and vans, bicycles and people and the noise of their business filtered up to Jenny's ears like smoke signals. She missed her children, the morning rousing, cuddles and squabbles and her heart cried out to them across the channel. Her toes were freezing now and she hopped from foot to foot taking in huge lungfuls of air, before being forced to return indoors.

Bags of all shapes and sizes littered her dressing room, while a few items hung on the rails so, like a child at Christmas, Jenny spent her first morning in Paris delving into tissue paper and trying on her new clothes.

In a bronze Dior dress with matching shoes and jacket, her hair freshly styled by a hairdresser brought in by Angel, Jenny met Serge and Simone, had a late breakfast with Angel and then set off for the Opera District, the Place Vendôme, where fine jewellery boutiques rubbed their elegant shoulders with the Ritz Hotel.

Jean-Luc dropped them off in front of a large double fronted shop with canopies above the windows. The assistants seemed unhelpful. Even with Jenny's limited French vocabulary she could tell by the shaking heads and dour expressions that Angel wasn't making much headway but she persisted, her French flowing freely and expressively with frequent gestures and hand movements. Abruptly, Angel ceased her patter, nodded to the staff and she and Jenny were at the door as a small lady, dressed plainly all in black, emerged from a side door to way lay them.

Angel smiled and bowed. "Madame Chevalier," she said.

The lady nodded and smiled and beckoned them to follow her through the side door. The room was draped heavily with curtains and wall hangings and the three chairs round the fire looked worn and comfortable yet, there was an air of opulence and luxury like wealth that doesn't need to try too hard. Old money was the phrase Jenny recalled.

They sat and Madame Chevalier conversed with Angel. Jenny noticed how different Angel was. Quiet and demure she answered Madame's questions and within minutes, the two of them were smiling and laughing. Jenny looked at her feet, in shoes she didn't recognize and then, around the room. A baby grand piano, visible only by its legs was draped with a gold and white cloth, scattered with black and white photos, towered over by two magnificent lamps and, quite surprisingly, thought Jenny, interspersed with Egyptian figures in marble, granite and alabaster.

"Jenny?"

"Hmm?"

"Madame Chevalier would like to see your hands, if you please."

Jenny leaned forward but she wasn't close enough. Madame's eyes beckoned her and without thinking, Jenny knelt before her and held out her hands. Madame smiled broadly and took them, turning them over. She began tracing lines across Jenny's palm with a bony finger. Madame spoke quickly in sharp phrases and Jenny caught none of it. Finally, the old woman brought Jenny's palms together and held them as Jenny looked up.

"She says you are a pilgrim whose journey is beginning," said Angel, "That you must use your head but follow your heart and that it will be your heart that rules your hands. It is then you will produce the work she wants from you."

Madame Chevalier let go Jenny's hands and indicated for her to sit as she took the portfolio that Angel offered. Madame began leafing through but stopped, took a pad from the table next to her and began to draw. Minutes went by to the loud tick of the exquisite clock on the mantelpiece and the fire in the grate began to dull. Madame made comments in murmurs turned back to the portfolio and began to leaf through again, sometimes smiling and stopping, pointing, chattering to Angel and then sketching on her pad once more.

"Well, that was a result," said Angel as she and Jenny left the shop.

"Was it?" said Jenny.

Angel turned to face her and took her arm. "Jenny, I'm so sorry! You've no idea what's going on and I hadn't thought, please forgive me."

"Of course!" said Jenny, smiling. "I just feel a bit of a spare part, that's all."

"And it's my fault Jen and you're not, you're really not! You're a star! Come on. We need coffee."

The spring sunshine had brought everyone out for lunch. Car horns beeped as they dodged around the tables on the pavements, past tourists and Parisians alike, weaving through smaller streets until they found the place Angel was looking for.

They sat on a second floor balcony with two other tables, empty as yet of clientele, catching the sunlight and walled in by a vertical garden seemingly suspended from the sky.

"Wow!" said Jenny, "You'd never find this place on the off chance and these plants! It's amazing!"

"Aidan found the restaurant," smiled Angel. "It's the first living wall he did. He's getting known now and he's had a lot of interest from hotels, I believe."

Jenny felt like she was in a secret garden, suspended above all life below. She relaxed in her cushioned cane chair and slipped her jacket behind her.

"I took a chance today," said Angel, "and went straight to the top."

"I thought those shop assistants looked uninterested," said Jenny.

"Oh, they were," laughed Angel, "but my words weren't for them. I knew Madame would be listening out the back."

"So you asked to see her?"

Angel shook her head. "No, never so direct. I asked if Madame Chevalier might be interested in a new designer and they, of course, replied that they already had their own. I explained how you'd started working with silver and found a natural affinity and had only made gifts for friends so far but wanted to take it further." She laughed again. "But I hoped Gisele wouldn't be able to resist a look at you."

"Gisele? Madame Chevalier?"

"Let me tell you a story, a story of Paris," said Angel, settling into her seat and cradling her coffee cup, "After the revolution, many aristocrats lost their land, their titles and some their heads, but some, more in tune with the demands of the ordinary people, retained theirs. They'd been the people who'd provided good employment, fair pay and decent dwellings for their workers before the revolution and, they continued to do so. Many bought up huge tracts of land and real estate, having retained their wealth in secret caches and this new money improved conditions for everyone."

Angel sipped her coffee and Jenny tried to recall her French history lessons; crazy wigs, amazing gardens and palaces and the Guiotine.

"These old established families retained respect too and continued their good work, founding hospitals and orphanages all over Paris," continued Angel. "With the German occupation from 1940, most aristocrats were seen to be towing the German line, as it were, while all along coordinated the Resistance, protecting and helping people in need, wherever they could. Others spoke out about the regime and one child lost her whole family to over zealous German officials in a blood bath in front of her eyes. The child just fourteen years old disappeared into the French countryside and vowed to work for the resistance and fight for French Liberation, whatever the cost. That child was Gisele Chevalier."

"But that makes her eighty four or eighty five years old?"

"I know," said Angel.

"But she didn't look that old!"

Angel smiled and continued. "She moved back to Paris when the Germans left and, with the help of those who had had respect for her parents, picked up where they had left off. More to the point, she expanded everything they had started and she now owns as much of Paris as the Duke of Westminster does of London."

"That...that little lady?"

Angel nodded. "And," she emphasized, "she has a say in how every shop, bar, café, restaurant, hotel, every business that rents from her, is run and presented."

"Bloody hell!" said Jenny.

"Exactly," said Angel.

"So, hang on," said Jenny, "If Madame Chevalier says 'yes'..."

"Everyone else does!" laughed Angel, "And she's even made you some drawings to base further designs on! That's a first, Jen. She *really* liked you."

That evening, Jenny and Angel sat in the hotel restaurant. The afternoon had flown by amid coffees, salads, drawing and planning. Jenny had made more sketches, inspired by what she'd seen of Paris so far. They planned their next few days around sight seeing, leaving time for a final meeting with Madame Chevalier on their way to the station. The drawings made by Madame Chevalier were bewitching and Jenny couldn't wait to have time to sit and ponder them. They drank champagne from delicate flutes in their similar Valentino gowns, Angel's in red, Jenny's in blue.

"So how did you find out about Madame Chevalier?" said Jenny, dipping her fork in fresh spinach and rocket leaves with just a hint of dressing.

"She found me," said Angel, "I was barely eighteen when I first came to Paris..."

"On your own?"

Angel nodded. "I was alone then. I fell in love with a piece in one of the windows, a cabochon sapphire set in white platinum, surrounded by tiny diamonds on an exquisite chain."

"I've seen you wear it!"

"Though the staff in the shop were rude to me, a scruffy little thing with my schoolgirl French, Madame appeared and spoke gently to me. She took me under her wing and I've got to know her and her family over many years. She has a daughter, though her husband passed away eight, maybe ten years ago. I spent time with her then and see her when I'm in Paris."

"And yet, you wouldn't ask for her direct?"

"Ah, but this is business. I would not presume anything and why should Gisele feel obliged to help me? It would put her in an awkward position."

"And, this is how you do business?"

Angel smiled. "When I can, Jen, when I can. You see..."

Their plates were whisked away with a flourish and a bow by a young, dark haired waiter and Jenny watched with interest as he walked away.

"It is a cute butt, isn't it?" said Angel.

"What? Sorry?" Jenny blushed. "That obvious?"

"No, don't worry. I had to have a look too!"

They both laughed. "Sorry, you were saying about the way you like to do business," said Jenny.

"Yes, well, it's also to do with the story this afternoon, about Gisele's family..."

"And the other wealthy aristocrats?"

Angel nodded. "Well, as succinctly as possible, they were wealthy powerful people and yet, they'd built their fortune on the ordinary people. Not by fleecing them or using them but by putting them first and that is the way I try to run my businesses. There aren't enough businesses run like that, in my view."

"Okay, so, in practice, what does that mean?"

"Take 'La Maison de la Lune', that's a good example. I met Simone and Serge about four years ago when I stayed in another hotel," said Angel. "That one was tired and unloved and though they tried hard to please the customers and make them welcome, because the owners didn't care and were, therefore, only in it for the money, Serge and Simone were unhappy and business was tailing off. We had dinner together one night. We talked about their ideas for a hotel, how they would run it and I gave them mine and we made a deal to find another hotel, refurbish and set it up for Serge and Simone to manage it for me. Part of the deal was also to find a much smaller establishment for them as a long term goal so that, in time they would own a hotel of their own and have someone else managing it for them."

"Just like that?" said Jenny, as a huge white plate was placed in front of her with a tiny stack of spinach, potatoes and lamb in the middle.

"Well, obviously there were numbers to crunch, budgets to be set but fundamentally yes, just like that!"

"But you didn't know them?"

"Well enough, Jen. Haven't you noticed the difference in people when they speak about what they care about, what they're passionate about? You looked so different this afternoon when we were working on your plans."

"Yes, yes I see, I think."

They ate their food in silence, the hum of conversation and the clink of glasses and cutlery all around them.

Jenny savoured every succulent mouthful before making a pink kiss on her napkin as she finished. "You said this was the way to do business that you preferred."

Angel nodded. "I deal with like minded people, people with energy, ideas, passion and open minds. The other way," Angel paused and sighed. "The other way is using the power of money, celebrity and glamour. I have to do a lot of acting. It's not really me." She smiled shyly, "Aidan loves it. I prefer to keep a lower profile."

Jenny nodded and sipped more champagne. "I like the first way best," she said, "But I could get used to dressing up and having my dinner cooked for me!"

"Then tomorrow, we'll walk through the Tuilères to the Louvre before taking you shopping again!"

"Ok," said Jenny, smiling, "But I'm going to pay you back, you know."

"You already have," said Angel.

"How?" said Jenny.

"Because your jewellery and your silver sculptures plus the ideas Gisele gave you will sell, Jen and not just sell to anyone," said Angel. She stopped as their plates were cleared and their glasses topped up.

Picking up her glass she continued, "But what you don't know are who the customers are who go direct to Madame Chevalier, whereas, I do. They're the very rich, Jen. Through her, I've had customers to my hotel, hence my interest in buying another and so, through your jewellery, there'll be a link to me…"

"And your other businesses," said Jenny.

Angel nodded. "Real estate, yachts, finance, insurance and Aidan too with gardens and landscaping."

"Everyone helps and cares about each other," said Jenny, "I can't wait to be part of this new family!"

Angel raised her glass. "I'll drink to that."

"She asks if you've enjoyed your stay," said Angel to Jenny as they sat in Madame Chevalier's parlour, bags packed in the car outside on their way to the airport.

"Very much," said Jenny, nodding "I can't believe it's only been days! We've done so much!"

Angel translated and Madame smiled and left her seat, talking as she opened a drawer of her bureau.

"She has a gift for you," said Angel.

Madame Chevalier returned to her seat, a small wooden box in the shape of a beetle on here lap. Her soft smooth face smiled gently as she handed the box to Jenny with a nod while Angel continued to translate. Jenny opened the box.

"This piece of lapis lazuli is for you to keep. It came from Egypt long ago, supposedly from a tomb of an Ancient Egyptian queen."

Jenny held the stone in her palm, bewitched by its colour and depth, a mini universe in her hands.

"The Ancient Egyptians regarded lapis lazuli as a stone of the gods, partly because it reminded them of the starry heavens but also because they believed in its medicinal purposes, to improve eyesight so, it was often worn in the eye of Horus amulet."

Jenny held up her hand so the polished lapis lazuli stood proud and glistening in the shape of a pyramid.

"Some associate lapis lazuli with the planet Jupiter and the air but for me, for Madame I should say, it has always symbolized Venus and water and so, she believes it to be a perfect gift for you."

Madame smiled at Jenny's face entranced by the crystal.

"So, why's it perfect for me?" said Jenny.

Madame spoke and Angel laughed before she translated. "She says she saw the moon in you as soon as she met you. She also saw a need for protection and healing. Kept close by you, the stone will relieve headaches and anxiety. The stone also brings courage which she feels you lack in some areas of your life but, most of all, it brings love. Meditate upon the stone and the queens of Ancient Egypt will find you the love you need."

Jenny stopped her star gazing and placed the stone in its scarab bed. On her knees before Madame she wept and Madame took Jenny's head in her lap, stroking her hair, soothing, and cooing away her tears. "With all my heart, I thank you," said Jenny.

The men were called in and took a seat around the long table in the dark wood panelled boardroom. Photos of Mr Aloroso and various foreign officials hung on the walls, smiling as they shook hands. What kind of deals had been forged in those pictures? What goods had changed hands? Mr Aloroso took his seat at the head, his bodyguards standing behind him on either side. The men round the table looked expectantly at him, waiting on his words.

"Operation Barley went well, gentlemen," he said, beaming down the table.

The men sighed and smiled and nodded to each other.

"Unfortunately, a man died."

The men waited. Some sipped water from glasses in front of them but no longer did they meet each other's eyes.

"Unfortunately, the night guard was diligent, in my experience a rare trait in night security, but our new member, Mr Rogers gave him the chance to run and he didn't take it. Decided to play the martyr." Mr Aloroso shook his head. "Wrong people to mess with but the idea to remove his head and use the petrol soaked body to start the fire was inspired."

He looked up. "Mr Rogers, welcome to the family."

March

21

The sun shone weakly on a bright cold March morning as Justin arrived at the site. Already, groundwork was in place and the foremen and his men were busy laying the under floor heating pipes. Justin pulled up at the site office, prepared for another day of meetings and paperwork when his phone began to ring. He answered it as he stepped into the chill air but stopped, listened, got back in his car and drove back out the gates.

He hadn't expected a greasy spoon café but he watched in admiration as Sophia tucked into her breakfast as she spoke. "Thanks for coming," she said, putting down her fork and lifting up a slice of crispy fried bread. "Hoped to catch you en route."

"No worries," said Justin, chomping into his bacon roll, "Hmm, good food."

"Isn't it?" said Sophia, "Can't beat a good breakfast before a walk and this place is the best round here."

As she spoke, a huge man in a navy apron appeared at their table.

"All is good, princess?"

"Yes, lovely Guido. Mr Preston?"

"Hmm fabulous, thanks."

"Anything else for you?"

"I'd love more of your grilled tomatoes please Guido and another tea would be lovely," said Sophia, smiling. Guido bowed as he went off to grant her wish.

"Granddad loved this place," said Sophia, "He said Guido made the best lasagne in the world."

"Really?"

"Mmm and the best tiramisu. Granddad loved his food."

"And you?"

"I have my moments," Sophia laughed, "You were going to be your honest self there a moment and then changed your mind." She grinned at Justin, her eyes twinkling, sparkling wickedly under her perfect blond fringe.

"I was," said Justin, mopping his plate of ketchup with the remains of his roll, "I'm just a little surprised that such an important man would eat here but then, thinking about it, I shouldn't be."

"No you shouldn't," said Sophia, "Great food can come out of all sorts of places. Granddad knew Guido's parents and his grandmother before them. A hospitable, generous and kind family. Granddad didn't judge by appearances and nor should you."

"I know. You're right," said Justin.

Guido arrived at the table with tomatoes and tea.

Sophia slid the glossy steaming fruit onto her plate and cut them into quarters before popping one in her mouth. "Bella!"

Guido's grin was so wide, you could have driven a hummer through it.

They turned up their coat collars and Sophia produced a peach knitted beanie hat as they began their promenade along the front. The bracing wind bit into exposed flesh and Sophia took Justin's arm and questioned him as they walked. He was impressed by her ability to hold all the latest developments in her head and her keenness on detail. He answered as best he could without his notes and they soon covered the required distance. An 'about turn' sent them back again, the wind behind them, gusting now, sending Sophia laughing and off balance as she clung to his arm.

Back at Guido's, they ordered milky coffees and sat warming their hands as Sophia finished her quizzing. "Granddad always liked to walk and talk," she said, as their fingers fizzed and their faces tingled. "He taught me a walking meditation too, though no talking allowed with that one!"

"He's obviously been a big influence in your life, Miss Anderson and still is. I'd have liked to have met him," said Justin.

Sophia smiled gently. She'd kept on her peach hat and Justin thought she looked like a glamorous sixties hippy, a model maybe. "Do you like to walk?"

"Go out for walks you mean?"

Sophia nodded.

"Can't say I've really thought about it." Justin imagined Tiffany's response if he suggested they went for a walk.

"It's a wonderful way to get close to nature," said Sophia, "You can walk the same path twelve times in a year, but every walk will be different as the seasons change and the weather bestows it's varied gifts. The ocean too," she said, her face brightly animated, "Each time you visit it, it sings a different song."

They sat in comfortable silence, people watching as the café filled up, until the coffees were drunk.

"So, the deadline for the first phase is 21st March. Will you make it?"

Justin came back with a jolt. "That's only two weeks!"

"I know, doesn't time fly!"

"I'm not sure, I hadn't realized…"

"You've got the schedule, Mr Preston. There's a list of dates for completion of each phase. I'm sure you'll be fine," said Sophia, smiling.

"Yeah," said Justin, smiling back, "'Course I will."

Rob pulled at the waistline of his trousers and grinned at Teresa. "Reckon we should have a weigh in, don't you?"

Teresa brought the scales from the bathroom and put them in the middle of the kitchen floor. Rob thought about removing his rings but his first weigh in had been fully suited so, he tentatively stepped onto the scales while Teresa read the verdict. She wrote the evidence in Rob's diary and handed it to him.

"Twenty six pounds?"

Teresa nodded. "You've lost nearly two stone in two and a half months. No wonder your trousers are loose! Better put a belt on!"

Rob beamed at Teresa and went in for the hug. "Thanks, Trees. Thanks for helpin' me."

"You're the one that's done it," said Teresa, laughing as she pushed him back, "I fink you've done really well, Dad. What a brilliant birthday present to give to yourself! We should celebrate!"

"Yeah, yeah we should. I've not got work 'til 10pm tonight. One beer won't hurt."

Teresa pulled a face, twisting her mouth as if she'd a lemon bonbon lodged within. "Okay," she said, at last, "But just one, ok, with our lunch. I've work 'til late after so won't be in 'til 9pm. Spike said he'll give me a lift back."

"Dad! Wake up! Dad! It's gone 9pm!" Teresa shook the crumpled figure on the sofa. "Dad!"

She looked around at the empty bottles on the table and the floor, did a quick count and shook her head. "Dad! Come on! I'll make you coffee!"

Rob woke up on his back, felt sick, turned over and fell off the gurney.

Teresa bit her lip, tears in her eyes as she recounted the previous evenings events, as told to her by Shirana. "You fell asleep in the car outside the club and forgot to lock the doors, Dad. Two guys dragged you out and hit you, I don't know how many times. They'd followed Shirana and Carmen as they came out of the club. One grabbed Shirana but she fought back screaming and the club security intervened."

Rob lay on his back, peering at his daughter through one half closed eye. The other and his head were heavily bandaged. The room was dark with only a sidelight by his head but he saw the monitors and wires and drips. Pain pulsed through every vein as if he'd been crushed by a steamroller and he found it hard to swallow, let alone speak but he did. "I'm sorry, Trees, I'm so sorry."

Justin sat on the bed, papers strewn around him, tapping on his laptop. He'd dropped into the site on leaving Miss Anderson and had a meeting with the contractors before speeding back home. The weather had changed by the time he hit the motorway and shafts of sleety rain had slowed his progress. Luckily, the house was empty because this, more than ever, was a time he did not want to be disturbed.

He scrolled through the contract and there it was; deadlines for the four phases and the penalties and costs for not meeting the dates. He changed the font size to 150% and stared at the screen as the rain hammered on the bedroom window and sleety gusts bombarded the house. He reached for his mug on his bedside table but opened the top drawer instead. He found, lit and inhaled on a cigarette. He hadn't smoked since New Year but now seemed a good time to start again. He sat and stared at the screen, his head pounding and sweat running down his back. How could she have done this? He shook his head. But she hadn't, had she? He was the one who'd read and signed the contract. He was the one

who'd insisted he didn't need a lawyer. Fuck! Bollocks!
Arse! Shit! Justin lay back on his pillows and smoked.

Though rain teemed down the windows and grey clouds
buffeted the sky, nothing could wipe the sunshine from
Vincent's world.

The laptop hummed, keyboard tapping, emails flying,
replies, bookings, sales, deals, ks; Vincent was ecstatic. He
sat back on his sofa a moment and breathed deeply,
wallowing in the joys of real business. He'd bitten his
tongue, passed the test and was now part of a new family
and he was relishing every second. He was aware there was
danger of course, but the excitement thrilled his blood,
motivating him like nothing ever had. His confidence filled
the room, turning to smile and congratulate him and he, in
turn, smiled back; a success, a winner, a conqueror.

Panic subsiding, Justin began to work out the costs, the new
time frame and most importantly, the necessary path to take
to meet three further phase deadlines. All the while his mind
scolded him for his stupidity but he quashed it; it's not my
fault, one of those things, lot to deal with, biggest project,
bound to be problems, until he'd reached a compromise with
himself.

Calmly, carefully, he calculated the shortfall. Then he
worked out how to fund it.

22

The two couples sat on sofas opposite each other as the fire
roared and crackled and the wind outside stormed.

On the low table between them, tea was set and Angel played 'mother' as she spoke. "Congratulations! That's wonderful news!"

"You're the first people we've told," said Danielle, "There's no ring yet 'cos I'm hoping to…I'm going to lose more weight." She looked up at Zac.

He smiled gently. "It's been fun being a couple. I like having someone to share with, share everything with, both good and bad. Helps put things in perspective."

Aidan nodded. "You can't beat coming home to the little woman." He grinned as Angel raised her eyebrows.

Angel turned to Danielle. "Ignore him. So, tell me what's been happening with you since the party?"

"Well, where to begin! I've been working in the gym with Zac. I'm just getting to feel confident there," said Danielle, squirming in her seat a little, "Everyone's so fit and well, I thought they were but, that's the point, isn't it? You go there 'cos you want to get fit and the more I went, I met other people like me, well not exactly like me, and…sorry."

Angel looked up from her tea. "What for?"

"Oh, me waffling on."

"No, not at all. It's hard to make the words fit when you're excited about something." Angel's kind words had the desired effect and Danielle relaxed. "Do go on."

"Well, I've been to the gym and sorted my eating…"

"How?" said Aidan, "Sorry but I'm presuming there was a problem, if you don't mind me asking."

"No problem, no, yes I had a problem but I don't mind… whatever," said Danielle, smiling and running a hand through her newly coloured and styled hair, "It's been everything else that sorted my eating! I'm busy and positive and…looking to the future. Zac's got this brilliant idea…" She looked to Zac and he nodded his go ahead, "We want to take fitness out of the gyms, you know, out of that world and into real life; schools, clubs, on to the street to help young people." As Danielle continued, her pale cheeks glowed with passion and her pretty face stood out even more from the rolls of unwanted flesh that restrained it. "We've been working on a plan and…I've taken up belly dance!"

Conversation bounced back and forth and tea and cake were consumed.

"So, if you could name one thing that was the catalyst to this new life, what would it be?" said Angel.

"Zac," said Danielle, without hesitation.

"And my life's changed too," said Zac, reaching for Danielle's hand, "You've both been amazing friends, still are, but I've gotten closer to Danielle than anyone, ever and she's let me in, even with her problems and I, in turn, have been able to confide in her."

"I'm so pleased for you, Zac," said Angel, her eyes conveying love and respect. "Sounds to me like you've met your soul mate."

"Well, of course I'm a bit pissed off!"

Aidan pulled her closer as they lay on their backs under the covers. "But you always knew this might happen."

"Of course I did and, all credit to Danielle. She grabbed the opportunity and took it, good for her."

"You don't mean that."

"I'm trying to!"

They laughed and snuggled closer. The warmth of him, the smell, lulled Angel and her calmness returned. "Our path is to offer the choices and Danielle made her choice. A good one, especially if it helps Zac," she said.

"But to lose him from the ritual too," said Aidan.

"Hmm and with the Spring Solstice nearly here and plans for Wales already made…"

"Hmm, I'm a bit pissed off!" said Aidan, grinning.

"You are intolerable!" said Angel, straddling him and pinning him down with his arms above his head.

"I know," said Aidan, smiling, "But you love me."

Angel looked down into the beautiful carefree face, blond hair tousled, green eyes sparkling, jaw line proud and strong and lips of succulent sweetness. She brought her lips a hairbreadth from his lips, breathing over the skin of his face and whispered in his ear. "More than you'll ever know."

"It felt too big, Mads. I'd get lost in it," said Sophia, bench-pressing as Maddy spotted.

"But you'd have room for a full size gym," said Maddy, grinning, "And a spare room, in fact a few!"

"Enough," said Sophia, straining on the final rep. Maddy seated the bar in its holder. Sophia sat up and reached for a towel, legs in Lycra swinging on either side of the bench. "Like I said, I didn't like it. Anyway, it was miles from yours." She got up and stepped away from the bench.

"I know," said Maddy, removing weights from the bar and re-tightening the cuff before lying down. "But it was beautiful and the stream running along the boundary..."

"True, but I can't buy a house for a stream," said Sophia, lifted the bar down to Maddy.

"You could," said Maddy, pushing up, thin white scars all over her arms, shining as she strained.

"I could live anywhere in the world but I'm not going to and I'm not going to buy a house for a stream either!" said Sophia. She paused a moment. "I might for a woodland *and* a stream!"

Workout complete and bodies showered, Sophia and Maddy snuggled into the plum coloured velvet of Sophia's sofa in their pyjamas, bowls of steaming stir-fry in their laps. A fire blazed in the grate of Sophia's ground floor apartment while a tribal beat rumbled in the background from the music centre.

"I'm sure you'll find the right house," said Maddy, "What are these flat things?"

"Mange tout."

"Eat it all! How funny!"

"I suppose it means you eat the pod too. You not had them before?"

"Not sure. I like them in the stir fry though."

"Good job or you can cook next time."

"Me!" laughed Maddy, "You *are* joking."

"It's easy, Mads."

"I'm sure it is but I love you cooking for me."

"And when I'm not here?"

"I manage. I'm never hungry on my own."

Bowls cleared to the sink and with carrot cake between them, Sophia and Maddy sipped their coffee.

"You heard any more from the charming Mr Rogers?"

"No and I'm glad," said Maddy, "He was a creepy man. Ughh!" She shuddered and brought her coffee cup closer. Her red checked pyjamas matched her cheeks as the glow from the fire flickered in the dark room.

"And you're not bothered what happens to him?"

Maddy shook her head. "Why should I? I gave him the choice and a good one at that. Brian Foxleigh is a cool guy, really happy to advise, you know. Mr Rogers would have done well to call him."

"But he didn't?" said Sophia, stroking the moonstone at her throat.

Maddy shook her head again. "Saw Brian for lunch Tuesday last week, or was it Wednesday? Anyway, he'd had no contact."

"So, it seems the greedy Mr Rogers has picked the dangerous path?" said Sophia, balancing her cup on a pink fleecy knee.

"Who knows," said Maddy, "I never want to see him again! Do you know, he tried to put *me* down and then started on Eli and Zac? How *dumb* is *that*?"

Sophia nodded. "Yes, you said."

"So, how's your Mr Preston doing?"

"He's…well he's…trying."

Maddy giggled. "Can he handle it?"

"Mads, he's already in so deep. I feel sorry for him."

"*Sorry!* You're not serious!"

"I am. He's a nice guy."

"Sophia, get real here. You *know* what he did to Angel."

"Yes, but only because he was led by Rogers."

"He could have said no," said Maddy.

"But they were a gang, Mads, how could he lose face? Anyway, it was *years* ago!"

"Then let's hope he's changed and he'll own up to not being able to cope with the job and he'll have learned his lesson," said Maddy.

"Yes, let's hope."

"You like him, don't you?" said Maddy, "I don't think you're supposed to."

"Who says?"

"Well, Angel says we're to be the catalysts, remember. Set the scene rolling and then walk away."

"But I have to *work* with Justin!"

Maddy raised her eyebrows at the red glistening face of Sophia. "You've not…you're not…"

Sophia laughed. "Mads, don't look so worried. There's potential below the surface in Justin, I'm sure of it. I suppose I don't want his world to crumble without him having a chance."

They sat gazing into the glistening jewels of the fire. Maddy thought about Mr Rogers and the relief she felt having finished playing her part while Sophia constructed a plan to help Justin, giving him a second chance.

"Maybe you should speak to Angel," said Maddy.

"No, Mads," said Sophia, "I can handle it. How are you getting to Wales?"

"Jed's taking me. We've both got business in London then we're at mine for the evening and coming up the next day. You? Do you need a lift?"

Sophia shook her head. "I'm driving. I'm bringing Jenny."

The squally rain had made the walk home from school a wet one. Jenny peeled off Scarlett's snow suit and her own jeans and socks and while Finn undressed himself, Jenny ran upstairs for dressing gowns. She started the bath before she rejoined them.

"I'm fweezin'," said Scarlett, her bottom lip trembling.

"I know babe, I know," soothed Jenny, peeling off Scarlett's final layers. "Bath's running. You 'n' Finn can get all warm, don't worry."

"Don't know why we had to walk," said Finn, "I'm saturated!" He turned his back as he finished undressing, making Jenny's heart miss a beat. He's growing up so fast and won't want to bath with Scarlett soon. How can I tell him there's no money for petrol because I've spent it on his birthday this Saturday?

Jenny thought quickly. "Shall we have bubbles?" she said, "We could play 'Dinosaurs in the swamp', what you reckon?"

"Bubbles!" squealed Scarlett, "And 'sores! Big sores!"

Finn turned back and smiled. "Okay," he said, "But I get T Rex."

Bath time mayhem followed. Dinosaurs bit babies, which made Scarlett cry but then, Happy Turtle came to the rescue and spun the dinosaurs back into the swamp. Warm and washed, Jenny went straight for pyjamas for them all.

"It's too early!" said Finn.

"It'll be cosy," said Jenny, "Shall we have seaside chips for tea?"

"And ice cream?" said Scarlett.

"I think that'll make your tummy cold again, Lettie," said Jenny, "We've got Nana Mo's apple crumble and custard."

"We can have seaside chips though?"

"Yes, Lettie. Any homework Finn?"

"Yeah, spelling and a map to fill in and then colour."

"I'll set you both up at the kitchen table then, while I'm cooking. Do you want your crayon tin, Lettie?"

"No, I want sprinkles."

Jenny and Finn shared a puzzled look before Finn understood. "Glitter! She wants the glitter box!"

"But you're all clean!"

"I'll be vewwy careful," said Scarlett, her bottom lip trembling, "I gotta do a surpwise."

"All right," sighed Jenny, "You get the box then."

Scarlett ran into her bedroom and Jenny heard a drawer being opened, as she attempted to dry the bathroom.

Scarlett returned behind an armful of boxes. "Sprinkles 'n' clarge 'n' glue 'n' crayons!"

Finn appeared in his Buzz Lightyear pyjamas and navy gown and rescued the boxes from Scarlett. "I'll carry them for you, Lettie, 'cos you gotta be careful on the stairs."

"I gotta do a surpwise," said Scarlett in her best stage whisper, "Gotta count now," and she began her descent of the stairs. "Leleven!..."

"Twelve," prompted Jenny, as she and Finn waited in procession behind Scarlett.

"I know!" cried Scarlett. She backed up one step and then stepped down, "Twelve," she said, smugly. "Tirteen!"

"Well done, Lettie," said Jenny. "To the table..."

"And beyond!" shouted Finn, running to the kitchen.

As the home-made chips sizzled in the pan, Jenny cut up fruit and carrot sticks for snacks at the table. Entrusted with one cocktail stick each, the children stabbed and ate. Finn filled in the states and coloured in his map of America while Scarlett made her 'surpwise'. As the chips were draining in the basket Finn asked to be tested on his spelling and soon, homework done and glitter removed, at least from hands, the three of them snuggled on the sofa. They each had a plate and a paper bag containing chips which they nibbled and blew on as they watched an episode of Dr Who, Finn's choice, Bagpuss, Scarlett's choice and, now with apple crumble and custard tickling their tongues, finally Jenny's choice, an episode of the Herbs.

Even Dill the dog's antics couldn't keep Scarlett awake so, Finn paused the DVD and took Scarlett's half eaten crumble bowl to the kitchen while Jenny persuaded her upstairs. Scarlett whimpered and begged to be carried but Jenny knew Scarlett needed to be awake enough to use the toilet and so began helping her count the stairs up. Finn joined them and Scarlett's progress quickened until, teeth cleaned, toilet successfully used, Jenny and Finn tucked Scarlett into bed.

"Storwy," whispered Scarlett.

"Once up a time," said Jenny, "There was a beautiful princess called Scarlett. She had blond curls and bright blue eyes and she lived with her Mummy and her brother Finn, who was training to be a knight of the round table, in a castle in the clouds. One day, it rained so hard that Princess Scarlett got soaking wet. She didn't feel like a princess any more but, after her bath, in her pink pyjamas, Princess Scarlett..."

Scarlett purred a snore in response.

"More Herbs or did you want to do something else?" said Jenny as she and Finn went back into the lounge.

"I wanted to ask you something," said Finn.

"Of course, anything," said Jenny, wondering if this was heading towards a birds and bees talk and beckoning Finn onto the sofa.

"You still *want* me and Lettie, don't you?"

"Of course!" cried Jenny. Finn backed away a little. "Sorry Finn, sorry, it's just…of course I want you! Sweetheart, have I given you any reason to think I didn't? Want you, I mean?"

Finn slowly shook his head. "But Dad said that you going away is you needing to get away from us because we're in the way. He says you've got a new life now."

"I see," said Jenny, feeling the colour rising to her cheeks, desperately stifling the anger, trying to prevent it seeping into her voice, "So, what do you think?"

"You said you were working."

"I was."

"I know. That's what I told Dad and, well, he, err, he said…"

"Tell me, Finn."

"He said you were lying and that you'd got a new love and that you wouldn't want us any more."

Jenny held her arms open to her son and drew him into her lap, stroking his hair and speaking softly. "I want you both more than anything, Finn. From the moment you were born and I looked into your calm blue eyes and Scarlett's. Hers were already naughty!" They laughed together. "I've told you the truth before and I will continue to, Finn. I went away with Auntie Angel to help me start setting up a new business, making jewellery and sculptures. Nana Mo and Granddad Colin love looking after you and they know that, now I'm on my own, I need to have a career and they want to support me, us."

"So why does Dad say all this rubbish?" said Finn sitting up, his face pinched and angry.

"I'm not sure," said Jenny, "I think partly it's to get at me for saying I couldn't be married to him any more. He liked things the way they were and often people don't like change."

"But you said there was no love left?"

"There wasn't Finn, just familiarity but that has nothing to do with my love for you and Scarlett. It won't change, or if it does, it will only get bigger!" She smiled at her son and pulled him to her again.

He happily nuzzled close and kissed her on the neck. "You're getting bony," he said, poking her ribs and shoulders.

"I ate my tea!" said Jenny, mock huffily.

"But you're a growing Mummy," said Finn, mock scolding and they laughed and snuggled up some more.

"I don't mind if you spend time with your friends or a boyfriend, Mum," said Finn, "I like hanging with my mates too. I love you and Let but it's different with your mates."

"It is," said Jenny, "Thank you for that."

"No worries," said Finn, more grown up than he'd ever sounded, "Dad told me why you really made him leave. I reckon if you find a nice boyfriend, you'll stop fancying women."

Finn chose to finish the evening with a chapter of Lemony Snickett and he was soon sound asleep like his sister. Jenny checked on Scarlett, tidied and cleaned the bathroom and went down stairs, automatically counting in her head. She smiled at the bottom and then frowned as Finn's question popped into her brain. Want them? She adored them, they were her life but, she was entitled to some life of her own too and, any break from them did her so much good. She remembered how full of energy she'd been less than a month ago on her return from Paris.

In the kitchen, she cleared the drainer. Her career plans weren't much further forward though. She'd sketched a few ideas, but the house sale and the children had consumed the past few weeks, especially as the sale had proceeded so swiftly; a young couple, coming out of rental to buy so, with no chain, her own purchase was moving just as speedily. She smiled as she ran half a bowl of water to wash up the plates and mugs. She'd known the new house was perfect as soon as she'd stepped inside. Mum and Dad had been happy to lend her the money for new wiring, central heating and plastering and were happy to put them up in the meantime. Angel's contractors were confident they could work together and complete the basics in four weeks and then, it was up to her and the children. So, Finn's birthday this Saturday, Scarlett's two weeks later and then furniture divided, boxes packing for storage, suitcases and crates to pack to take with them…Jenny leant on the sink and sighed. And Scott feeding the children such terrible lies! Her anger bubbled and she clenched the icy stainless steel trying to cool her head. *Me* fancying *women!* How *could* he? Don't act rashly. Think first. Don't want any repercussions for Finn. She sighed again. Doing it all was one thing but trying to do it all at once left her weak and dizzy. But it'll be over in a few months, she tried to convince herself, just a few more months. Be strong, Jenny, they need you.

Her phone buzzed in her handbag on the microwave. "Hi Angel," said Jenny, "Yes, good thanks."

"You sound exhausted."

"It's been a long day, that's all. Just one more and then it's Finn's birthday Saturday but, I think I'm organized for that." Jenny moved over to the kitchen table as she talked and began to collect usable card together.

"Jen, you're doing too much."

"I know, really I know, but it has to be like this at the
moment." Jenny put the tops back on the glitter tubes and
the crayons in the box.

"Okay, well, I was going to ask about the business plans
but it sounds like you've enough to think about."

"Oh no!" cried Jenny. "It's in my mind all the time!" She
cleared away the debris until she was left holding Scarlett's
surprise. A shiny moon face glistened from the paper
surrounded by pink, purple and orange stars all bathed in a
peachy glow. The moon smiled with generous benevolence,
almost winking at a best kept secret.

"So, you've not come up with a name yet?"

"Oh, I think I have," said Jenny, smiling, "Juniper Moon."

23

The house clung to the Welsh mountainside below road
level, hugging the hillside, suspended over the river that
mirrored the road above. Grey slates and chimney pots were
visible as they turned onto the narrow driveway and Sophia
backed the Forester into a narrow gap in front of the house,
finishing neatly up against Aidan's Land Rover and next to
the oak front door. As Jenny alighted she smelt the warm
dampness of the earth and the honeysuckle beginning to bud
on the thick stone walls and she heard the rumblings of the
river below them.

Angel hugged them both in the hallway of the house and
showed them to their room, requesting their presence in the
lounge once they were settled. Jenny felt relaxed yet excited
as they chose a bed and freshened up before joining Aidan
and Angel.

The vast beamed lounge took up one side of the house,
while on the other side, meandering through narrow
passages, was a mishmash of extensions and styles

incorporating bedrooms, bathrooms, kitchen and conservatory.

Jenny entered through massive doors hung on hinges with burnished peacock tails and was launched back in time to a medieval hall with a vaulted and beamed ceiling. The broad fireplace, as tall as she, stacked and crackling with chunks of timber within the claws of its wide log basket, welcomed her with its rustic warmth. It's mantle, barely visible beneath drapes of greenery, was a massive slab of regal oak. High windows circumvented the room, heavily draped, while at the far end were a solid wooden table with high backed chairs around it and the customary Welsh dresser. Around the fire a long low sofa and chairs, slung with throws and blankets and dotted with cushions, urged the new comers to be seated and Jenny took a place as her eyes caught a glimpse of a towering standard lamp, its base a fabulous carved dragon, also wound round with bright succulent foliage.

"What a room," said Jenny, still turning her head, catching things she'd missed.

"The original house," said Angel.

"You made good time," said Aidan, poking the fire and sending cascades of fire fairies up the chimney.

"Jenny didn't mind an early start," said Sophia, "So we were ahead of the traffic all the way."

"Kettle's on," said Angel.

"I'd love a cup of tea," said Jenny.

"Absolutely and then we'll show you round and you can help us finish the decorating if you like," said Angel.

The wind creaked and buffeted around the house as more guests arrived. Storm clouds had been channelled over them and brought rain that hammered on the roof above and added sustenance to the seething river. The surge of the torrent was audible in the stone built house so, with the fire blazing, all the elements were present and Jenny felt energized and a little scared by their power and potency. She was glad of Sophia's reassuring smile amidst the industry all around her, as daffodils were added to swathes of greenery, people came and went in tunics of green and white and cloaks of black, green, lavender and sky blue, logs were heaped by the fire and covered plates and platters emerged from the kitchen and took their place on the table. Jenny's head hummed. She knew the Spring Equinox was a fire festival and festival of new life, fertility and birth from her conversation with Sophia in the car but the anticipation of the ritual, sent shivers down her spine.

As the buzz of preparation slowed, Sophia took Jenny and dressed her in a white tunic, a cloak of lavender velvet and gave her new flat sandals as a gift. Sophia painted Jenny's face with spirals and flowers before they adjourned to the conservatory where they sipped a cleansing drink of apple, carrot and lemon juice mixed with spring water and thyme and Jenny constructed her first floral crown. A base of soaked willow was made first and then entwined with plants and herbs that the wearer felt sang out to them so Jenny was soon the proud owner of a crown of lavender, violets, lilac and trefoil, a delicate purple clover, and all the while the preparations were made, Jenny could hear the wind blowing and the excessive rainwater tumbling down the river.

The raging weather forced them inside for the ritual so, as the birds began their lullabies, seven figures, cloaked and sandalled descended the stone steps beneath the hallway into a cellar beneath the house. As Jenny's eyes became accustomed to the darkness, she saw that the room continued, spreading out into a cave below the mountain and she was glad of her warm velvet cloak.

Two lighted braziers cracked and shot sparks in the gloom, taking off the damp chill of the air while chunky candles in nooks in the cave walls warmed to their task, dousing the assembled party with a golden glow.

A table, covered with a green cloth stood in the circle marked on the floor and as she took her place, Jenny noted all that was upon it. First, the abundance of candles in white, black, yellow, green, pink and red and then a chalice and a wand and dishes of earth and seeds as well as tiny smoked glass bottles, a vast bunch of daffodils and tulips, a basket of painted eggs, some fur and a long stick.

Aidan and Angel stepped forward to the altar and a hush fell upon the figures in the cave. As the ritual began Jenny's skin began to prickle and scraps of phrases sang in her head as she breathed in the power of nature and sighed at the beauty of her world.

"Faery Queen Blodeuwedd, join us in our circle and bring to us the delights of Spring…", "The power of fertility…", "Blessed Ostera, Queen of Spring", "Empower the children of the Earth…"

As Jenny watched, Angel planted seeds into the rich earth and Aidan charged the water with his blade before Angel sipped it saying 'the waters of life' and then poured some onto the seeds. A tingling in her chest like a spark igniting for the first time made Jenny's ears buzz and when the fur was blessed, Jenny saw the lambs in the fields and the buzzard soaring above the mountain peaks, wrapped in their own bubble of protection, bestowed upon them by the Goddess Ostera.

As the energy in the circle heightened, Jenny saw the procession of laughing, smiling faces, walking between the sacred stones; mothers, children, fathers, grandparents, all decked with flowers, their faces painted and their feet bare to the earth. Upon the sacred hill top, between the tall standing stones the procession circled and called upon the Goddess and when the Priestess beckoned them, as the laughter and singing stilled, they took a seed from the blessed basket and planted it in a clay bowl and watered if from the flask from the sacred well. Jenny saw herself take her turn, feeling the wind whipping her simple shift and the tendrils of her hair. As she planted her seed in the earth, she felt the vitality of new life surge through her fingers, filling her body with light.

"We send this magic to the winds of change, to protect and revive the Earth, our home. So mote it be."

Aidan carried the basket to each of the friends and they chose an egg beneath the straw, while Angel anointed each forehead with Ostera oil. Jenny caught the scent of lavender and patchouli as she chose and turned over her egg.

Angel smiled. "You've chosen stars, Jen. Well, there's a surprise. It's the Silver Wheel, the Goddess Arianrhod."

The sea was divided by a rivulet of molten silver as the moon beamed down her light. Jenny flexed her toes in the fine white sand as she watched the sky glistening and twinkling its welcome. Lights began to join together, moving across the sky, collecting more stars like a runaway snowball as they arced and soon, a disk of silver light spun in the darkness above her. She lay down on the sand as the wheel grew, adding more stars until it filled the sky above her head, turning slowly. At its hub two shining figures appeared and the first stepped forward.

Blond and smiling, fun and mischief sparking from her skin, the face before Jenny was ageless, sometimes maiden, sometimes crone. "I bid you welcome, Jenny," said the figure and she bowed. "You see before you the wheel, ever turning, the wheel of time. There must be death for there to be new life but time is a great healer. Honour me, Arianrhod, the Silver Wheel, at the place of the Full Moon and I will protect you and your children and support you in your work."

"I will," said Jenny, as the figure stepped back and the other forward.

"I bid you welcome, Jenny," said the tall figure with dark hair and blue eyes, "I too am a goddess of the Moon and embrace you as my sister." She held out her hand to Jenny. "Take this gift and when all around you is confusion, you will understand."

Jenny reached up to the glittering sky above her and woke up.

As she unpacked her bag from her weekend away, remembering the ritual, the feast of a multitude of quiches and salads and the games, Jenny found a stone wrapped in her spare socks. It was dark grey, almost black and when she turned it a certain way, it looked just like an Egyptian cat.

Justin awoke to a misty cold morning with those flickers of light in the cloud that you hope are heralding a fine, crisp spring day. He dowsed the persistent alarm so as not to wake Tiffany, reached for his robe at the end of the bed, before shuffling quietly to the en suite. Only upon his return, with light seeping through the curtain gaps, was he aware that Tiffany wasn't there.

At the kitchen table, now fully dressed, he ate his toast while consulting his laptop and finishing his coffee. A glance at the kitchen clock caused a sigh and then a thumped fist on the table before he tapped at his keyboard and then shut it with a snap.

At the bottom of the stairs he sighed again and began to call as he ascended. "Chloe! Harry! Chelsea! Wake up! Breakfast in ten minutes!"

Justin sat in the anonymous coffee shop in the service station next to the motorway. The school run had put him two hours behind but he'd rescheduled his three meetings and had felt the need to take a break.

Where the fuck was she? Her mobile was off and there had still been no message from her. Despite his anger, he was a little worried. He'd never deprived her of evenings out so long as they didn't affect him, but he realized she was out most nights now, once Chelsea had been put to bed.

They rarely went out together in the week and, since December, their regular Saturday evenings with friends at a club or bar had also dwindled to rarely. But to leave him to sort the kids without a word and with all the pressure he was under! Justin watched as two men and two women in smart suits and camel coats queued for their beverages and, not for the first time, compared Tiffany to the women and then to Sophia. Why *did* he stay with Tiffany? In many respects, she made his life easy. The house and kids were her domain, leaving him time to interact with his children when he wanted to and relax, eat and sleep in an equivalent four star hotel, but at what cost? He never saw her credit card bill, just the debit from the account when it was paid and he'd sometimes wondered what the money was spent on but then figured he had no idea how much beauty treatments and cosmetics cost and didn't care. There was enough money to pay the mortgage, bills and a chunk in his pension and savings. They could meet the payments but was Tiffany really worth it? He tried to visualize a scenario where she wasn't there and he struggled. He sipped his coffee and imagined, instead, a lifetime of just him and Sophia.

April

24

"So, how are you feeling?"

"Ashamed," said Rob.

"I meant physically," said Jed, watching the face of the man in the bed.

Rob sat propped up with pillows behind and around him and the brown floral duvet cover over his chest. Any skin that was showing was bruised and raw and he looked far more wolf than grandma.

Rob dismissed the enquiry with a shrug and a wave of his left hand. "I'll heal," he said, "But the pain of letting y'all down is far worse. Teresa spoke to the office for me, to make sure the girls were ok."

"I know," said Jed, "They told me. She was very upset."

Rob's face contorted and he nursed his broken hand to his chest. "I know, what I've put her through…"

"But you tried, Rob…"

"No, no," said Rob, shaking his head, "I was an idiot! I've ruined everything! How stupid to think I could just have one drink on my birthday!"

"Hmm, maybe not your best idea," said Jed, sipping tea from a stripy mug.

"Fuckin' understatement!" said Rob, "Never again! I've had it with alcohol!"

"Really?"

"Oh yeah," said Rob, "I was responsible for them girls and you trusted me, Mr Carter. Now, I've let them, Trees, you, everybody down, just for a bloody drink! It could've been so much worse too! I've learned my lesson."

Jed nodded. "So, what are you going to do, once you're well again?"

Rob took his glass of water from the cabinet next to him and sipped before replacing it, his pudgy left hand shaking with the effort. "Start again," he said. "Start again but different. I stuck to the diet, I can stick to no alcohol and I'll have to start looking for work again, regular work, not just when somethin' lands in me lap."

"So, you don't want your old job back?" said Jed.

Rob's face pinked beneath his bruises, his eyes widening with amazement. "What? You'd take me back, Mr Carter? Really?"

"Yeah," said Jed, his hazel eyes softening, "I wasn't sure before we spoke but, I think you deserve a second chance, don't you?"

Tears ran down Rob's cheeks and he hurried to stifle them. "Sorry, really sorry, it's just…I didn't imagine for one second you'd…Thank you, thank you Mr Carter."

"But this time Rob, it really is up to you. It was a close call. You, the girls, it's a dangerous business out there unless you're diligent. No room for any more mistakes."

Rob sat up in bed now, his chest no longer caved in and his shoulders back. His tear stained face was slapped with a huge grin as he nursed his hand to his chest. "I promise, Mr Carter. I'm done playing the idiot. I won't let you down."

Vincent's mobile began to buzz as the doorbell rang and he signed the courier's chit as he answered it, the phone on his shoulder.

"All arrived safely, excellent," he said, thanking the courier with a nod and shutting the door. "Yeah, just arrived. By noon, excellent, I'll keep an eye on the account." He opened the packet and scanned the transfer deeds and documentation. "All looks in order. I'll check through and then fax my signed receipt. Really? Well, my man in Poland is good, very good. Really? Well, of course…by next Friday? No, it's not that…I can't, it's just cutting it a bit fine…No, it's the legal paperwork over there…okay, yes, I'll get onto him straight away…Of course, I see, right, okay…Well, of course, a regular order of that size…Of course, I'll get back to you today, no problem."

Vincent ended the call, grabbed his laptop and began tapping, a smirk on his lips becoming a grin in moments. The money was already there, in the account, winking at him. He'd worked out the profit last night, a nice round 15k and the client wanted more and not just once more, but a regular monthly order. If Ofim could sort it, this would be a great little earner for not much work. What a start and all above board too! Vincent sat back in his chair, ran his hands over his bristly, cropped auburn head and grinned while all around him danced thousands of little ks.

"It's up to you, Aidan. We could do them both with some help. We could take Luke and Clive, maybe John or were you going to hire from Rome?"

Jed and Aidan stood in Jed's office, papers spread over the desk.

"Not sure yet. Let's have a think. Mrs Spellman's is ongoing. She'll have the wall this time but she has homes that need gardens too while Georgio just wants the glass wall in the foyer. It'll be tricky making sure the plants take evenly and on both sides." Conversation continued, becoming more technical and then financial as the men talked time and money.

"Well, if you're planning to start 1st September, I can give you more or less a straight eight weeks but, I've been invited to France after Samhein and I might go for a few weeks, always a good time for reflection," said Jed.

They drank from beer bottles and clinked them in the air as they sat on opposite sides of Jed's desk.

"You seen Mr Manning yet?" said Aidan.

Jed nodded.

"So, you'll need another driver?"

"Not necessarily," said Jed, "Mr Manning was really sorry and so, he remains in my employ."

"You are kidding?"

Jed shook his head. "His words were true Aidan, they had depth and I believe him. He wants to make something of his life for himself and his daughter. He's giving up the drink."

"But, can you risk it? You don't have to."

"I know," said Jed, "But I've been there, remember. If you're trapped in a corner and can't see a way out, it's a frightening existence."

"You were different Jed and surely Manning has no one to blame but himself for his own stupidity?"

"Maybe but remember, he's never been a leader, only a follower. He's not used to making his own decisions and getting them right. Until his wife left, he'd gone along with her every whim. Sound familiar?"

"Jed," said Aidan, leaning forward, "It's not the same, mate. You suffered, were suffering at the hands of others while Mr Manning…"

"Is suffering through lack of opportunity and good guidance. Anyway, he's on his final chance. It's up to him now."

Aidan nodded. "Fair enough. How've you been?"

"Okay, hard to get motivated some days I'll admit, but rugby training seems to shift the feeling and I'm keeping busy. Wales really helped."

"It's amazing, the power in the support of friends."

"To be honest, I haven't given it much thought. I know you mentioned it before…"

"We don't have to have a party if you don't want to."

Angel and Jenny sat on beanbags in Jenny's sparse lounge, nursing coffee mugs, boxes, bubble wrap and tape all around them.

"I don't know," said Jenny, shaking her head.

"Right now, you've enough to worry about, I'm sorry," said Angel.

"I'm just not sure that this old brain can make a decision about anything!" said Jenny, tapping the side of her head. "Anyway, I don't have many real friends. Not any more."

"No?"

"Well, I didn't see my college friends once I started work and work friends departed once I had Finn. I suppose there's a couple of girls from antenatal I see and a few from the school…"

They sipped at their mugs.

"I guess you and Scott didn't socialize much as a couple?"

Jenny shook her head. "He didn't like any of my friends, he said. There was the occasional kids birthday that was extended for all the family, you know, barbecues but not many and these past few years, he refused to attend any. Funny that?"

"Why so?"

"I'd never thought before but I guess he didn't want to be caught out. Hasn't been to any parent evenings, sports days…He's really missed out."

Angel nodded. "Caught out?"

"Mmm," Jenny stifled a nervous laugh. "He's got a lot…gayer, you know, more camp."

"Since he moved out?"

"Yeah but it'd already started." She viewed her left hand. "His nails are far better than mine."

And they laughed, really laughed. Laughed so much that the tears flowed and they put down their mugs and Jenny crawled into Angel's arms until they were done.

"Thanks so much for coming over," said Jenny, cuffing her eyes and sitting up. "These last boxes seem to be taking forever."

"But you're doing it," said Angel, "It's all happening thanks to you and there you were worrying about running your own business! It'll be a proverbial piece of piss compared to what you've achieved!"

"Thanks, thanks Angel but it's been…manic!"

Angel watched the gaunt figure of her friend take the mugs to the kitchen and begin rinsing them under the tap. Jenny's skinny limbs worried Angel and a furrow had begun to form between Jenny's eyes as she wrestled with a head full of problems these past months. Helping to pack boxes was all very well, practical and useful but she wanted to ease the pressures from Jenny's mind and take some of the tiredness away.

"What can I do?" said Angel, appearing by the drainer and picking up a tea towel.

"There's only these few bits and we'll need breakfast bowls," said Jenny. "Just two more boxes should finish the lounge and then they're ready for storage and then, tomorrow, while Finn's at school, we've our bits to pack into crates and suitcases to go to Mum and Dad's."

"I meant for you," said Angel, drying the mugs.

Jenny gripped the sink. "I'm fine."

"No you're not, you're exhausted."

"Well, there's a lot to do," said Jenny, releasing her grip and cleaning round the sink.

"And while you're so busy, there's no time to think and you fall into bed exhausted so you've a good chance of sleeping?" said Angel.

Jenny turned and smiled at Angel. "You got me."

"But you need time to think, Jen and let some of this out. You're saving up trouble for later and you don't want that. Let me help," said Angel, "I'll run you a bath. I've some oils in my bag and while you're soaking, I can finish the final boxes and…oh, Jen!" Angel hugged her sobbing friend to her and held her.

Jenny came up for air, grinning. "It was the bath Angel, sorry. Good dad, useless husband but he ran a lovely bath!"

It was midnight as they lay in Jenny's bed.

"But you're bound to miss him," said Angel, "Anything that becomes habit will be missed."

"And he never hit me and rarely shouted, in fact, it was all quite pleasant in some respects. Easy," said Jenny, staring up at the fitted cupboards above her.

"And the children," said Angel, "You've two beautiful children."

"Yes, I have," said Jenny.

"So it was worth it," said Angel, "Not what you'd hoped for but worth the struggle."

"Yes," said Jenny.

"But everything changes, Jen. Nothing stays the same," said Angel, turning on her side to face her friend, "People change, work, friends, everything and, as long as we learn from our experiences, we can move on with hope and excitement."

"I *am* excited," said Jenny, turning to face Angel, "It's just hard, with the little ones too."

"I bet it is," said Angel, "But they're wonderful. They seem very normal balanced kids to me. I might not have vast experience with children but I know people and I sensed a little worry and concern, but they're excited too and looking forward to their new home."

"We've at least four weeks with Mum and Dad first," said Jenny. "They're great but they do fuss."

"But it'll be worth it," said Angel, "All the wiring, plumbing, plastering all done and you and the kids can decorate when you like."

"I've asked for magnolia throughout as a start," said Jenny, "Except the kitchen and then we can choose colours when we're in." She rolled onto her back. "I can't believe I'm leaving here tomorrow."

"It's been your home for a lot of years, Jen, but it's only bricks and mortar. Remember all the good times, carry them in your heart but leave the sadness and disappointment behind you. Jen?"

Purred rhythmic breaths came from Jenny's side of the bed. Angel leant up and kissed her cheek. "Night Jen."

Angel stood in the sphere of power, her golden amber shift to her toes and a simple circlet of pink flowers upon her head. With Lilith beside her she watched the Tree of Life, the witches Qabalah, hanging in the air before her.

Shapes began to form within the Tree, triangles, diamonds and squares, each tipped by a Sephirah and linked by a numbered pathway. Angel saw the spheres of Netzach[16], Hod[17] and Tiphareth[18] gleaming from the Tree and she knew this to be the Magical Triangle and Chesod[19], Geburah[20] and Tiphareth and she knew this to be the Ethical triangle. Out of these shapes, one began to glow and resonate the brightest of all, in the centre of the Tree, linking the pathways together, golden and majestic beamed Tiphareth and Angel knew this to be her destination.

Thoth, the Dweller on the Threshold appeared as the Tree began to fade and she opened her mind for his scrutiny. Convinced of her intent, the lunar disk and crescent upon his head began to glow and he welcomed her onto the Path as the Doorkeeper, reassuring her of his duty to protect her.

---

[16] See Glossary
[17] See Glossary
[18] See Glossary
[19] See Glossary
[20] See Glossary

Angel stepped alone onto the silver thread before her, her sandals tracing pathways that she recognized. First, a pathway overhung with oak, beech and ash, a blue black world where she felt the sorrowing Isis and understood the pain of death but also the bliss and hope of resurrection. She walked on and shed the weighty blue of sorrow and replaced it with a world of violet and crystal where Levannah ruled. She opened her Treasurehouse of Visions for Angel to behold and Angel understood the link between the earth and the moon, the inspiration and the manifestation, the chaos and the calm. On she walked through a landscape of rushes and reeds, the air around her pulsing dark vivid blue and centaurs galloping beside her, laughing as the arrows they shot exploded into green and yellow sparks above her head. Angel understood the centaurs firing their Arrows of Swiftness Willed Force and within the colours she could see the conscious and subconscious, the Force of life and the original spark that began it.

The Angel Raphael, cloaked in green, welcomed her as she climbed the golden steps to the Temple and she entered through the portico to a majestic building lined with further pillars, where the breeze sang in harmonies within. Angel walked amongst the columns, studying the pictures and symbols engraved upon them while the fragrance of frankincense, cinnamon and Egyptian Kyphi filled her head. She saw plants and herbs; gorse, laurel, rosemary and twisting vines and a lion and a phoenix. On another pillar she saw the rosy cross while on another, cubes and hexagrams, grouped together in sixes.

At the end of the Temple was a square table covered with a golden cloth upon which were six vibrant sunflowers in a vase and an incense burner. The wondrous smells expelled filled her senses and opened her mind. Behind the table, backed by a vast stained glass window was a high backed wooden chair. The light shone through the glass, bouncing warm honey around the Temple.

A single flash of intense white light illuminated Angel and she saw the journey she had travelled so far. Ra, the Sun God, sat upon the throne, a man with the solar disk upon his head surrounded by the sacred asp. He, Ra, The Creator, Great Father, god of magic, prosperity, destiny and truth looked down upon his child and smiled upon her and with his golden smile, the Temple shone like a beacon, the central point of existence, the point of transmutation between the planes of Force and Form. The light from Ra, the intense pure yellow light, entered Angel's head, not to see with by her physical eye but to illuminate the body of images she had stored from her mystical experiences and she learned from them. She saw in the face of Ra, the qualities of earned success, material success, victory and joy and she understood that sacrifice brought forth new life. As her mind opened up to the possibilities on this plane, she fell to her knees with the enormity of the knowledge and, in a blinding white flash, the Temple vanished and she was on her knees within her circle of protection, in the basement of her home once more.

As Angel drifted off to sleep, the Sun God Ra stood before her and gave her a message. "You've reached the Sun, the central point, the beginning of life and I say to you, do not journey further! Dwell in Tiphareth and honour her codes. Learn from her beauty and harmony, recoup your energy and abide within these golden walls until you are healed. Before you venture further up the Tree, complete the Magical Triangle Angel, for I know your true destination and, without the gifts of Hod and Netzach, you will be destroyed!"

"I'm good, thanks. How's it going?"

"Good, yeah," said Jenny, leaning back in her dad's chair, the phone on her shoulder, a notepad on her lap. "Just come back from the house. It's all happening there!"

"Good, good and remember, it'll look a heap for a few weeks yet and then suddenly, it all comes together!"

"But they've done so much in a week!" said Jenny, "It's amazing and I've had some ideas too."

"Brilliant, well, best say now if you want any changes to the spec…"

"No, not the house. I've had a bit more time to think, since we've been here, about other things, you know, work, friends and birthdays."

"Your mum looking after you?" said Angel.

"Oh yes," said Jenny, "Food keeps appearing in front of me and I'm not even allowed to wash up!"

Angel laughed. "Make the most of it, enjoy it!"

"Oh, I am," said Jenny. "A few weeks break from chores will be great and dad's taken over bath and bedtime and the children are loving it!"

"Good for them!" said Angel.

"So these are my thoughts for starting the company," said Jenny. She'd had rough ideas in her head but, as she talked and Angel asked questions, a plan began to form and soon, Jenny was scribbling in the notepad as she talked. "So, if I give myself a few months, start college in September, while getting under way with the ideas I've got, I reckon I can get enough for the display cases in Paris and New York by November, hopefully in time for Christmas."

"Sticking to the unique pieces for now?"

"Mainly but I'd like to target a slightly cheaper market too so, still hand crafted but less expensive materials and less fiddly so I can produce more."

"And there's a real variety of markets on the net now so, you need to find your niche and then it's much easier to sell…"

"But I'll need help with the marketing…"

"Then you're talking to the right person, my love."

"I know, you're wonderful! I think I may have a lead for the less expensive pieces too. Sarah, Oscar's mum, one of Finn's friends, her brother's friend has just opened a shop in Manchester."

"Go on."

"Well, she says it's a real mixture of east meets west, with a bit of the occult thrown in."

"Sounds interesting," said Angel.

"I'd taken a photo on my phone of your Christmas present and when I was telling her about Paris and the jewellery, I showed her the photo."

"And she loved it, of course. So when can you get up to Manchester?"

"I may not have to. It seems her brother's friend is down in a couple of weeks for a few days so, I'm hoping to arrange a time to meet with him then."

"Sounds perfect," said Angel, "You *are* getting yourself organized! You mentioned birthdays?"

"Yeah, I've been thinking, what I would like and I've got a big favour to ask."

"Ask away."

"Well, given the choice, I'd like to celebrate my 30th with you and Aidan, Mum, Dad and the kids and Tim, oh, and Sophia. She's called a couple of times and Maddy. So kind of them. Well, whoever but I wondered if we could have a day at your house? It was the pool you see. I can't afford to take the kids away and Mum and Dad are selling the motor home as it's just too much for Dad, so they're not going away…"

"What a brilliant idea!"

"Do you think so?"

"Absolutely! Come and stay over! I'm...I'm so glad you asked."

"You okay?"

"Yes, I'm fine. Let's talk birthdays!"

25

The sun was having a lazy morning as Sophia and Justin set off for their walk. It dallied behind the puffy cumulus clouds, winking out occasionally before retiring behind another fluffy bank for a snooze.

The beginning of the wood was dense and damp and Sophia held Justin's arm as they tramped uphill along a muddy path, deeper into the undergrowth and, as they walked, Sophia marvelled and pointed at the natural world all around them. "Oh, just look at those oxlips!" she said, "Native British flower and yet, so much rarer now. Careful!"

She held him back and Justin looked down at the ground where regiments of wood ants crossed the path to a mound just off it. Diligent and determined the ants ignored the human giants, intent as they were on their tasks of cutting, carrying, climbing and building. With every step, all around them, the birds conversed across their heads and every tree and shrub was bursting with buds and the ground zinged with tiny industrious life.

Sophia stopped him again. "Listen."

A ricochet of tapping afforded Justin his first sound of a woodpecker.

At the top of the hill, the path bent left and down and as they followed it the sun emerged from its reverie and Justin's senses were bombarded by every green on the palette. Twinkles of sunlight lit up patches of ferns and bracken, shining through fresh new leaves and the luscious earthy smells rose up to tickle the smelling senses which, in turn, delivered tastes, flavours and textures of spring. On a narrow path, leading the way, around another corner Justin gasped and stood rooted to the ground by the sight before him. Sophia came up and took his arm. Waves and swathes of bluebells painted the forest floor. Around the trees and up the banks encircling the dell, fountains of softest blue burst forth among the ferns. Every patch of bare earth was colour washed by the blooms like a delicate, scented carpet of tiny, juicy bells.

As Sophia watched, smiling at Justin's awestruck face, the sun, now showered, clothed and with it's trainers on, beamed down onto the glade and, through the abundant green leaves, shafts of yellow light illuminated the scene like bars of gold descending from the sky. Sophia nudged Justin forward so, close together on the narrow steep path, they descended under the canopy to the ground below, rubbing shoulders with the foliage as they went.

As they reached the bottom, at Sophia's request and watching carefully where he put his feet, Justin ascended a bank, ducked beneath the foliage and emerged into another dell, totally enclosed by the mammoth presence of the rhododendrons. A rustic wooden bench was set to one side on the grassy earth within the circle and they sat down, unfastening their coats as the sun chased away the clouds and came back to warm their cheeks.

"I'm rarely lost for words," said Justin, removing his coat and pulling his fine knitwear sweater over his head.

"I've noticed," said Sophia, laughing.

"Yeah, yeah," said Justin, "But I mean it. This place, the dell, it…it took my breath away."

Sophia sat back into the corner of the bench, her padded lilac body warmer unzipped over her cream jumper. Her hair was tied in a spiky knot on her head so, as she turned to speak to Justin, only the fringe of her hair was visible, giving the viewer no distraction from the sparkling blue jewels of her eyes. "I'm glad it moved you."

"Are you?"

Sophia nodded and turned away to the shiny succulent walls that surrounded them.

Justin felt his heart beating through his white t-shirt, filling his body with vitality, every beat pounding blood into his senses, heightening them all.

He edged closer to her on the bench. "Tell me why," he said.

"Nature gives me my inspiration," said Sophia, "Tiny seeds and shoots spreading roots into the earth, growing and rejoicing in the beauty of the world. Plant now and who knows what will grow in the future." She paused a moment. "I wanted you to see and feel what motivates me, Justin. When I see all this," she spread out her arms, "I believe I can do anything!" She turned to him, eyes blazing. "Do you understand?"

"I think so," said Justin, "And you can. Do anything. You, you know so much. I try not to," he ran his fingers over his spiky head, "But I often feel out of my depth, when I talk to you."

"Do you?" said Sophia, her blazing eyes enquiring for the truth.

Justin nodded.

"About the hospice?"

"Oh no!" said Justin, "I'm on safe ground there, I know my trade. No, about nature and the world, you know, I've never given it much thought before."

Sophia nodded. "But, going back to the hospice, you'd say if you were out of your depth, wouldn't you?" Sophia turned her eyes to Justin, serious and intense.

He was glad that the sunlight was glowing on his face. "Of course!" he said, smiling, "All under control and now the weather's brightened up, it's full steam ahead!"

Sophia's face softened as she returned her gaze to her surroundings. A squirrel appeared at the far side of the circle, sat up on it's back legs to get a better look at them and then scampered away. Sophia laughed as its tufty tail disappeared into the undergrowth.

"Granddad brought me here often from when I was a tiny child," said Sophia with a sigh, "I was on his shoulders the first time I remember the bluebell glade. He lifted me down and sat me in his lap and told me, if I was quiet enough, I might see a fairy."

"And did you?" said Justin. His words surprised his mouth and his mind couldn't believe what he'd just asked.

In reply Sophia turned to him and looked straight at him. "I was three years old and as we sat, the sunlight glittered through the leaves and in every patch it lit, I saw a fairy," she whispered.

"And what did you do?" whispered Justin back.

"I named them," whispered Sophia. "Blossom and Fifi, Tilly and Rosie, Eva and Columbine and Honeysuckle." A tear trickled down her cheek, a single fairy tear and Sophia turned her head away from him.

Justin moved closer and put his arm across the back of the seat, barely touching her shoulders. "Go on."

"My life…my childhood…it wasn't easy growing up but Granddad was always there. He'd tell me stories about fairies and angels and how they were always there to help us, if we'd only ask. Such a practical man," she said, brushing away the tear, "And yet, so spiritual."

"Sounds like a well balanced combination," said Justin.

"Yes, yes, you're right," said Sophia, turning to him. Justin made to retrieve his arm but Sophia stopped him. "You're fine," she said, "I needed to tell you. Where it all comes from, my drive, my zest, my…"

"Spirit," said Justin.

Sophia nodded and as they sat with the April sunshine warming their bodies, their minds were at peace. Sophia looked contented and Justin felt closer to her than at anytime since they'd met. She'd shared a favourite place and a special link to her Granddad with him and his chest glowed with pride at her acknowledging his worth to her. And yet, he'd not been totally honest and that bothered him…a little. But everything was back on track now; he'd cruise to the June deadline if the weather stayed like this. And why spoil it? Sitting on a bench in the middle of a wood with his arm around Sophia, Justin was happy. I never knew bliss could be so simple, he thought.

"You sure you just want us to turn up?"

"Of course!"

"And stay over?"

"Jen, it'll be fine. Everyone can have a drink if they want one, get a good night's sleep and then set off home, relaxed on Sunday morning."

"Thanks, Angel. It'll be a relief to not have anything else to think about."

"That's what I thought. Shame you won't make Beltane though."

"I know," said Jenny, "But its moving day!"

"And a very auspicious day to move too! We'll send a lantern up for you and there's always next year."

"Thanks and who knows where I'll be next year!"

"Uh yuk! That's gross!"

Tim turned round, wiping his face with his towel as three women, meticulously clad in the latest workout gear stood around the machine he'd just vacated.

"Sorry ladies," he said, stepping forward, "I should have towelled it before I walked away." He wiped the padded leather on the seat of the machine, cleaning away any traces of sweat.

Two of the women viewed him like a slug, wrinkling their perfect noses, as he apologized again and turned to walk away.

"It's disgusting! Sweating all over the place! Fat people shouldn't be allowed in the gym!"

Red and embarrassed Tim glanced over his shoulder as two of the slender young women carefully laid a towel on the seat before one of them sat on it. The third woman looked at him, her brown eyes blazing. She turned away when he caught her eye.

Tim continued his circuit of the gym, the word 'fat' resonating in his head. He wasn't fat, he insisted to himself, just out of condition and that's why he was here, after all, to get back into shape. Since Jenny's invitation to her birthday party at Angel's, Tim had been to the gym every other day, swimming thirty lengths on the alternate day. Was it vanity? Yes, a little but more that he knew he wasn't in the best shape and the party was a good target to aim for but, he wasn't expecting miracles in seven weeks and, with Maureen's cooking, he knew he'd not appear in his shorts an Adonis. As he piled on the weights for the bench press, he imagined Aidan's torso, the chest Angel curled up to ever night and he felt close to giving up. He leant on the machine and took a deep breath before lying down and getting on with his programme.

Under the shower in the changing rooms, he soaped away the sweat and smiled. Four straight weeks and he could feel the difference. His muscles on his arms and legs pushed tight against his fair skin and the flesh around his middle had dissipated, beginning to give him a waist again.

Back in jeans and t-shirt, he decided to treat himself to a fresh fruit smoothie before going home and he perched on the stool in the juice bar, chatting easily to the staff. He took a sip through the straw.

"Pineapple smoothie please," said a voice behind him.

Tim turned at the voice, and then quickly back to his drink.

"I'm sorry," said the voice coming closer, "For my friends, well not my friends, people I work with. I'm sorry they were so rude."

Tim turned to face the owner of the voice, feeling embarrassed and shy in the face of such kindness. "Err, it's okay," he said.

"But it's not, is it? You're not fat, not in the least and everyone sweats for goodness sake!"

"I believe ladies glow," said Tim, reassured enough to take part in the conversation.

"Oh, that's what it is," said the young woman, laughing. "I'm Isabelle." She held out her hand.

"Tim," said Tim, taking it and looking into the face of the young woman whose hand he held. With him perched on a high stool and her standing he had to look up so Isabelle was at least 5'10" tall and well built. Not muscular as such but toned to perfection.

Her rich brown eyes were complimented by fine chestnut hair that sat on her shoulders softening them and Tim almost reached out to the shiny curls as Isabelle took a stool and flicked her hair from her shoulders and continued the conversation. "Been coming to this gym long?" said Isabelle, taking a long slurp on her straw and sighing with satisfaction as the straws worth filled her mouth.

"Is that the modern slant on the 'do you come here often' line?" Bugger, he thought, what an idiot.

Isabelle laughed. "Sounds like it doesn't it! Sorry."

"No really," said Tim, "I was being facetious and I shouldn't. Yes, I have. Regularly until September last year.

There's been family stuff," he said. "Anyway, been back in the gym four weeks straight now, every other day."

"Cool. Got a special holiday coming up or is there a special woman?" said Isabelle, eyes wide with questions.

So Tim told her about Jenny's birthday and the pool party, leaving out any mention of Aidan. Isabelle asked questions and soon he was telling her about Finn and Scarlett and his dad's heart attack and the minutes rolled by. He offered her a smoothie as their drinks were drained.

Isabelle declined. "I'm juiced out," she said and looked at her watch. "Oh bugger! I'm supposed to be home by now!" She grabbed her phone from her holdall and then looked at Tim. "If I can square this, would you like to make an evening of it?"

Tim didn't know what showed on his face but by Isabelle's reaction he was concerned it had been dismay.

"I'm sorry, forget it," said Isabelle, picking up her bag, "You've probably got to get back."

"No, no wait," said Tim, touching her arm, "Isabelle, I'd love to. I was surprised you asked, that's all."

Isabelle smiled and the little blue flames in Tim's stomach burst into orange. "So was I! I don't make a habit of asking men out, truly but, I'm enjoying myself and I…I didn't want it to…" She was blushing now.

Tim held her arm more firmly. "It's fine, really. I'd be honoured to take you out for dinner."

"Wow," said Isabelle, "Now that's an offer I can't refuse."

"I can't believe we live on the same side of London! All the people I know live out west!" said Isabelle, dipping peshwari naan and scooping up dhal. "What a small world!"

"I know," said Tim, laughing. He felt relaxed and contented and thankful he'd added jeans and jumper to his sports bag at the last minute.

"So do your family live nearby?" asked Isabelle.

Tim nodded. "I moved back to my parents after, well, a long term relationship ended and Jenny's only a few miles."

"Me too, though I live with grandma. Not as bad as it sounds," said Isabelle, "It's a massive house and Gigi has her own self contained flat. My parents live in Canada…" and the evening went on.

"So, this pool party," said Isabelle, sipping coffee as the sleek waiters removed the dishes and warming plate, "Is it in England or abroad?"

"Oh no, over here," said Tim, "Angel's house is in Surrey."

"Weather dependent then?" said Isabelle.

"Well, part of its indoors and it can be covered. It's an amazing pool by all accounts." He described it as Jenny had done.

"An infinity pool," said Isabelle, "Awesome! I swam in one in a hotel in South Africa when I was a junior. International meet, may have been the junior worlds, must have been seven maybe eight years ago."

She looked up into Tim's bemused face, "I'm a swimmer," she said, "Only county now but I was a world class junior."

Tim couldn't stop himself. The exercise, the juice, the easy, friendly companionship of a beautiful woman left him so relaxed, he had to ask. "Fancy coming to a party?"

Vincent was on the landline when the other phone rang but he finished the conversation and caught the mobile call.

"Family meeting, tonight 7.30pm, usual place." The caller hung up.

Vincent felt his heart begin to race and his palms moisten as he shut up the mobile. He'd been busy with the import work from Poland as well as other projects and hadn't noticed the weeks pass by since the warehouse job but now a meeting had been called and he reckoned that this could be the big one, the biggest job of his life, the Mother load.

Vincent arrived early at the offices to find the street door locked to any of his knocking. He hadn't needed to gain his own entrance last time as he'd arrived at the door with three other suits but now he stomped around in the alley, checking his watch, his pulse beating in his ears, angry to be left outside waiting. A car drew up in the road, dropping off a passenger who walked down the alley towards him. At the door, the newcomer glared at him with narrow suspicious eyes.

"The meeting," said Vincent, "I can't get in."

Without speaking the man knocked on the door with three separate patterns of beats. The door opened immediately and Vincent went to step forward but hung back letting the man take the lead. He muttered something to the shadow that'd let him in and, receiving confirmation, he turned and nodded to Vincent.

The boardroom was already nearly full as the latest arrivals took their seats. Young Mr Aloroso explained what was required from each man the following day.

"As far as anyone at the docks is concerned, this consignment will be signed for by Mr Bellman," he said, nodding to a small, grey haired man on his right, "And be unloaded and packed onto lorries by his men. However, each of you is to be responsible for one container. There are eight in all. Load up your vehicles and take the merchandise back to your depot for safekeeping. Keep it dry and then, you'll be contacted again when we begin redistribution. Everyone clear?"

Clear as fuckin' crystal, thought Vincent. Another fuckin' labouring job! All his hopes for the big job were dashed and he scowled at his own stupidity for believing.

"Half a day to load up," said young Mr Aloroso, "Keep the merchandise for a few weeks and then, another half day job unloading where we tell you. Mr Aloroso will pay each of you twenty thousand. Simple. Couldn't be more straight forward. Any questions?"

It was nearly two weeks later when Vincent got the call to drive his consignment to a warehouse site near Leicester and he duly obeyed, arriving on his own in grey bleak drizzle around midday. He scanned the rain spattered plan at the entrance to the site and eventually found 'Harwood Gardens Ltd 60' and drove to the offloading bay at the far corner of the complex. One lorry was offloading and another waiting so he sat, watching the minutes tick by and the rain streaking down the windows. He noted that, like him, the lorry owners had brought unmarked vehicles.

When it was his turn, the rain was slanting like stair rods and he was glad the bay was under cover. He gave a man in navy overalls his code and the man nodded and ticked on his clipboard. As the cartons and crates were unloaded, Vincent glanced into the warehouse beyond. It was stacked wall to wall with anonymous crates but a few items had been unpacked and he saw Eastern looking statues, water features and urns. His mind registered his initial disgust - a fuckin' chinky garden centre.

One of his crates, from the middle of the load had been left to one side and he was asked to wait while it was scrutinized on the outside and then carefully opened. The urn that emerged stood on a broad base with three claw like feet. He saw the man in blue overalls unscrew one foot and Vincent caught a glimpse of a packet, hastily stuffed back into its hiding place. The man picked up his clipboard, scribbled a few notes and then gave Vincent the thumbs up.

As Vincent drove off the site, the weather was worsening. The wind had picked up and bucket loads of rain were intermittently dumped on his windscreen and he could see very little so, he pulled into a service station to get some coffee and ride out the storm. He was angry and just wanted to go home but a young woman interrupted his mood with her smiles and flirting and, within the hour, he'd booked a room at the adjoining motel and was parking the lorry in their car park.

The next day as he drove home, traffic building and slowing as the rain continued, his anger and frustration returned and, even when he arrived home and found an envelope stuffed with notes on his mat, Vincent was seething. He thumbed through the notes and this soothed him a little but his mind would return to the package in the urn, the basis of his anger. *How big must that drug haul have been to pay one hundred and sixty thousand pounds for its safe storage?*

Rain bleached the windows of the little coffee shop as Tiffany sat in a corner stirring her cup of black coffee. Though in a village, the motorway was only five minutes away so, this coffee shop had proved ideal as a meeting place. This would be her third meeting, a businessman from Birmingham.

She'd learnt from her previous encounters and, though wearing a short skirt and blouse as before, this time she'd brought condoms. She shivered a little as she recalled the battle she'd had, insisting liaison number two couldn't come inside her, supposed vasectomy or not and she'd vowed not to make that mistake again. Anyway, this new bloke seemed nice. A bit bald and thin, but not bad looking from the photos and newly divorced so, there might be more to it than a shag in the car. His emails had been chatty and flirty and had made her feel girlie again. He'd been disappointed she had no web cam, having met up with a woman before, he'd said, who was four stone heavier than her photos but Tiffany had assured him the photos were recent and he'd particularly liked the one of her in her red cat suit before the Fancy Dress party.

Tiffany glanced up at the clock on the wall. Not late yet, she'd been early and with the thought of the party last October, thoughts of Clare echoed in her head. Such a shame Clare had let herself go and lost all her confidence. She'd not been exactly full of it at school, Tiffany recalled, but at least she'd known how to stick up for herself. Tiffany sipped her coffee. But then years of living with a mother like Clare's would wear anybody down. Tiffany was glad her mother wasn't like that. At just forty-seven, Mrs Hagger was more like a sister than a mother. And how alike they were!

A bell rang over the door of the shop and a man entered backwards, battling with a black umbrella. Once under his control he glanced around the shop and, spotting Tiffany in the window, treated her to a beaming toothless grin.

May

26

Jenny watched the first day of May dawn from the bed she'd slept in as a child. As fuchsia light streamed across the sky, dianthus clouds disappeared and the morning blossomed bright and fresh. It seemed that her wish for a dry moving in day had been granted.

"One more trip I reckon, Jen and this is the last box in the car," said Tim, carefully sliding a large carton into the lounge.

"Great," said Jenny, "Can you pile it with the others? Thanks."

"What time does the storage load arrive?" said Tim.

"They said between twelve and three. I hope it's not three," said Jenny, shaking her head. "I'd like it a bit sorted before Finn and Lets get back."

"Well, its only ten. We can get to Mum and Dad's, load up the final stuff, unload and be sipping tea by half eleven. What do you reckon?" said Tim.

"Brilliant," said Jenny.

"You alright?"

"Yeah, sorry, it's all a bit weird, you know." Jenny stood and looked at her brother. "Tim, this is *my* house."

Tim nodded and they both broke into a grin.

Tim and Jenny sat on the floor, backs to the cream lounge wall dunking plain chocolate digestive biscuits in large mugs of tea.

"Thanks for getting us away from Mum's."

"'S all right."

"Couldn't relax until I was back here."

"I know."

The large brass letterbox clanged.

"Is that them? I didn't hear a lorry!" cried Jenny, nearly spilling her tea.

"Nope," said Tim, leaning up to see out of the bay window," It's a delivery."

"It's a shrub," said Jenny, bringing the box into the lounge to Tim, "No, hang on, it's a rose bush."

"Who's it from?"

Jenny opened the card. "It's from Angel. The rose is called 'Healing hands', a pale yellow rose tinged with pink. A new plant for my new garden. That's so thoughtful."

"She always is Jen."

"I know," said Jenny, tears in her eyes.

Jenny was grateful for those chocolate biscuits as the hours from noon flew by in a haze of boxes, furniture, children, parents and unpacking. She knew she was growling at everyone but somehow, this wasn't how she'd wanted the taking possession of her own house to go. Yes, she was grateful for the help but she wished everyone would go away and leave her on her own. Tim was ok. He always knew when she needed space to think. Maybe he should teach the others!

By the time the children had passed through excitement, impatience and hunger, grizzling and bickering had turned to pinching and screaming. "Will you both shut up!" cried Jenny, "You ungrateful children!"

Maureen arrived at the door as the children both burst into tears. "Oh, come on, Mummy didn't mean it," she said, opening her arms.

"No!" yelled Jenny, "Mummy *did* mean it! Do you know how hard everyone has worked to get this house ready for you? Do you?"

Finn looked up and shook his head. Scarlett mewled and whined and headed for Nanny. Jenny grabbed her arm, gently but firmly and turned her to face her next to Finn. Jenny took some breaths and knew this was the right thing to do.

She was also aware of the looks her Mum was giving her. "Scarlett, Finn, I'm sorry I shouted at you but I want you to understand. You can't have what you want, when you want, all the time! Scarlett, I'm sorry that we can't find the box with the Spider in the Bath book and Finn, I'm sorry we can't find the box with the X men lamp in but does it really matter? Does it?"

Scarlett and Finn looked into their Mum's face with glistening eyes and trembling lips and shook their heads. Jenny drew them to her. "What's really important is that we have each other," she said. "You can borrow my lamp for tonight, Finn. Scarlett, I'll read you two stories to make up for not having Spider in the Bath, okay?" The children nodded and wound soft chubby pink arms around her neck.

"I love you so much," said Jenny, into soft clean heads.

"Love you."

"Wuv you."

"Thanks for sitting tonight, Tim. Bet it's the last thing you feel like," said Jenny, running a finger over her eyebrows and fluffing up her hair. "Do I look alright?" She wore a simple cotton dress over black leggings and centurion sandals.

"Fine," said Tim, "A bit tired, perhaps."

"I'm shattered, really I am," said Jenny, "But this is business. If I don't see him tonight, I'll have to drive or train it to Manchester and I've neither the time nor the money to do that."

"You know Mum thinks it's a date," said Tim.

"Mmm," said Jenny, squirting perfume behind her ears, "She's not very happy with me at the moment but I'm determined to do things my way and the kids earlier, well, they've been spoilt at Mum's and I can't let that continue."

"She worries, take no notice," said Tim, "What time you back?"

"10.30, 11.00, something like that."

"Got your portfolio?"

"Shit!" said Jenny, "Where have I put *that*?"

Jenny hurried into the wine bar on the high street, fifteen minutes late and peered around bodies, trying to locate a man on his own.

"I think you're looking for me," said a voice over her shoulder, making her jump. "Gosh, sorry."

Jenny turned and there was Ryan Carvell and all she could think was they were the bluest eyes she'd ever seen. He wore a psychedelic t-shirt over black skinny jeans and tartan converse boots. His mousy brown hair didn't quite meet his shoulders and he held his head on the side as if keeping his heavy side fringe from his eyes.

"You must be Jenny," he said, with a grin.

Jenny smiled in response and they stood still for a moment as the clientele in the tiny room towered above them on impossible heels. They shouted and guffawed at each other, even though there was no music.

"Ryan," said Ryan, holding out his hand. "Shall we find a pub?" he suggested, calmly holding onto Jenny's hand when she took his and secreting it in the nook of his arm. "I thought a bar with no music would be quieter," he said, as they took a side street and walked away from the main road.

"You would have thought," said Jenny, "Why do they have to shout at each other?"

For the first but not the last time that evening Ryan laughed and Jenny loved it. A little elfin and mischievous but soft and warm like a favourite blanket, it quelled her trouble mind and relaxed her.

"Sorry I was late," she said, as they found the pub in the next side street.

"You did well to get here, with you moving an' all. Thanks so much for coming. Well, here we are. Not quite so salubrious but a bit quieter," he said, holding the door for her.

Drinks bought, they settled into rather sticky seats with a wall to one side and a settle on the other, affording a little privacy. The table too was wet and sticky and Jenny held her precious portfolio close to her chest.

"Hang on," said Ryan, getting up. He returned moments later with a cloth and dry tea towel and began to clean the table. "And me without me marigolds," he muttered, making Jenny giggle.

Re-ensconced next to her Ryan began. "Right, at last, what a faff! Hello!"

Jenny smiled. "Hello!" she said.

"So, how did the move go?"

And that was it. Two hours disappeared in minutes as they chatted, laughed and looked at Jenny's portfolio. Ryan was interested in her future plans too, admiring her courage to go back to studying.

"I just think it'll give me more choices," said Jenny, as she drained her third orange juice, "Angel's convinced I have the talent to do anything but I'd like the opportunity to put real knowledge behind my work and I'd rather study part time now for three years, than do a job I hate just for the money and then have to retrain at some point to be equipped for a job I *do* want to do. Sorry. That was waffle."

"You're tired," said Ryan, running his hand through his hair, pushing his fringe back and revealing a pierced ear beneath. "But I get it. Still very brave with two small children."

"I know," said Jenny, "But I've wasted so much time, I need to get on with my life."

"But it's hard fitting the little ones in," said Ryan, gently touching her arm. "I've a son, he's eight now, Kai and even making sure I see him in the week and have him with me every other weekend is a challenge."

A bell clanged into their conversation and Ryan looked up. "Another?"

Jenny shook her head, the sheer length of the day caught up with her, aching her muscles and paining her tired feet.

"You must go," said Ryan, looking worried. "You're exhausted but we should talk more. We hardly got started."

"I know," said Jenny, "Yes, I'd like that."

"Do you have Skype?" said Ryan, as they made for the door and he opened it for Jenny.

"Well, I will have," said Jenny, smiling to herself as Ryan tucked her arm through his as before.

"Of course, you've just moved in! What's the matter with me? Are you in the multi storey?"

Jenny nodded and they walked in that direction. "Maybe you're tired too?"

"Yeah, maybe, just trying to think of everything…and everyone…"

"Oh, I know about that!"

"I bet you do!"

They arrived at Jenny's car and Ryan let her have her arm back and then extracted a card from his wallet. "This is me," he said.

"Thank you, thanks so much Ryan," said Jenny.

"Do you have a card?"

Jenny shook her head. "It's on the 'to do' list. Not that high up it, if I recollect, now where's my keys?"

"Would you like me to follow you, or will you be okay?" said Ryan.

"Sorry?"

"You look shattered, really pale."

"No, no, I'll be fine."

"Sure?"

"Of course!" laughed Jenny, "I'll put the blowers on full blast in my face and wind the window down. It's only twenty minutes."

"Well, if you're sure."

"I'll be fine, but thank you."

"You couldn't just, you know, text me to say you've got home safely?"

Jenny looked into a concerned tired face with the most caring eyes she'd ever seen. "I will," she said. "Promise. Now, you drive carefully."

Ryan shuffled a little, looking at his shoes and then up at Jenny. "'Bye then," he said and leant forward quickly and kissed her cheek.

"'Bye," blushed Jenny, as she watched him walking away, turning every three steps to wave and smile at her. But something tells me we'll see each other again soon, she thought, fastening her seatbelt and making her weary way home.

"Mama! Mama! Wake up! We made you bweckfast!"

Jenny began her first day in her new home eating soggy cornflakes with a teaspoon on a mattress on the floor and sipping a mug of cold milk with a hint of tea, as Scarlett and Finn bounced excitedly around her and all the while she was thinking of a pair of caring blue eyes and the message on her mobile.

"Night, night. Sweet dreams, Jenny."

"It's a blessing the sun's out this morning," said Tim, unwrapping plates and passing them to Jenny.

"I know!" she laughed, stacking the crockery in the cupboards, "And Mum had made a picnic, which was kind. Thanks so much for this."

"No problem," said Tim, elbow deep in the packing box, "Glad to help."

"And with the kids at the park for a bit, I can get organized and try and take it all in," said Jenny, "I'm well chuffed with this kitchen!"

"It's a good job," said Tim, "Well fitted."

"It wasn't expensive but Angel's fitters were great. Don't you, well, don't you ever…?"

"What?" said Tim, passing up the final plate from the box and straightening his back.

"Well, don't you ever think about a place of your own?"

"Yeah," said Tim, "On and off." He turned the carton over, ripped off the thick tape and flattened the box against the wall with the others. He stopped, Stanley knife poised above the final carton. "I just, well, after Vanessa, I didn't want to live on my own." He split through the tape and opened the box.

"I can understand that."

"But recently, I've been considering taking the plunge."

"Yeah?"

"It has to be done," said Tim, passing out Pyrex dishes and mixing bowls, "I'm thirty three, Jen. Too old to be at home."

"Yeah, but circumstances…"

"I know, but its time I stopped wallowing," said Tim, "I've made a fresh start already. Been back to the gym…"

"Yeah, thought you were looking trim," said Jenny, looking at her brother, "You look well too."

"Thanks," grinned Tim, "But that could be Tink."

"Tink?" Jenny raised her eyebrows.

"Isabelle," said Tim, blushing a little, "Bell as in Tinkerbell. I, err, met her at the gym."

"You sneaky rat! You didn't tell me!"

"Well, you've been busy. Anyway," said Tim, returning to his unwrapping, "It's early days, you know, didn't want to tempt fate but…"

"Yes?"

Tim looked into the desperately curious face of his sister and smiled. "I really like her."

"And Tink?"

"Err, I think she really likes me."

"Tim, that's wonderful," said Jenny, throwing herself around his middle.

"Steady on!"

"Hey!" cried Jenny, pulling back and lifting up his t-shirt, "You have abs!"

"Well," said Tim, covering up his middle, "I told you, I've been back to the gym and, err, been swimming a bit." He delved back into the box.

"So, what's she like?" said Jenny.

"Look, I, look I hope you don't mind but…"

"What?"

"I kind of invited her to your birthday party," he mumbled, eyes busy on his unwrapping.

"Oh, you did, did you?"

"Err yes. Err, she's a swimmer you see…and, well, it just came out and…"

"And what am I supposed to say?"

"Err, look…"

"Tim?"

"Hmm?" Tim looked up.

"Of course she can come, you idiot! If she makes you happy, she's very welcome," said Jenny, diving in for a second hug.

Tim held her, his cheek on the top of her head. "Thanks, sis," he said.

27

Two men sat on low bar stools opposite each other across the table like fighters about to start an arm wrestling contest. Pints contained in their right hands, they'd be set to proceed if the contest had been for strength of arms as opposed to strength of wills.

"But the weather last month must have set you back?" said Vincent.

"Well, of course it did," said Justin, "But the crew has worked weekends if the weather's been fine."

"But that's time and a half," said Vincent, smirking, "Bet that's eating into your profits."

"Not really," said Justin, "I'd built in contingencies for extras and with the weather picking up…"

"Tomorrow's dry but they're forecasting rain Monday onwards," said Vincent.

"Well, you know me, Vince. Always look on the bright side! Cheers!" said Justin, raising his glass. If only the words he spoke were how he really felt. He could put on this bravado all day and night for Vincent but the sinking feeling in his gut betrayed the true state of the building project. The problems were mounting; concrete that wouldn't go off and part of the site had flooded even with the pump running day and night and it was slowing work down. And the windows! Hand made they may be but considering the time they were taking, surely not hand tooled! Everything was behind and Vincent was right about the overtime. Meeting with the bank on Monday. Justin breathed a deep sigh. He'd sort it out.

"So, you seeing anyone?" said Justin.

Vincent shook his head. "Not really," he said, "There's this girl I met up north who I might see again, but nothing serious."

"So you not been flashin' ya cash now it's rollin' in?"

"No, Just. You know me," said Vincent, smiling "Never like to make a scene about money but I picked up some new wheels last week. Ex army land rover."

"Not exactly new then?"

Vincent looked Justin straight in the eyes. "No," he said, "But with a tuned V8, it beats the shit out of your truck."

Here we go. Mines bigger and better than yours. Let's try to get away from money for a change. "Sounds awesome," said Justin, "Any plans for the summer? You taking your boy away?"

"Nothing booked," said Vincent, "If I do it'll be spur of the moment. Has to be with business as it is. Had another big job for my new client the other week. Hard work, have to put the hours in but it's worth it." He smiled with satisfaction and drained his glass. "Another?"

"Yeah, why not," said Justin.

Vincent stood at the packed bar, a purple note between index and middle finger, elbow leant on the wood while he looked at his friend from school. Justin had always had the looks and the charm but the years, or maybe this job, were stripping away the former. Still had the gift of the gab though but Vincent wasn't falling for it this time. Whatever he said, Justin was worried, probably in trouble, quite big trouble if the scale of the project was to be believed. Perhaps he could lend him some money at a very reasonable rate? No, he looked a pretty bad risk. Vincent stared at the gaunt face and bagged eyes of his friend, temples rifled with grey streaks and grey dots showing through the stubble and shook his head. Of course, *he* wasn't doing quite as well as he was bragging. The event company was ticking over and he'd had the cash from the last job but the Landrover and late night online poker had made a pretty big dent in that but surely the next job would be the big one? He gave his order to the barmaid. Or not? Would he just be kept as the tiny fish in the big pond? Sure, the 20k was easy money and he'd met Lizzie. He licked his lips as he thought about the night they'd spent together. Maybe he'd try and get some more work up that way anyway. He wouldn't mind spending another night like that.

As he walked back to the table, he had trouble dismissing the image of Lizzie from his head, gag in her mouth, spread-eagled and tied to the bed. "So how are Tiffany and the kids?"

"Fine, fine," said Justin, "Don't see a lot of them to be honest. It won't be for long," he added, visions of his children's joy when he'd promised to take them to Disneyland bouncing round his mind. Why had he told them? Why had he bloody opened his mouth?

"At least we've women to look after the kids," said Vincent, "Though it can't be easy working with them around. Darren's alright in small doses, but sometimes!" He raised his eyes and shook his head, "The bloody questions! I don't think his mother talks to him at all! I seem to be the only parent concerned about his mental welfare."

"It's fine," lied Justin, "I get loads done on site or in the truck so, its just a few phone calls and bits at home." I wish my woman *was* looking after the kids! Two mornings this week he'd done the school run as Tiffany hadn't come home. Did she think he was too preoccupied to notice, silly cow? He sighed, just another problem to sort out but he didn't have the energy right now. "Have you heard from Rob?"

The gym cradled shadows in its corners, saving its light for the centre ring, and smelt of warm wet dog. Three small boys thumped at punch bags while older lads held them and two lean young men were skipping, light footed and smiling. A small grey haired figure in the ring held up a punch guard as a stocky young man jabbed and punched to a rhythm banged out on a drum. Tap, tap, boom, tap, tap, boom. As the ring fighters turned, the grey haired man spotted him and raised a hand to cease the beat, squinting into the doorway. "Manning?"

Rob stepped closer, nearer the light.

"Hey! It *is* you!" The grey haired man grinned with empty gums, giving his flat nosed face the impression of a happy gargoyle.

"Hi, Mitch," said Rob, "Long time no see."

"Ya tellin' *me*!" laughed Mitch. "Hang on. Be right with you."

"So, ya wanna get back trainin'?" said Mitch, handing Rob a mug of muddy tea in a not too clean chipped mug. "There's biscuits in that tin."

"I'm good," said Rob, accepting the tea, "Look, I'm not sure what I want, okay, but I've had physio since, ya know, the incident and well, I kinda enjoyed workin' out. I mean, I'd done a bit of weights work and treadmill stuff when I went on my diet, ya know…"

"Rob, lad," said Mitch, scratching his head and then flicking the residue from his nails, "Get that chin up! From what ya say, ya tried and ya fucked up but this Mr Carter now, he has confidence in ya…"

"He's given me one final chance…"

"Well, that's still more 'n a lot o' people would lad so, he believes ya can crack this and *you* gotta believe it too."

"I know," said Rob, "But it's all so bloody hard! The diet, no drinking…no sex!"

"No sex?"

"Well, I never get out to meet anyone!"

"And whose fault's that?"

"Well, I've been workin' and then in hospital and…"

"I repeat, whose fault's that?"

"Yeah, I know," said Rob, "But it's like ya said, Mitch, I gotta have confidence in meself and its drained away since I took that bashin'. Look, I just thought, well, I was always happy here, ya know. Home turf."

"Yeah, I know," said Mitch, screwing up his nose and smiling like a good-natured old terrier that'd been given a biscuit. "I think you've done right, lad, in fact, I'm sure ya have. Ya were a good boxer, Rob."

"Thanks, Mitch."

"Look, what I mean is, ya can be good again but, more 'n that, if you pull this off, kick the booze, get in shape *and* keep ya job, ya 're a good role model for the kids in 'ere. They'd learn a lot from ya."

"Ya reckon?"

"I do," said Mitch, draining the dregs from his mug. "So, drink up lad and let's see what ya made of."

As Rob lay in bed that night every inch of his body throbbed with pain. He was convinced that his kidneys and liver were about to explode as he gently stroked his bruised and battered belly but he was happy. He'd a lot of work to do for sure; he'd barely managed a minute on the rope, every punch at the bag had sent pains up his arms into his shoulders and he'd been slaughtered in the ring by a thirteen year old but he was still standing. Well, not physically at the moment but, metaphorically, he was still giving it a go, taking on the fight, giving it his best shot. Not metaphorically but physically he lifted his chin before he fell asleep.

28

Rain was hammering on the bedroom windows, muffled to thumping by the heavy drawn curtains and the fire in the grate crackled as stray drops from the storm clouds fell down the chimney. Sophia and Maddy had helped clear up once Jenny and her family had left and then gone to Maddy's house to talk about the horse she was desperate to buy and chill out with a movie and a bottle of wine.

Angel and Aidan lay in bed on a Sunday afternoon, the scent of sex on their limbs and contented smiles on their faces. A white light that seared through the curtains as if they were tissue paper was quickly followed by a ferocious rumble and crack from outside.

Angel stroked Aidan's chest as she nuzzled into his flesh. "Glad it didn't do this yesterday."

"Absolutely," said Aidan, stroking her hair, "Imagine the kids with a free run of the house!"

"But they were good though," said Angel, "It was a lovely day."

Jenny and her mum and dad arrived with the children at 10am on the dot and were ushered to the pool room to enjoy the morning sunshine. Within seconds, Finn had stripped off and was in the pool, the brunch buffet and drinks holding no attraction for him. Jenny had barely two minutes to inflate and affix armbands before Scarlett launched herself after him and, without a word, Aidan had removed his shirt, grabbed a beach ball from the side and joined them.

"They'll keep him happy for hours," said Angel, as they watched the game begin and heard the squeals of delight as Aidan lifted Scarlett out of the water, toes wriggling, to catch a particularly high throw from Finn. "So, how are you, Mr Parkes? Mrs Parkes? What can I get you to drink?"

An hour passed in comfortable conversation, the sun growing brighter and tea, scrambled eggs and muffins soothing their stomachs.

"You've a beautiful house," said Maureen, "And the gardens! Oh, I wish my borders looked like that!" She looked a little hot in her dress and cardigan but had given in a little to the warm weather by wearing pop socks rather than tights.

"True, I designed the décor for the house," said Angel, "but Aidan must take the credit for the grounds and our friend Jed, of course. I swear Aidan makes him do all the donkey work!"

They laughed and watched Aidan and the children. "So, are you and Aidan engaged?" said Maureen.

"Oh no!" laughed Angel.

Maureen and Colin both frowned.

"I love him deeply," said Angel, "But neither of us feel the need to get married."

Colin nodded. "Well, as long as you're happy, that's what counts." He smiled at Angel, the caring fatherly smile, the one that said, 'I may not approve but you must live your own life'. He looked relaxed and happy in his white polo shirt and long khaki shorts and obligatory socks with his sandals.

Maureen was less tactful. "Well, I don't understand you youngsters sometimes. I loved your dad, Jen, and he loved me so we got engaged and married and have been happy ever since. Can't see what's wrong with that." She sipped at her tea leaving a sharp, acrid taste in the conversation.

"There's nothing wrong with it Mum," said Jenny, "but I loved Scott. Maybe if we'd lived together first…"

"No, no, you can't say that! Your marriage blessed you with children and you wouldn't have wanted them out of wedlock!"

"Jenny just meant that things are different, Mo. Their choices are different," said Colin, "Things are more acceptable."

"I know," said Maureen, "I meant no offence, Angel."

"None taken, Mrs Parkes."

"Maureen, please, I just…it all seemed simpler for us. You fell in love, got married and worked at it. It was important. Nowadays, well, it seems more haphazard, you know," said Maureen, getting flustered and red in the face. She unbuttoned her cardigan.

"Mum, I know it's hard for you, the divorce and everything but you know I had to end it," said Jenny, touching her mum's arm.

"Yes, yes I do, Jenny," she said, smiling at her daughter, "and it wasn't your fault that Scott turned gay or bi-sensual or whatever. No, nothing you could have done but I worry."

"I know you do, Mum," said Jenny, "But look." She turned to the figures in the pool. Scarlett was doggy paddling frantically after a ball and Aidan was launching Finn into the water off his shoulders. "The kids are fine and we've a lovely new home and I'm fine too. I've my place at Uni confirmed, I've already orders for my work and I'm happy enjoying my 30th Birthday with the people I love most!"

"Well said, Jennifer Juniper," said Colin, "Well said!"

Maddy and Sophia joined the party and took over from Aidan in the pool. Scarlett made an instant friend in Maddy, even letting her put on more sunblock without a fuss as they swam out into the midday sunshine and Maddy's was the lap she wanted to sit on when they'd all dried off and Tim and Tink arrived.

"Amazing physique that girl Tim brought, what was her name?" said Aidan.

"Tink," said Angel.

"Such a defined shape considering she's not training every day any more and absolutely fits the phrase 'Leg's up to her armpits!'"

"Yes, she is beautiful, fantastic figure," said Angel, "but you don't have to go on about it."

Aidan grinned. "Not a tiny bit jealous?"

Angel took and twisted a nipple until he yelled. "Not in the least," she said, stroking the offended appendage and moving to his soft downy belly, "I love my breasts and curves, and my legs are perfectly long enough, thank you. Of course, if you don't like them, you're free to move on."

"Never, my sweet," said Aidan, kissing her head, "Never, but I wonder what Tink sees in Tim."

"What do you mean?" said Angel, "He's a poppet."

"Exactly," said Aidan, "Who wants a man like that?"

Angel smiled. She knew she was being wound up, it was part of the game and she duly played her part. "But he's lovely! He's kind and gallant and thoughtful. I bet he's a real man in bed."

Tim had got lost finding Tink's flat and then stuck in traffic on the way to Angel's house, as the whole of the south east went out to play in the sunshine.

Relaxed and smiling in white cotton shorts and t-shirt, her swimsuit visible beneath, Tink was introduced and she easily conversed with everyone around her. A simple knotted ponytail held her hair from her neck and the only hint of make-up was a gloss on her lips.

She presented flowers to Angel and then hugged Jenny and handed her a small parcel. "Happy Birthday," she said, "Tim told me you just moved so, I thought it might be something you'd like for your bedroom."

Jenny unwrapped a glass and chrome incense burner, much wider than any she'd seen before.

"It burns really slowly," said Tink, "So you can leave it alight all night and it won't dry out. Sorry. I was bought one and I get so excited about things that work well!"

Jenny smiled. "Thank you, Tink, it's beautiful. Work well?"

Tink smiled back. "Fill up the top with water, two drops of lavender oil and I sleep all night!"

"Cool," said Jenny.

"Well, if we're doing presents," said Maureen, "There's two bags somewhere..." She looked hopefully around her. Maureen Parkes had relaxed comfortably into a sun lounger now the Pimms and lemonade had been distributed. She'd even abandoned her pop socks.

"In the hall," said Colin, making to get up.

"I'll get them," said Aidan.

All eyes were on the birthday girls as they unwrapped their gifts. Jenny uncovered kitchen items; a handsome set of free weight scales, sandwich toaster and kettle while Angel found a delicate crystal bud vase and a fabulous fine glass jug. They finally opened the gifts from each other; a bundle of silver and a tiny pack of gold for Jenny and a statuette of two silver filigree hearts embracing an emerald for Angel.

"Let's fill up my new jug and get the party going!" declared Angel, brushing away a tear and smiling. "Tim, Tink, help yourself from the buffet won't you. I can highly recommend the salmon and cream cheese wraps made by Sophia. Melt in the mouth gorgeous. Drinks anyone?"

"I'd love another cup of tea," said Colin.

"I'll do drinks," said Maddy.

"I'll have another one of those fruit drinks, love," said Maureen to Angel while Colin behind her mouthed 'no' and shook his head, grinning.

"Extra lemonade this time, Mads," whispered Angel, "I'll bring out the children's table," she said.

"I'll help you," said Sophia.

Food and drinks co-ordinated, everyone content, they sat looking out over the garden as the sun, hitting its peak beamed down on them, then another flurry of activity in which more sunshades were erected and finally, the party were settled.

"So, where did you two meet?" said Colin, smiling at Tink.

"We go to the same gym," said Tink, sipping iced water, "Started chatting one night at the juice bar." She smiled at Tim, sat on the blanket next to her.

"It's a very odd name," said Maureen.

"Oh, it's a nickname really but I really like it! I was christened Isabelle, that became Tinkerbell and the Tink stuck!"

Maureen frowned. "Nothing wrong with a god given name, can't see why you need to change it."

"Mum!" said Tim.

"Isabelle's such a pretty name." Maureen took a long slurp of her drink. "Had a girl at school called Isabelle, I remember. Pretty girl, bit dim though. Ended up falling for the charms of a traveller when the fair came to town."

Tim hung his head, reddening with embarrassment. Tink smiled unbothered and tried not to laugh as Colin pulled faces behind his wife's back.

"So what do you *do* exactly?" said Maureen, the glass rapidly losing its supply of liquid.

"I work in HR at a large stock brokers in the City," said Tink, "It's okay, pays the bills and I like working with people, trying to help them, sort out their concerns, that sort of thing."

"You should work for our bank then," said Maureen, "You wouldn't believe how hard it is to get through on the phone and when you *do* get through, your account numbers not enough any more! They won't talk to you without passwords and special words and knowing what you had for breakfast!"

As Maureen droned on, the children, Maddy and Aidan made a break for the grass, while Sophia sat with Jenny and Angel. Football on the lawn and hopscotch on the path, drawn by Maddy in pink chalk, amused them for a while but either the heat, the excitement or both, soon led to squabbles, pinches and squeals so, Finn came to sit with Tim on the mat with his box of Lego while Scarlett was scooped onto Colin's lap and soon, gentle snoring from them both betrayed their contentment. A sudden lull in conversation confirmed that the alcohol had finally done its work and Maureen dozed in a peaceful fruity haze.

"Shall we adults swim? We can play tennis later when it's cooler," said Angel, looking at Jenny and Sophia.

With Finn content to build the two storey space launcher for play later, Tim and Aidan joined the women, gliding up and down in the water. Angel took note as Tim shyly removed his t-shirt, where a buff taught chest betrayed his efforts at the gym and smiled at him as he entered the cool water beside her. He returned her smile but he soon sought out Tink's brown eyes in favour of hers, swimming slowly towards his girlfriend and lifting her up out of the water as he reached her. As he lowered her down, he kissed her mouth, then her nose and then her forehead as they came to him. Angel saw Tink's eyes and gestures in return; the depth of her gaze on him, the slightly parted lips and the way she held the back of his neck as he swam her to the edge of infinity.

Aidan flipped Angel onto her back. "Not enough of a real man for you now, is that it?"

"You'll do."

"Is that right?" he said, pinning her arms behind her head.

"Well, a real man would go down and make a pot of my favourite tea for me while I stoke the fire and then gently cover me in kisses until I'm begging for him to make love to me," said Angel, looking up into Aidan's eyes.

"I see," said Aidan, "That's what you want, is it?"

"Mmm."

"But maybe this real man wants to lick you now." His face came close to hers. "Lick you and bite you and then take you, his superior strength forcing you to his will."

Once the sun's warmth had left the garden, Sophia, Maddy and the children came in from the tennis courts and everyone else from the pool room and they all adjourned to the large conservatory to eat fresh vegetable soup and crusty bread and a magnificent apple and blackberry crumble made by Sophia. While Aidan and Sophia cleared away, stacking everything onto a robust trolley to be taken to the kitchen, Angel showed her guests their rooms so they could freshen up and adjourn whenever they wanted.

Scarlett had a pale lilac room off Jenny's, really a dressing room but Angel had thoughtfully decided she'd be best close to her mum but not necessarily in the same room. Finn had his own room and was thrilled to find an electric racetrack set up in it.

"Aidan dug it out," said Angel, "He's had it for years! Could do with a good playing with!"

"Where's Uncle Tim?" said Finn, making for the door. "I *have* to show him!"

"In a mo, Finn," said Jenny, "Let him and Tink settle in first. Come on," she added as Finn's face forewarned a moan to be on it's way, "You've been entertained all day. Give him a minute."

"Tell you what," said Angel, "We're all going in the lounge soon. Why not have your bath and get your pjs on and then, we'll play a board game downstairs and I promise Aidan or I will play with the racetrack before you sleep."

"Okay," said Finn, "Sounds fair. Do I just put the plug in and turn on the hot?"

"Yes," said Angel.

"Can we give Scarlett a quick dunk first?"

"If you must," said Finn, bouncing on the bed.

"Nap!" yelled Scarlett,

"No it isn't!" cried Finn, "They're not the same! You can't say 'snap' to everything!"

Scarlett burst into tears and Jenny moved to quell the flood.

"Have you got your own room?" said Maddy, joining Jenny.

Scarlett ceased sobbing and little wheezy cries ensued as she nodded.

"How exciting!" said Maddy, "Would you like to show me?"

Scarlett's face brightened and she nodded again. "And Bagpuss is in my bed."

Maddy smiled and giggled. "And I bet Bagpuss likes a story before bedtime?"

"Yes! Yes!" said Scarlett, taking Maddy's hand. "He likes da elephant stories best and I've got fwee of dem!"

Scarlett and Maddy made their way upstairs to cries of goodnight from the rest of the company and Jenny followed close behind. She took Finn's hand as she went and he came reluctantly.

Aidan stopped them at the door. "I'm sure I was supposed to do something before you went to bed, Finn. Just can't remember what it was, exactly." He over acted a puzzled face.

Finn grinned. "I reckon you were going to get thrashed on the racetrack."

Aidan laughed. "We'll see about that! You too, mum. We've three controllers."

While Maddy read to Scarlett, Finn, Jenny and Aidan raced the cars around the track until Finn started to get grumpy, especially when Jenny and Aidan both overtook him on the penultimate bend. Aidan wished Finn goodnight and Jenny settled him into bed.

"The sooner you get to sleep, the sooner you can get up and play tomorrow," said Jenny, "May even have time for more swimming."

"You say that on Christmas Eve and every night you want me asleep," said Finn.

"Well, it's true," said Jenny, kissing his forehead, "And its been a long day and you're tired."

"You say that too," mumbled Finn, reaching for teddy and snuggling him under his chin.

"Night, night, sweet dreams."

With the children settled, it was only a milky drink and a biscuit later that Colin and Maureen went up to their room. Aidan lit the fire and conversations started up all over the lounge. Jenny's mobile tinkled and she retrieved it from her bag and read the message, a smile spreading across her face.

"Everything alright?" said Angel, coming over to sit next to Jenny by the fire.

"Mmm fine," said Jenny, blushing a little.

Angel raised her eyebrows but said nothing.

"Just a 'happy birthday' text," said Jenny, thumb moving hastily across the buttons and winging a reply back in seconds, before putting the phone in her bag. Moments later it went off again. Jenny pretended to ignore it.

"You've another message," said Angel, tucking her feet under her on the sofa.

"I'll get it later," said Jenny, not looking away from the fire as flames soared up the chimney. The phone tinkled again.

"He's very persistent," said Angel.

Jenny turned and met her friend's eyes. They were both smiling now as the phone tinkled once more. "He is, isn't he?" said Jenny.

"I'm not complaining, I'm not," said Angel.

"Sounds like it to me!" said Aidan, throwing on his robe and leaving the bedroom.

Angel got out of bed and began laying in the fire. It wasn't what she had said that had upset Aidan, she was sure of that, but she had to admit that her timing had been a little off. She enjoyed Aidan's flirting and teasing but, recently, as soon as sex was a definite, his insistence on domination and taking her forcefully had become the norm and this was beginning to worry her.

She reached into the log basket and produced more kindling, which she expertly stacked, ready for lighting. Heat in her head and hands demanded that she light it herself and she felt the power sizzling in her fingertips but she declined and reached up for the matches on the mantelpiece. Her fingers touched Jenny's entwined heart sculpture and she brought it down with the matches. As flames shot up the chimney, Angel stared at the intricate filigree in her hands and turned it slowly, watching the way the light caught it, changing its shape and casting shadows. Should she have said anything? Probably not, but seeing Tim and Tink and then seeing Ryan's texts to Jenny had made her crave that sense of shyness, tenderness and intensity that always starts a new relationship. But Aidan *had* changed. More confident for sure, then his trip to Rome had brought three huge contracts for more living walls so he had a right to be and, at the beginning, it had been fun to indulge him, allowing him to be the master but was he taking too much control? They'd talked about the power and she'd thought he was happy handling it as she was, but maybe it *was* taking him over. A burst from the fire sent the emerald glittering in the centre of the two hearts and for some inexplicable reason, Tim's face came into her mind. And Tim's body.

"It was fine, stop worrying," said Tink, laughing as she wrapped her long legs around him and pulled him to her. "All your family are lovely."

"But Mum does go on," said Tim, leaning up on one elbow and stroking Tink's hair from her face onto the pillow like a rich brown halo. He felt his body stirring against her and a moan issued from his lips.

"I think, DCI Parkes, that you should stop this worrying at once and give this suspect a thorough examination," said Tink, trying not to laugh.

Tim replied just as seriously, "Do you really think so? Well, lets just warm my hands a little…"

More than an hour later, Timothy Joseph Parkes lay on his back in bed with his beautiful girlfriend dozing on his chest. His mind fizzed as he stroked the downy soft flesh of the arm flung across him and his heart fluttered as she took his hand and linked his fingers with hers. It had been a brilliant weekend and he felt slightly ashamed that he'd worried that Tink might not fit in, recognizing it had been his own inadequacies that he was really worried about but he'd felt good. A little shy at first but he felt like that in front of Angel at the best of times so, in her own home, her own pool and naked to the waist, who wouldn't be a bit nervous? But Tink had made it all better. Her gentleness and kindness, touching his arm and holding him in the pool, her smiles of reassurance when his mother went on, she'd just fitted in and taken him with her. Oh, to have that confidence! But why didn't he? He was looking good, really good in fact. Healthy food and exercise had made him feel amazing too and he knew that shone through in his face and, if the past hour was an indication of his manly prowess, he was pretty sure that was on the mark and that's why his mind fizzed. This was it, here and now. The man he wanted to be with the woman he wanted to be with, facing the world and the future together. This was happiness, true contentment and as Tink turned over, rubbing her soft peachy bottom up against the top of his thigh, he rolled over with a smile and caressed the warm flesh of her buttocks and proceeded to turn contentment into ecstasy.

"I'm sorry I lost it," said Aidan, pouring tea in front of the fire.

"No, I'm sorry Aidan," said Angel, "I wasn't complaining, really."

"I do know what you mean though," said Aidan, passing her a mug, "Probably why I overreacted. I've noticed it myself."

"What's that?"

"The burning. It's like electricity in my blood," said Aidan.

"But that's just passion and lust surely," said Angel, watching him, the flames causing shadows to appear and merge across his face.

"But is it?" said Aidan, facing her. "I've always been passionate about you, Angel, but it feels different now."

"Really?" said Angel, her heart beating loudly in her ears, "Is this all the time or just in bed?"

"It's not all the time," said Aidan, dropping his gaze to his cup, "But when I'm with you, or at least close to you…"

"Yes?" said Angel, her mouth drying and heat rising from her toes. With every word he spoke, he fanned the flames and they rose to her waist.

"I want to have you, I need to," said Aidan.

"But surely that's passion…" said Angel.

"*No!*"

The room was silent save for the hum and crackle of the fire as it drew air from under the bedroom door. The heat traversed Angel's limbs rising to her throat.

"I want to possess you, Angel," said Aidan, "No, not possess. Consume."

The final words completed the transformation and Angel let Lilith take over her body. "And why should that be a problem, husband? We are as one and either or both may consume," she rose to her knees, "devour," she dropped the wrap from her body, her belly at Aidan's lips, "and possess the other."

Aidan looked up at her, white light surrounding him, his skin taut and glistening against his muscles. He dropped the cup on the rug and rose onto his knees before her, white light screaming from his eyes. Rich red heat surrounded Angel, flames licking at her limbs and curling around her flesh and as she lifted her arms and Aidan embraced her, red and orange sparks glinted off into the shadows. As their auras combined their bodies jerked as if a bolt of lightening had shot through them both and then their bodies grew, filling the room with their power. On her back, Lilith smiled up at her husband, her red hair spread all around her, her body pale save for the flames that licked at her legs. Asmodeus slowly filled her and as they joined, he covered her mouth with his, every part of them sharing, entwining, consuming but sustaining the other and all around them the room was a whirlwind of colours, shadows and fire.

June

29

"Thanks for coming up, Jen," said Angel, sipping jasmine tea, "It's lovely to see you!"

Jenny laughed, her blond curls dancing and her eyes twinkling even more brightly than usual against the soft pastel blue of her wrap over dress. "It's only been two weeks!"

"I know," said Angel, smiling "But I missed you and phone calls are never the same."

"It was a lovely weekend," said Jenny, "A really memorable birthday."

"Most definitely," said Angel.

A waiter came over and Angel watched as Jenny engaged him with her natural smile and began asking about the food. "Shall we order a few dishes to share? The tofu in black bean sauce is a special on today," said Jenny, "I'm not sure how hungry I am but I'm sure I can be tempted!"

"Whatever you like," said Angel, "I've had coffee and biscuits at three different meetings so I'll eat anything! How's the house?" she added as the waiter drifted away.

"Brilliant," said Jenny, pouring herself more tea, "Though it's going to take a while to get completely straight."

"But it's liveable?"

"Oh, yes!" said Jenny, "You and Aidan must come over."

"We'd love to," said Angel, "So you're already planning a dinner party?"

"You're kidding!" laughed Jenny, "We've only three chairs at the moment! You'll get bangers and mash on your laps and like it!"

"I'm so glad you're happy," said Angel.

"Yes," said Jenny, seeming to surprise herself, "I really am. You know, I've so much to do, to take care of, the house, the divorce, the kids, college, the company but it's okay. I feel...able, you know. As if it'll be alright."

"The love of a good man can do that to you, you know."

"Aw, I don't know about that, " said Jenny, a blush rising, "But the fact that someone likes me again, likes me as a woman...oh, whatever!"

"No, it makes sense, Jen. Scott took that away from you. He broke the bond that allowed you to be his woman."

"I didn't know who I was any more."

"*You* got lost."

"And Ryan found me again," said Jenny.

"I think you were already finding yourself, Jen," said Angel, flicking back loose hair from her face and lifting it off her neck, "but Ryan's shown you to yourself."

"That's a good way of looking at it," said Jenny, as the food arrived.

Thick linen napkins on their laps, they picked up their chopsticks and began to lift, dip and eat.

"Do you think that's what's happened to Tim?" said Jenny, "I mean, the day I moved in he was talking about getting a place of his own again."

"Who knows," said Angel, "Did the working out at the gym and taking charge of his own destiny begin before or after he met Tink?"

"Hmm, not sure," said Jenny, tofu poised, "You know, *I* think it was before, maybe seeing me going for it. Not that I'm taking any credit," she added, popping in the mouthful and chewing, "Tink's wonderful and it's good to see the real Tim back. I hadn't realized how much losing Vanessa had taken out of him."

Angel nodded. "He seemed bold enough at the Fancy Dress party but there was a shyness, a restraint underneath."

"Last October?"

"Hmm," said Angel, "It felt like *he* didn't matter, as if he'd given up. He was at the Fancy Dress party for *you,* to support *you.* He's good at that, putting other people first."

"Easier to worry about other people and get involved in their lives than to sort your own mess out," said Jenny, "I know all about that!"

"Yes, but you've both come through, haven't you? Look how your life has changed in a year!"

"Only a year? You're right. Bloody hell! No wonder I'm shattered!"

They laughed and dipped eagerly into the tempting morsels on the table.

"Mmm, that bean curd is awesome," said Jenny.

"Are you sure?"

"Yes, I'm in awe of the bean curd!"

"You turning vegetarian?"

"Do you know, I reckon I could," said Jenny, twizzling her chopsticks, "Meat is so expensive and I've always loved my veg."

"Ryan a vegetarian by any chance?"

"Well, yes, as a matter of fact," said Jenny, smiling "But he's made me think."

"Good," said Angel, "New people bring new ideas and they're what keep you young and gorgeous. How are the kids doing? You said Scarlett hadn't been well?"

"Just a nasty cold," said Jenny, putting down her chopsticks, "but that's the trouble with play school and school. Breeding ground for germs. She had a day in bed, much to Finn's chagrin, but that got her over the worst and she picked up quickly from then on."

"Your mum and dad collecting them today?"

"No, Tim said he would and they love him making tea for them."

"How are your mum and dad?"

"They're fine and Mum seems better now."

"She not been well?"

"No, just grumpy and difficult. No, that's not fair," said Jenny, pouring tea for them both, "The whole Scott thing has been very hard for her and I know she's done her best to support me. I mean, when your whole being believes that marriage is sacred and divorce the work of the devil, it must have taken enormous strength to support my wishes to split."

"True," said Angel, "True and then you staying with them and the new house, Uni and your chosen career. I bet what you're doing isn't what she'd hoped for you?"

"Oh, definitely not!" said Jenny, shaking her head, "She'd have me back at church, pairing me off with someone's bible bashing geeky son! Oh bugger, that was a bit strong," said Jenny, putting her hand to her mouth, "You know what I mean though?"

"Absolutely, yes, been there, remember?" said Angel.

"Of course!" said Jenny, "I *do* remember! Hey, do you remember that missionary's son? The one with the eyes? You must do?"

"Oh yes! Oh fuck, those wandering eyes! And while you talked to him, each of them was determined to seek out the huge mole on his nose!"

"Cross eyed Christopher! That was it!" said Jenny. She bit her lip, "Oh, that's a bit wicked."

"Wicked? No way!" said Angel, her eyes blazing, "If you remember, Cross eyed Christopher was eighteen while I was fourteen. Now he may not have had control of his eyes, but he certainly knew what his hands were doing! Ugh, yuk! Makes my skin crawl even thinking about it."

"Parents," said Jenny, "How misguided they are, thinking they always know what's best for you."

Angel smiled and looked her best friend from school deep in the eyes.

"While I, of course, " said Jenny, retaining eye contact, "am a perfect parent."

They dissolved into hoots of laughter as the smiling young waiter approached and began to clear the table.

"So, can you make the end of the month to come up to Wales?" said Angel.

"Yes, yes, I meant to say," said Jenny, "I tried to swap weekends with Scott like we'd said but he was just being bloody minded so, Tim and Tink are booked to stay at mine. The children have already started a list of things they want to do including swimming, of course and marathon story sessions so, I can come away with no worries."

"Excellent," said Angel, "I can't wait."

The sun shone down like a benevolent Cheshire cat, purring on their skin as they walked hand in hand through the park. She loved to feel his hand in hers, so strong and broad, like having a hug all over and she looked up at him as, at the same moment, he smiled down on her.

They picked a spot with shade under a large spreading oak and Zac lay out the picnic cloth and began to take plastic boxes from the bag. Mayflies and insects whizzed and buzzed all around them and crickets sang in the grass as they tucked into strawberries, grapes and fresh pineapple and tiny brown triangular sandwiches. Another box contained celery and carrots and a small carton of home-made low fat cheese dip. They talked quietly about their day so far, sharing their news and listening intently to each other as the picnic food slowly disappeared.

"So, what do you think?" said Danielle, "My first pair of shorts since, well, I can't remember. Do you like them?"

"They look lovely, sweetheart. I had noticed," said Zac, "and I would love to take some photos of you when we're finished."

"Oh, I dunno," said Danielle, face falling to her knees, hands wringing in her lap. The mirror was one thing but you could walk away from that. Photos were scary, your image captured in time for anyone to see.

Zac took her hands and held them, stroking her fingers, "And why wouldn't I want a photo of my fiancée in her summer shorts? I rather like that apple green top too," he said, "Really suits you."

"Does it?" said Danielle, looking up.

"Danielle, you are beautiful," said Zac.

Again, Danielle tore at her hands, "I don't know."

Zac stood up. The muscles on his limbs stood proud in the sunlight and his white t-shirt and gym shorts made him seem even darker but his smile was bright and sincere and he took Danielle's hand and helped her up and out into the sunshine. Turning her around so her back was by two young silver birch saplings, he stepped back quickly and snapped two photos of her.

Danielle began to cry and two strong arms held her and soothed her. "But you have to see, my darling. You have to," and he led her to the blanket beneath the vibrant green of the oak and sat her down in dappled shade and showed her.

Danielle looked in astonishment at the photo of a woman she barely recognized. Khaki cargo shorts revealed defined strong calves and tight thighs while a bright green top mimicked the shape of her body; a definite waist and gorgeous curving breasts. Zac zoomed in on the photo. Five stones of fat had disappeared from that body and finally, in close up, her true face was revealed at last. Zac kissed her and she knew she'd found herself again.

Tiffany hurried along the street, occasionally swaying in her wedged sandals. The sun was blazing down and she could feel sweat gathering between her breasts but she kept the pashmina over her head and shoulders as she walked, eventually ducking into a welcome cool doorway. She pressed the third button down on the intercom on the wall, glancing at the street to see if anyone had noticed her entering and gave her name as the receptionist answered. A buzzer sounded, she opened the door and made her way up two flights of open stairs, clinging to the banister rail, her knees at odds with her ankles.

Bruce had been nice. He'd been happy with a kiss and a grope on their first meeting and it had been exciting in the woods, although a little disconcerting when that huge grey dog appeared, eventually running off to a whistle from it's owner. But he hadn't replied to any of her emails since. Alistair had been nice too, though sex in his work van had been a bit uncomfortable, what with the paint fumes and the paste brushes and sandpaper reels falling off the racks. He didn't reply to emails either and his mobile didn't seem to work any more. Trevor had been too old and she'd managed to get out of any sex when her phone began to ring and she was able to plead an emergency with the children. Thank goodness she'd asked Farrah to call her in case she needed a 'get out'! Andy hadn't been nice. Nasty, sharp, vicious man. Of course, the sex had been intense and fulfilling, she had to admit, but she'd felt that the situation was so firmly in his hands, that it had scared her and she didn't like being scared. And finally Billy. Well, Billy and Kieran, as it happened. He'd brought his mate along for moral support and she'd thought, why not? You don't get a threesome with twenty somethings every day of your life. She'd never forget their skin, so tight and firm and young, oh and their…

"That's it, Mrs Preston" said the nurse, closing Tiffany's legs and pulling down the white shift. "You can get dressed now and join me at the desk."

"So what have I got?" said Tiffany, appearing from behind the curtain, wincing a little as she put one foot in front of the other.

"Please sit down," said the nurse.

Tiffany sat carefully on the edge of the chair.

"You've a very nasty infection," said the nurse, "You'll need strong antibiotics, maybe even two courses and, of course, as the infection leaves, you must replace the good bacteria you are also losing."

"Of course," said Tiffany, her brain oblivious to the words she was hearing, "So I take the tablets and it'll go away?"

"Yes, in time Mrs Preston but you must have been feeling really unwell in yourself too?"

Tiffany looked bemused.

"Well, I mean, the infection is affecting your whole body. I'm sure you haven't felt quite yourself?" enquired the nurse again.

"I've been okay," said Tiffany, "Just this pain in me fanny that's the problem but I'll take the tablets…"

"I trust Mr Preston is aware of how you're feeling?" said the nurse, writing on labels on clear plastic tubes as she spoke.

"Not likely!" said Tiffany, "This ain't man's business! Anyways, he's busy. He's a very important building project he's managing."

"Well, he ought to get checked too," said the nurse, finishing her writing.

Tiffany ignored her. "What're they, them applicator things?"

"Swabs, Mrs Preston, to be sent to the lab," said the nurse, filling out a form on her desk, "Now, take this with you and wait in the corridor and you'll see the doctor shortly."

"Doctor! I thought that was it!"

"Mrs Preston, please calm yourself. With my diagnosis and recommendations, it's unlikely Dr Schaffer will need to examine you again."

"Thank fuck for that. I've gotta get 'ome!" cried Tiffany, her orange face puckering with anger.

"Mrs Preston, please understand. You've a *very* nasty infection. The tests will be back from the lab in ten days to two weeks. We'll need to review the situation then," said the nurse.

"What do ya mean? Won't the tablets make it go away?" said Tiffany

"The tablets will help but, even once the infection has gone, your body needs time to repair. When we feel you're infection free, we'll do the tests again. It's usual procedure."

"Okay, look. I've got 'alf hour, then I gotta go. I just want my tablets 'cos I'm fuckin' sick o' me fanny bein' on fire, ok but then I want to go," said Tiffany, getting up.

"I'm not sure you understand…"

"Look, you tol' me, I get it, okay!"

The nurse sighed and handed Tiffany the paperwork and an appointment card. "Go to the reception on your way out to have these confirmed. I've written in an appointment for two weeks. It'll give the results time to get back and one in three months for…"

"Yeah, yeah, okay, look can you see if the doctor's free now, *please*? I don't wanna leave Chelsea waiting."

30

Justin sat on the beach alone. He'd passed a couple of families and a few fishermen as he'd walked but he was at the end of the bay here and alone, bar the odd wheedling seagull.

He'd set out very early, leaving Tiffany snoring, safe in the knowledge she'd be there to see to the children. He'd driven north, up to the coast, away from home and as far away from work as he could manage. With just the wind and the sea for company, he could let his mind wander, clatter, fill and spill in the despairing hope that he could find a way out, a way to make what was happening not happen.

He got up and stood on the shoreline watching the ebb and flow of the tide flooding the sand and then retreating, leaving it clean and gleaming in the sunshine. He wished the water could do that to him. He shook his head and stood up, scuffing his shoes in the sand as his mind whirred. Why hadn't he told Sophia at the beginning, or at least in March when the project had been put back so far by the weather? She'd have listened. She'd have understood. Maybe. But he couldn't. His pride wouldn't let him. No, instead, he'd re-mortgaged the house and, on paper, that had looked okay. With his earnings from the job, he paid off a straight 30k but there was still more than a quarter of a million owing and he'd put nothing aside for tax and VAT.

Justin bent down and picked up a flat stone, which he attempted to skim across the waves. It landed with a wet 'plonk' and he scuffed his feet in annoyance. And yes, they'd had some dry days recently but the excessive rain had put them so far behind. And the windows! Those bloody windows! So much work had been ruined when plastic sheeting had come away from holes where windows should have been! But even then, he'd been confidant they'd make up the time. Windows in, wooden floors laid, walls plastered and then rain, rain and more fuckin' rain! He'd been on site yesterday and the landscaping looked like a motor cross track but worst of all, yes, there was even worse than turf and paths sliding into the lake, worst of all was his own short sighted, idiotic decision to ramp up the under floor heating to dry off the plaster. He'd been told before and after the floor was laid and he had it in writing, to leave the heating on very low but constantly for at least a fortnight before attempting to turn it up.

Justin watched as the sea lapped round his ankles. But he hadn't, had he? Without the plaster dry, they wouldn't get the decorating and finishing done by the end of June and he hadn't been able to face the thought of that. Justin took another step into the sea, water lapping at his calves, his canvas shoes squelching into the sand. No, rather than face the possibility of another unmet deadline, rather than own up and say 'the weather has beaten me' or say anything, no! He'd done the one thing he'd been told not to do in the blind hope that they didn't know best and that he did.

Justin stepped further into the sea, oblivious to the tide lapping at his knees; the only picture in his head was the inside of the hospice. The floors to be precise. Wooden floors; beech, oak, wenge, wooden floors in every room and every corridor. Wooden boards lifting, separating, drying, cracking and peeling. Ruined wooden floors.

"Throw it harder, more direct, use your shoulders like this," said Rob, taking the medicine ball as if it were a grapefruit. He placed it on his chest and pushed out with his arms. The speed and force of the pass nearly bowled over the catcher.

"Okay Rob," said the lad beside him, "I'll have a go."

"Better, much better Errol, my man," said Rob, grinning and moving to the next part of the circuit training where boys were skipping, red faced and sweating.

"Relax boys," said Rob, "It's all about the rhythm, ya know? Keep it even and sweet, just let your feet skim the floor. Relax. Hey! That's better, good work!"

Planks had been set against the wall bars in another corner of the gym making crunchies really tough, while the final step on the circuit was the punch bags.

Rob blew his whistle.

"Water break boys! Get plenty down ya then move to the next circuit clockwise. Sam, in the ring with me please lad. Okay, keep moving boys! Thirty seconds more then back to work!"

The gym buzzed with excitement and hummed with endeavour. Back to their training, boys from six to sixteen, smiling and sweating, took up the strain and put in the work. Both the inner and outer doors had been propped open, affording any draught they could muster but even at half past six in the evening, the sun was burning down outside and the air was still and humid.

Having finished his tutoring in the ring, Rob blew his whistle again. "Rest boys! Well done everyone!"

He took a swig from a water bottle and climbed down into the mêlée of excited boys. "Hey Miles! Good work on them crunchies son! I saw ya! I saw ya Greg! Excellent work! Jim, Phil, keep at it lads, it'll come, no worries. Everyone, quiet!"

Silence fell like a fire blanket on the gym as Rob stepped back up onto the ring apron. "Let's finish in style, ok boys! Grab a partner, get gloved up or take the pads. Ya know the drill."

Into corners the boys dived, chattering and laughing like macaws, emerging with gloves and pads. They helped each other lace up and spread themselves into every available space, including two pairs in the ring.

Rob walked over to a battered CD player. "We all ready?"

"Yes, Rob!"

"Keep to the rhythm, boys. Here we go."

A familiar rhythm filled the gym and the boys began - jab, jab, punch, jab, jab, punch - their ears filled with 'We will rock you' by Queen. As parents arrived and crowded into the doorway, the gym was working in unison, every face intent and concentrating on keeping their time in the orchestra. As the music finished, a roar and a cheer went up from boys and parents alike, the latter applauding the sight they had witnessed.

Rob, face red and glistening, blew his whistle from the ring. "Good work, everyone! Brilliant session! Really proud

of you all!" He smiled at them as he continued, "Have a
stretch and make sure you pair up before putting away and
I'll see you Thursday or next week."

The boys cheered and began removing gloves while Rob
wandered over to the parents, happily accepting slaps on the
back and acknowledging cries of 'Big Man!' with high fives.

Mitch came out of the office smiling like a contented
gnome. "I'll put the kettle on," he said, as the final parent
left, "Got 'alf an hour before the next lot."

"Be lovely, Mitch," said Rob, "I'll jump in the shower."

As Rob sat on a milk crate in his shorts, towelling his
shoulders and head, Mitch talked. "It's unbelievable! I'm
turnin' kids away, Rob. Just not enough places to go round!
You've worked a miracle, mate."

"Nah," said Rob, "I ain't done it, the boys have."

"But words got around; Big Rob is back! And they all
wanna be coached by you!"

"I'm chuffed," said Rob, "Really am Mitch but, this is
your gym and, I'm happy to do two nights like we agreed."

"But I'm makin' money, son, good money. I've rent
money for the next six months already put by!"

"That's good, Mitch. Good for you and good for me,
feeling useful, ya know."

"Useful? You're a bloody lifesaver! And the music!
Inspired that was."

"Well, all kids like music," said Rob, "'N I know Queen's
a bit ol' hat to them but it's a classic and ya can't beat a
classic, I say!"

"Inspired," said Mitch again, handing Rob his tea. "Look
Rob, will ya not reconsider? I know you're working an' al
but, we could really *do* somethin' wi' this place. I'd love to
smarten it up and get some new gear, maybe hold a
fundraiser in August. But I ain't getting' any younger. I can't
do it alone. I need a partner. What do ya say?"

Rob sat back, the towel round his neck and sipped his tea. "Tell ya what, Mitch," he said, "Give me a few more weeks. I'm only just gettin' back to full fitness meself, ya know! I'm enjoyin' me job too, ya know and I don't wanna let Mr Carter down. And there's Teresa. I've others to consider as well as meself."

"Anythin' ya say, Rob. However ya wanna play it but my offer stands. I'd be happy to set up a partnership, everythin' 50/50 and, of course, I ain't gonna go on forever so..."

Rob listened to Mitch's words and every one of them made his heart purr. To be part owner of a boxing club, coaching boys and young men to be fit and disciplined, strong and respectful and to achieve anythin' they set their minds to be was an exciting idea and gave Rob a glimpse of a possible future.

"...Bay Road Boxin' Club will belong to you."

The cell door clanged behind him, the key grating in the lock. Vincent stood for a moment, letting his heartbeat quieten before sitting on the edge of the bed. Questioning today had been the same as yesterday. With a bit of luck, he'd be out by tonight, his twenty four hours up without any charge being brought.

"So you don't remember who got you the job?"

"I'm sorry, I really don't," said Vincent, running his hand over his ginger cropped hair.

"But you were in the Railway?"

Vincent nodded.

"Please speak for the tape, Mr Rogers."

"Yes, I was in the Railway."

"But you don't remember who gave you the job?"

"No I don't. Like I said, I only found the slip of paper in my jeans the next day."

"So, you went to the docks not knowing who you were working for?"

"Yes."

"Bit unusual?"

"Not at all. I may have been told but there was a match on. Had quite a few beers before I walked home."

"And the match?"

"Barcelona, Man U."

"And the score?"

"2-1 to Man U. It was the first leg so, two away goals was…"

"Thank you, Mr Rogers. So you remember the score but not the person who told you about the job?"

"Yes," said Vincent.

As Vincent ran through the questioning in his head, he was sure his story was unshakeable. He'd made sure the man at the docks had a baseball cap and sunglasses and wore overalls so, no chance of describing him further to the police and the garden furniture to be taken to the Midlands warehouse for distribution on the date given and the code to confirm the consignment were verbal instructions so, that dismissed any worries re phone calls and he'd been paid in cash so that couldn't be traced either.

He stood up and stretched, arms above his head. But someone had squealed. To have the Leicester warehouse manned by police, someone knew the whole drill and Vincent tried to remember the seven faces around the table that night, trying to recall if anyone had looked strained or shifty. It would always be hard to tell though as nerves always kicked in, in the presence of Mr Aloroso so, he tried to recall who'd been at the docks loading up. He thought he'd seen three other lorries but then, others may have been there earlier or later and anyway, anyone with any sense would continue with their part of the plan if they'd grassed or their absence would just stand out, making them the guilty party. But who would *dare* cross the family?

He lay out on the bed with his arms crossed behind his head, his brain whirring with possibilities. Maybe they would charge him but what for? If he didn't know there were drugs in the crates, they couldn't get him for that or could they? Or maybe the statues themselves were stolen but that was unlikely. Had someone named him? Now, that would be a tricky one to get out of. Nah, he shook his head. Stick to your story, don't grass on anyone and you'll be home by teatime.

31

The air con cooled their limbs as they sped down the motorway in the Land Rover. Outside the midday sun had bleached the sky to grey as it blazed in its summer glory. Aidan and Angel, both clothed in white cotton, sat back, sunglasses on, Bangra on the ipod, as the miles disappeared beneath their wheels.

Aidan pulled onto an A road and slowed their speed as the landscape changed around them. Factories, girders and steel turned to green as trees and fields came closer and the towns they drove through became villages. Onto B roads, sheep and calves in the fields, poppies fluttering in the breeze as they drove past and finally, up an unnamed track, bumpy and rutted in the dry searing heat, to a rumpled and dishevelled stone built farm house in a courtyard of other small stone buildings.

"And here we are," said Aidan, turning to smile at Angel. He left the engine purring, keeping them cool as he spoke. "My latest purchase," he said, his arms opening in an expansive gesture. "Needs some work of course and have to do *something* agricultural here, stipulation of the contract but, it doesn't have to make money as such and there'll be no problem putting up poly tunnels."

Angel smiled at the excited face beside her. Aidan's green eyes flashed with joy and pride as he described his ideas and plans for the future.

"But enough of that," said Aidan, taking her hand. "I brought you here as a surprise and to treat you and spoil you because," he looked up into her eyes, "I've never thanked you enough for saving me. I love you, Angel and I want to prove it."

"Aidan, really..."

"Please let me," he interrupted, bringing her hand to his lips and kissing it, "Let me be the master in this house but in the way I've always wanted. Let me be your man."

Angel smiled and lowered her eyes, glancing up at him through lush thick lashes. "Of course."

Aidan turned off the engine. He led Angel to the door of the farmhouse, opened it and then swept her into his arms. He held her tightly to him. "I've always wanted to do this, Angel. We don't need a ring or anyone's blessing but I want to carry you across *our* threshold."

Angel's heart expanded in her chest, her head and heart full of joy and love. Inside, hand in hand, they explored the house.

The lounge was long and low, a whole wall taken up with the magnificent inglenook fireplace and the rest, minimally furnished providing the most comfort possible but keeping the room open and spacious, despite the low ceiling. Two and three seater battered brown leather sofas, dolloped with cushions, were placed adjacent to the fireplace and a long low table sat on the rug in front of them. A low wooden oak chest of drawers with a lamp on it and a battered wooden box were the only other furniture. The massive log cradle in the hearth was laid ready for a fire and at the sides of the inglenook itself, logs stood to attention, awaiting their command to warm the house.

Angel ran a hand across the back of a sofa. "It's beautiful, Aidan."

"And in here," Aidan lifted the lid of the wooden box, "The softest, warmest fleeces and throws for my beautiful queen."

"You've thought of everything," said Angel, draping her arms around his neck.

"Ah, but there's more," said Aidan, peeling her from him, "Come upstairs."

They went into a cupboard that concealed the stairs and Angel followed Aidan up to a small square landing.

Aidan opened the door on the right and Angel gasped as her senses were swamped by a mass of voile and organza in pastel shades. Seemingly draped and hanging over every surface and from every beam, the material danced from the draught of the open door. The ceiling had been removed revealing the beams supporting the roof and its height shone through the voile making the room feel light and airy. A robust yet delicate four-poster was draped and swathed in white and lilac, its canopy finished with four gold owls at each corner. The bed was made up in rich Egyptian cotton, a leopard skin print throw over the end. Windows on two sides were swathed in green and lilac while the vaulted ceiling had been draped with pale blue, meeting in the centre at a modern crystal chandelier.

"Aidan I…its…" Angel wrapped her arms around him and they stood. "But how…I mean, when…?"

"I had some help," said Aidan, smiling, "Sophia's been brilliant and came with me to set this up but, I bought everything myself. I chose it all so, if it's not right, it's my fault."

"Not right! It's beautiful! It's a wonderful surprise!" She held his face and kissed him.

"Now, there had to be some compromises," said Aidan, taking her hands and holding them to him. "It couldn't all be finished, the whole house I mean so, the kitchen's pretty basic, the bathroom's *very* basic and the dressing room, utility room and spare bedrooms don't exist yet! However, I have another surprise."

"More! But you've done so much!"

"I wanted this done for us for this summer so, I hope you'll like it," said Aidan, leading her back downstairs.

Through the small kitchen and into the dining room and then through a back room with old French windows, Angel stepped out into the blazing sunshine onto a deck, the biggest deck she'd ever seen.

The farmhouse was built on a small hill so the back of the house fell away but this was no longer visible as below Angel's feet, shallow steps took them down to more decked areas and off onto grass or into dead ends with benches or shallow pools. There were plants in pots as well as in the soil, layers and layers of leaves and fronds, finally arriving at the bottom where a grassed area had been planted all around with shrubs and new saplings; birch, rowan, ash and by a large pond to one side, willow.

"Gardens are never instant," said Aidan, smiling "but it'll be fun to watch this grow and, in years to come, this will be a wonderful fairy glade, don't you think."

Tears fell beneath her sunglasses and Angel dropped to her knees on the dusty grass. Aidan joined her and they lay together, Angel crying quietly into his neck.

"I'm so sorry," she whispered.

"My darling, why?"

"Because I thought you'd changed, that you couldn't control it and all the while…"

"Yes but it *was* changing me, Angel and that's why I bought this place. Here, I feel like me and I wanted you here with me so, I made this garden for you, for us. A place to be just us. I use my skills for everyone else and I know I've done your gardens but I wanted to landscape *our* home, use all I've learnt about irrigation and living walls on *our* hideaway. Now, don't get me wrong, I love living at yours and in London. I love my work, travelling and lunch at the Savoy but I love this too."

Angel nodded. "So do I and Aidan," she held his face again, "You've been so wise, so clever to realize there was something missing. A real place, a natural place. Thank you, thank you so much." She kissed him.

"Of course, there has to be some boys toys, right?" said Aidan, lying flat on his back.

"Oh yeah?" said Angel, sitting up and cuffing her face with the back of her hand.

"And I've not tried it out yet," he said, grinning up at her.

"No time like the present," she said, getting up and reaching down for him, "What is it?"

"Not telling," said Aidan, accepting the hand up, "I'll show you," and he sped back up the steps with Angel close behind.

Angel and Aidan sat naked side by side in the sunshine in the whirlpool hot tub in a wooden room half in and half out of the garden. A garden room. The 'in' part had been kitted out with bar, television and music centre. They lazed back in the frothing water, sunglasses on, sipping champagne from wooden goblets as the sounds from the garden and the occasional 'baa' from the hillside merged with Miles Davis easing through the speakers.

Angel loved the way the bubbles buffeted her flesh, kneading the muscles and then resting them in the warm scented water.

Aidan reached over to the control pad and turned the bubbles down. "I do have an ulterior motive however," he said, "There's a rugby match on in a bit."

He looked across at Angel, her head back, her lips gently parted and he felt the familiar yearnings for the woman he loved. "I can put the music through the speakers by your head, if you like."

"That's fine, I don't mind," said Angel, smiling, "You know I don't mind rugby."

Aidan clicked on the television and, as he turned up the volume, the news was just finishing. "And the headlines again, eight men have been arrested and charged with the illegal importation of cocaine with a street value of nearly £5million, following a tip off to the police that led them to a warehouse site in the Midlands. The police say…" As the newsreader continued, the report flashed up images of the men leaving court, some hooded under blankets, others…

"That's Vincent!" cried Angel, dropping her goblet as she leapt up, "Look!"

"Are you sure?"

"Shhh."

"If the men are found guilty, each will receive a minimum sentence of 15 years in prison. Police are also looking into the possibility of a link between a warehouse fire at the same docks in February where a security guard was killed, and the activities of this possible drug ring. In Egypt…"

Angel looked at Aidan, her eyes wide, shock, wonder and hope betrayed across her face. "Was it him?" she said.

"We can check," said Aidan, reaching for the control pad, "I set the machine recording when I turned it on."

"Oh, right."

"Well, if my beautiful woman had required my attention, I would have had the rugby for later," said Aidan, with a grin.

Angel floated over to him, smiling. "You really *do* think of everything."

"Well, you know, wait, here it is. I'll get the freeze frame ready…okay…"

"Now!"

They both stared at the screen and then at each other, amazement turning to pure and unadulterated joy.

"Yea-e-e-s!" cried Angel, leaping up in the water.

"Yeah-h-h!" yelled Aidan, splashing his legs like a mermaid on speed.

As the sun tipped below the horizon and another champagne bottle stood half empty, Angel and Aidan lay inside in the hot tub, their backs to the entertainment wall, goblets full, looking out across verdant garden, their cheeks glowing and hearts light and dancing. They'd made love on a seat under a rose covered arbour, surrounded by delicate perfumed blossom, adding a luxurious freshness to their pleasure. They'd danced in the fairy glade, until the light had begun to fade, reminding them they hadn't eaten. They'd dined on fresh ravioli, salad and strawberries and they'd lit the fire in the inglenook to heat up the back boiler to give them hot water in the morning but they'd been drawn back to the garden room; an unspoken agreement to finish their evening at the place they'd heard the best of news. They lay back in each other's arms in the now still water, savouring the champagne but most of all, the company of the other. Night had fallen, an owl called and they heard the response.

"There is one thing," said Aidan.

"More! Really?"

Aidan smiled. "I could never buy jewels for you Angel. They'd never compare to your beauty, there's not a jewel in the world but this I *can* give you, my love. Jewels worthy of your company," and he pressed a button.

With a 'clink' and then a gentle whirr, a panel in the roof began to slide back revealing a sky full of stars for Angel.

GLOSSARY

1 Kyphi
One of the earliest and most celebrated aromatic formulas.
Though the exact ingredients are not known, most experts
agree that it contained myrrh, juniper, cinnamon, spikenard
(flowering plant of the Valerian family), frankincense,
saffron and cassia, amongst others.

2 Tree of Life
The Tree of Life, connecting all forms of creation and the
Tree of Knowledge, connecting heaven and the Underworld,
are both forms of the World Tree. Various trees are used
symbolically in world folklore. The Tree of Life is taken
from the form of the Flower of Life, a geometrical figure
composed of multiple evenly-spaced, overlapping circles.

3 Qabalah
This is a Western esoteric and mystical tradition, drawing on
many influences including Jewish Kabbalah, Western
astrology, alchemy, pagan religions especially Egyptian,
neoplatonism (religious and mystical philosophy based on
the teachings of Plato), gnosticism (religious beliefs and
spiritual practises common to early Christianity, amongst
others), freemasonry, tantra and symbolism of the tarot. It is
a syncretic system, combining different beliefs and often
melding practises of various schools of thought to provide an
inclusive approach to other faiths.

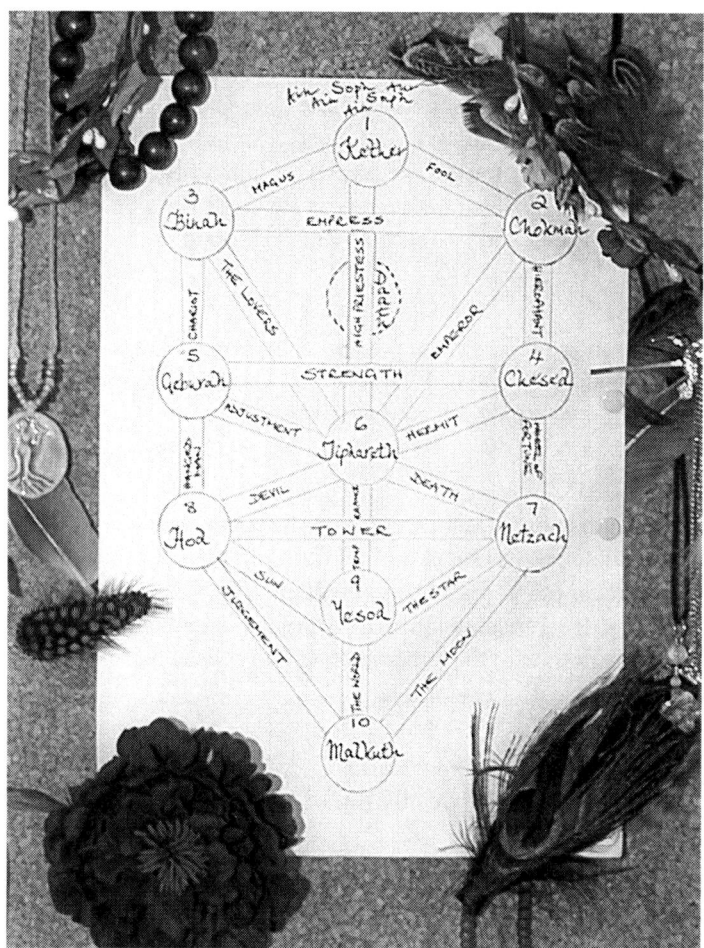

4 Sephiroth/Sephirah

Ten attributes/emanations in Qabalah, through which God
reveals himself and continuously creates the physical realm
and the chain of higher metaphysical realms. A step-by-step
process, illuminating the Divine plan as it unfolds itself in
Creation.

5 Lilith

In this story, Lilith is a symbol of oppressed womanhood in her role as the first woman. Unlike Eve, she was created at the same time as Adam as his equal. Her story has been shrouded with all negative aspects of humanity, especially the force of her lust and desires as the negative side of 'man' causing him to stray from that which is 'good'.

6 Thoth

An Egyptian God whose powers were greater than Osiris or Ra. Thoth is the God of knowledge, writing, inventions, astrology, mathematics and much more.

7 Malkuth

The tenth sphere, associated with the earth, crops, the immediate environment and all living things, is a sphere of consciousness, representing the beginning of the inner journey. It represents familiar, everyday consciousness and, as the entrance to the subconscious mind, is sometimes associated with Persephone.

8 Leviathan

Chief demon of the Deadly Sin of Envy.

9 Belphegor

One of the Seven Princes of Hell and Chief demon of the Deadly Sin of Sloth.

10 Mammon

One of the Seven Princes of Hell illustrating greed and material wealth as evil personified.

11 Lucifer
Also called the morning star or light bearer and symbolising the Deadly Sin of Pride.

12 Beelzebub
One of the Seven Princes of Hell and Chief demon of the Deadly sin of Gluttony.

13 Asmodeus
One of the Seven Princes of Hell and symbolising the Deadly Sin of lust and sexual desire.

14 Tzaphkiel
Dark Angel of the Soul of Man and Prince of Spiritual Strife Against Evil. An Angel of spiritual development, overcoming grief, balancing or changing karma.

15 Yesod
The ninth sphere, associated with the Goddess of the Moon, receives impulses and fluxes from the higher realms upon the Tree of Life. Yesod, associated with water, abounds in an ocean of astral imagery and is the symbolic centre of the sexual instinct.

16 Netzach
The seventh sphere, associated with the planet Venus, is the sphere of intuition, as well as love and physical passion. Netzach also represents the arts, creativity and the emotions.

17 Hod
The eighth sphere, associated with the planet Mercury, represents intellect and rational thinking. Mercury is a 'messenger' of the higher gods and so Hod represents the

lower aspects of the Great Father (Chokmah: Wisdom),
symbolising the sense of order that we perceive in the
manifested universe.

18 Tiphareth

The sixth sphere is associated with gods of spiritual rebirth
and resurrection. Tiphareth is symbolised by the Sun as a
giver of life and light and represents the mid-point between
the world of everyday reality and the realm of ultimate
spiritual transcendence on the journey of mystical growth.

19 Chesod

The fourth sphere, associated with Zeus and Jupiter,
represents the peaceful face of the ruler of the universe.
Chesod is protective, reinforcing and consolidating the
forces of Creation and has qualities of divine mercy and
majesty. From this sphere, Jupiter sits upon his throne,
surveying his kingdom, the entire manifested universe.

20 Geburah

The fifth sphere, associated with Mars, traditionally a god of
war, represents severity and justice. The destructive energies
of Geburah are intended as a cleansing, purging force and
are positive in their application.

Lightning Source UK Ltd.
Milton Keynes UK
UKOW042001120712

195898UK00006B/14/P